Praise for previous editions of

Fundamentals of Kayak Navigation

"This has to be a navigation classic—not just for sea kayaks but for all small boats. It is hard to produce original material on a craft that is as ancient as navigation. But I think Dave Burch has done it."

—John Dowd, author,
Sea Kayaking—A Manual of Long-Distance Touring

"This book . . . carries its reader into many practical realms where fingers replace dividers and kamals replace sextants. This fare is not for kayakers alone. It is for all serious coastal navigators, novice and old-hand alike."

—Roger Jones, director,
Foundation for the Promotion
of the Art of Navigation

"Immensely helpful to paddlers of every skill level."

—Ed Gillet,
expedition kayaker

". . . *Fundamentals of Kayak Navigation* is a must for any sea kayaker worth their salt."

—Mark Laiosa, WBAI-FM NYC

"Burch [is] the ideal author for this fine, comprehensive book. . . . Of particular practical value are the tips for figuring out where you are while keeping both hands on the paddle."

—*Islands* magazine

Help Us Keep This Guide Up to Date

Every effort has been made by the author and editors to make this guide as accurate and useful as possible. However, many things can change after a guide is published—new products and information become available, regulations change, techniques evolve, etc.

We would love to hear from you concerning your experiences with this guide and how you feel it could be improved and be kept up to date. While we may not be able to respond to all comments and suggestions, we'll take them to heart and we'll also make certain to share them with the author. Please send your comments and suggestions to the following address:

The Globe Pequot Press
Reader Response/Editorial Department
P.O. Box 480
Guilford, CT 06437

Or you may e-mail us at:

editorial@globe-pequot.com

Thanks for your input, and happy travels!

FUNDAMENTALS OF
KAYAK NAVIGATION
Third Edition

by

David Burch

Guilford, Connecticut

"Planning around Wind and Currents" in chapter 11 was published originally in the Spring 1989 edition of *Sea Kayaker* magazine. It appears here in modified form.

Illustrations by Stephen Davis
Cover photo: Outside Images/Skip Brown
Cover design by Laura Augustine

Library of Congress Cataloging-in-Publication Data
Burch, David, 1942–
    Fundamentals of kayak navigation/by David Burch; [illustrations by Stephen Davis].—3rd ed.
        p.   cm.
    Includes bibliographical references (p.   ) and index.
    ISBN 0-7627-0473-X
    1. Kayak touring.   2. Navigation.   I. Title.
GV789.B87   1999
796.1'224—dc21   99-23964
                                                                                              CIP

Manufactured in the United States of America
Third Edition/Fourth Printing

Contents

Preface

In the past 6-year's life of the second edition of this book little has changed in the fundamentals of traditional navigation that are the basis of this book. Several important things have changed, however, that require the attention of a new edition. One is the role of GPS satellite navigation, which has evolved from an almost novelty for kayakers to an almost commonplace aid to those doing long-distance or expedition paddling. The low cost and convenience of this electronic aid to navigation now makes it an attractive way to learn about paddling speeds, currents, and general navigation, even for those who are not planning long-distance trips. We have brought this section up to date and added a bit more detail since more paddlers are likely to take advantage of it.

We have also updated the inevitable name changing and re-structuring of government agencies and checked the other references listed. The federal licensing of portable marine radios has changed, for the better in this case, and there has been a consolidation of distributors for government materials that is also more convenient. Electronic charts are now discussed, and even though obviously not useful when one is under way in a kayak, they are a tremendous aid to the planning of a trip.

What is mostly new in kayak navigation — and in life in general — during the past six years is the role of the Internet. Navigation training and trip planning is much a matter of communication and information, as it is so in many endeavors, and the Internet has revolutionized these areas. We cannot talk responsibly of navigation, weather, and related matters without reference to the Internet. We have added useful Internet references throughout the book and compiled these along with a brief discussion of them and their use in a new appendix. These are very powerful tools for mariners. For those who have put off jumping into the computer world until the last minute, that minute is here. Internet resources are not just a novelty or alternative source; they are fast becoming the primary source of information in many areas, marine navigation being just one of them.

But to keep ourselves grounded and to not stray too far from the basics, we have added a brand new original piloting trick to the position-finding section (one that is uniquely suited to kayakers since it does not require much use of the hands to execute). It is a new way to locate your position on the chart without instruments by not much more than just looking at the shore.

With new technology, kayakers are confronted with the same dilemma navigators of much larger vessels have faced for some years. If the electronic approach is so easy and accurate, why bother with the traditional methods that take time to learn and practice and master? The answer is the obvious one. It is called prudent seamanship. No matter how well guarded or backed up, electronic equipment is simply too vulnerable in a small boat at sea. When safety is at stake, we cannot rely on any single aid in navigation, especially a little plastic box that runs on batteries. The marine environment is a harsh one (mechanically and electrochemically), and survival underway in tough conditions can result in the complete disregard of any material object when concentrating on the safety of the vessel. This is as true for 60-foot vessels as it is for kayaks.

Kayak navigation is unique, however, because kayaks are unique boats. They can go anywhere, but they do so only very slowly and only aided by the most basic navigation tools. Consequently, the level of navigation required in kayaking depends on the challenges put to the boat.

The fundamentals of chart reading, compass use, and speed, time, and distance reckoning are the same in a kayak as they are in the *Queen Mary*. Even further knowledge of basic marine navigation is required when sharing waterways with larger vessels. Vessel movements must be anticipated to stay safely clear of them. Kayaks are slow and difficult to see.

On the other hand, when paddling in and out among the rocks close to a beach, a kayaker is totally sheltered from other traffic. He or she is left entirely alone to face the navigational challenges of these special waters. Much of the navigation of these uncharted waters is actually being learned for the first time from kayakers; no other vessels have been there. A tide rip that poses no threat to larger vessels can be an important concern to a kayaker. Along low shores, the entire shape of miles of "navigable waters" can change for a kayaker with a 2-foot change in the tide. A kayak can go to places no other vessel can, but it also can get stuck in places no other vessel would—in the middle of a mile-wide mud flat or behind coastal rocks that were calm in the morning but covered with breaking surf in the afternoon.

The limited speed of kayaks makes them sensitive to wind and current, so knowledge of these topics is proportionally more important to kayaks than it is to faster vessels. Add to this that most of the underway navigation of a kayak must be done without the use of the hands, and you are left with good reason for a special treatment of navigation for kayaks.

There are many fine books on marine navigation, but they all include much that is not practical for kayak use and omit much that is vital to kayak use. Even those intended for small-boat navigation do not have in mind boats that are twenty-four inches wide and draw six inches of water. The goal of this book is to provide this information by compiling those parts of the topic that are useful to paddlers and to expand on those that are of special interest to paddlers. The topics of this book, however, are limited to navigational matters. Boat handling and other important topics of kayak seamanship are not covered.

Except possibly in the warmest weather, kayak navigation is done from the "seat of the pants"—meaning done in large part from careful looking and trained intuition. Done well, it appears not to be done at all. Although a watch and compass might be at hand, even those are often used by experienced paddlers without conscious thought of navigation. Some paddlers, who have covered thousands of miles in a kayak, have the same feeling that many mariners have—that they do not actually do much navigation under way. But to get by without much navigation takes much skill at navigation, even though it might not be thought of as such. In this sense, a goal of this book is to help new paddlers learn how "not to navigate," and to do so without the benefit of the years of time it takes a thousand miles of water to pass by. There is some paperwork and practice to do at first, but once the methods are learned, they somehow will not be needed any more. The net result will be the same.

Acknowledgments

Several topics discussed in this book first appeared in *Sea Kayaker* magazine. My thanks to the editors John and Beatrice Dowd for their encouragement and the many valuable discussions we had on these topics. John's book, *Sea Kayaking—A Manual for Long-Distance Touring*, provides a wealth of information, and I have learned much from it.

A special note of thanks goes to Matt Broze, kayak designer and safety columnist for *Sea Kayaker* magazine, and to Randel Washburne, author of *The Coastal Kayaker's Manual—A Complete Guide to Skills, Gear, and Sea Sense*, and *Kayaking Puget Sound, the San Juans, and Gulf Islands*. They read all parts of the manuscript and provided valuable comments and suggestions on each. They shared their experience in both writing and kayaking. It took a lot of time, which reflects their devotion to both sports. Their help was very much appreciated.

I also would like to acknowledge and thank several additional expert kayakers for the tips, details, and examples of practical kayak navigation that they have shared with me through discussions or in lectures they presented in various places. They include John Field, Bill McGowan, Lee Moyer, Tom Steinburn, and Kelly Tjaden. I have learned much from these discussions, and this book has benefited from their knowledge.

My thanks to Jim Green of the National Ocean Service, who helped me decode chart symbols of special interest to kayakers; to Dr. Alyn Duxbury of the Washington Sea Grant Program, University of Washington, who provided valuable comments on tides and currents included in Chapter 8; and to Douglas M. Fryer, attorney, for the discussions we have had on the rules of the road and for his comments on that section of this book.

My indebtedness to Stephen Davis is clear from the illustrations that follow. His skills as an artist and his knowledge of boats added content as well as form to the book. Thanks again.

It has been a pleasure to work with Carolyn Threadgill, Margaret Foster-Finan, Deborah Easter, and Judy Petry. Thanks for your skills, guidance, and patience.

CHAPTER 1

The Role of Navigation

Navigation means knowing where you are and choosing a safe, efficient route to where you want to go. These two skills are mandatory for long trips into unknown waters and are often valuable for shorter trips in well-known waters. For the most part navigation skills learned and practiced in one area apply to other areas as well; the fundamental techniques of navigation are universal. Safety and enjoyment are the main reasons to learn navigation. As opposed to wilderness hiking or ocean sailing—where the safety concern is getting lost—kayak navigation focuses more on avoiding hazardous areas that could be an immediate threat to a paddler's safety: waters with strong currents, strong winds, big waves or big ships. Discerning these hazards and knowing how to avoid them is part of navigation.

All kayak trips must be planned. A proposed trip must fit into the number of days you have allotted, and a day's run must fit into a day. If you do not make your destination by nightfall or in time for favorable tides at the landing site, the landing could be more of an adventure than you want at the end of a long day. In extreme cases it could be dangerous. A wrong turn made when paddling downwind might take a long hard paddle against the wind to correct. Poor navigation can turn a relaxed bird-watching outing into an athletic workout. With the basic navigation skills of nautical chart reading, estimating kayak speeds, and predicting currents, an itinerary can be set up and checked off underway that will help keep the experience in line with your intentions. Under any circumstances, however, the key to good navigation during the trip is thorough navigation planning before the trip.

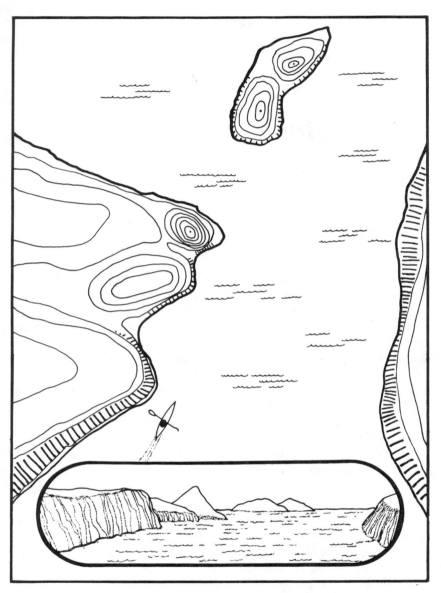

1-1. *Navigation from point to point. The inset shows the perspective from an elevated view. From the lower perspective of a kayak seat, the bases of the land masses appear more along a single straight line because the close horizon blocks the true view of the shorelines (see inset to fig. 2-8).*

Once under way on a well-planned route, navigation consists of keeping track of where you are along that route. The challenge of this task depends on prevailing conditions. When paddling along a shoreline on a clear day, keeping track means little more than just looking around. As one headland is passed, the next comes into sight. By identifying the next headland on the chart, you know where you are (see fig. 1-1). After passing a few prominent points, and noting the time it took to paddle from point to point, it is easy to figure out how fast you are progressing and decide how far or how long to continue on that day.

At night, in the fog, or when crossing large open waters, there is much less to see. Under these conditions, the value of practiced navigation skills is more apparent. If the only visible landmarks are far off, they will not help much in locating your position. In extreme cases, course direction must be read from a compass, and progress along that course reckoned from estimated paddling speed and predicted current flow. It is true that these skills are not often called upon, but your time on the water will be more relaxed if you are confident that you can navigate this way if need be. It pays to prepare for fog, significant currents, or nighttime paddling.

Even thorough planning, however, cannot cover all the navigational decisions a paddler confronts under way, even on a simple route along a shoreline. Should you, for example, paddle point to point straight across each bay you meet or follow the longer but less exposed concave route along the shoreline? And how should the point itself be approached: close in along the beach, or passed wide well away from waves and currents at the point? These and many other important decisions ultimately must be made underway, in the prevailing conditions of wind, waves, and current.

Although navigation covers a broad range of topics, all navigation decisions depend on knowing where you are. You cannot pick the best route to where you want to go without knowing where you are at the time. Good navigation and the safety it affords always boil down to knowing where you are at all times—being able to look at a chart and point to your position on the chart.

Crossing a shipping lane is one obvious example of how important it is to know where you are. Some waterways routinely traveled by large ships are divided into inbound and outbound lanes, which all large shipping traffic must follow. Though clearly marked on charts, the lane boundaries are not at all discernible from the water. They are effectively mile-wide invisible streets, which might lie a mile or more off the shoreline. If you detect an approaching ship while cross-ing the lanes, you have a quick navigation decision to make, but any choice of action must start with knowing where you are relative to the lane boundaries.

Types of Navigation

Finding and keeping track of position is done by one of two ways: pi-loting or dead reckoning. *Piloting* is the formal name for the usual way of getting around—using known landmarks and references. In boats, it means finding position using charted landmarks. Paddling past a buoy, you know where you are as soon as you locate that buoy on the chart. The same is true near any prominent landmark.

Well away from landmarks, on the other hand, it is not as simple to pinpoint your position on the chart by just looking. To find posi-tion with only one distant landmark in sight requires a compass direc-tion to the landmark and a measure of how far away it is. With two charted landmarks in sight, position can be found from the intersec-tion of the two compass bearings plotted on the chart. These and other piloting techniques are explained later.

With no identifiable landmarks in sight, position must be figured from speed and time. The procedure is called *dead reckoning*. The name probably evolved from the abbreviation "ded" for deduced. To navigate by dead reckoning, a present position is deduced from the distance and the direction paddled away from a known location. Paddling at a rate of 3 miles per hour toward due north on the com-pass, you can deduce that in thirty minutes you should be 1.5 miles north of where you started. With the known starting point shown on the chart, you can draw this route on the chart and point to where you think you are.

Although it may not be thought of in these formal terms, the nav-igation of any trip proceeds as a sequence of piloting fixes, with navi-gation by dead reckoning between the fixes (see fig. 1-2). Starting from a known position, you set off in the direction of your destination at some estimated paddling speed. From this you can deduce how long the trip should take and where you should be at various interme-diate times. Once underway along this route, whenever you suspect that winds or currents or any other factor might be influencing your progress, you take a position fix using piloting. Sometimes this takes no more than a careful look around and a quick note on the chart.

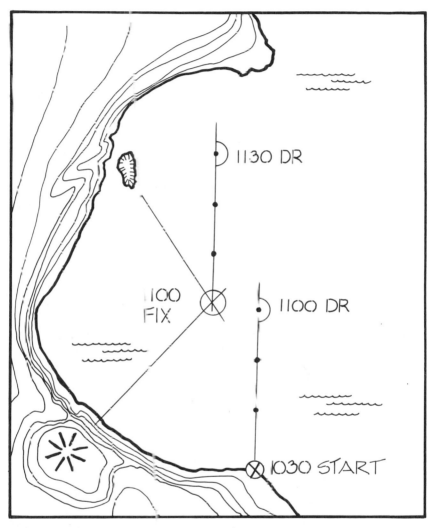

1-2. *Navigation by dead reckoning (DR) and piloting. Using estimated paddling speed, compass course, and time under way, the paddler thought he was at the 1100 DR position shown. He was actually located at the 1100 fix position as found from compass bearings to the island and peak.*

Other times it might require compass bearings and drawing a few lines on the chart. In any event, once you find out where you are, you mark it on the chart with the time of the fix and then figure the route that will take you from there to where you want to go. The several steps of this process are the subjects of this book.

Navigation skills are often distinguished by the waters they are used in. *Offshore* navigation usually refers to navigation out of sight of land, as opposed to *inshore* navigation, which refers to navigation in sight of or in close proximity to land and to established aids to navigation. The terms, however, are relative in kayaking; the centers of large bays, straits, or inland sounds can present conditions similar to those many miles offshore in the ocean, despite the visibility of land on either side. The distinction fades even more at night and in the fog. Furthermore, "in sight of land" is relative to the height of the land, as explained in chapter 6. A low coastline will slip below the sea horizon at a few miles offshore, whereas a coastal mountain range might be seen at 30 miles off on a very clear day.

For practical matters of kayak navigation and seamanship, a kayak is "offshore" in any waters whenever the nearest land is more than few miles off; this is, in part, because from this distance off, many lights, buoys, and other aids designed for the inshore navigation of larger vessels are simply not in view from the low perspective of a kayak. On the other hand, only kayakers can usefully distinguish the region of "close inshore" navigation, meaning right along the shore in and out of off-lying rocks and shoalings—a water realm of unique navigation and unique joys—reserved for kayakers. (See fig. 1-3.)

Navigation as a Hobby

There are two distinct aspects to navigation: knowing where you are and choosing the best route to where you want to go. The fundamental task of finding position is more or less straightforward. The techniques of piloting and dead reckoning that work in a kayak are readily learned and mastered with little practice. Planning the best route through various waterways and conditions, on the other hand, is not always so easy. This distinction is even more dramatic when using the electronic aids covered in chapter 7. With them, determining accurate position is simply a matter of pushing a button and reading a dial, whereas practical route selection is scarcely benefited at all.

The illusive factors that kayakers must always bear in mind when route planning are wind and current and their effects on waves. Big steep waves are potentially dangerous to a kayak, and strong winds make big waves. Current flowing against waves steepens them even

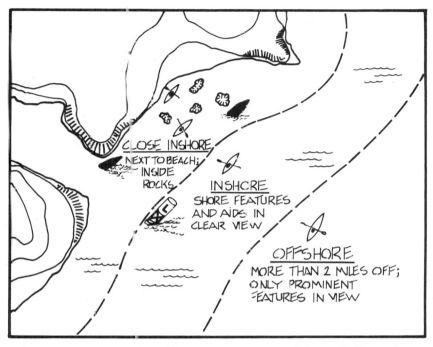

1-3. *A way to distinguish paddling regions in terms of the available naviga-tion aids. The terms and associated safety and navigational considerations are relative to the nature of the waterway and shore as well as the prevailing visibility.*

more—a lot more. So not only do adverse winds and currents hinder progress along some routes, their interactions are often an even larger threat to progress and safety.

Planning the best route, therefore, involves more than choosing the shortest distance between two points on the chart. You must con-sider which way and how strong the wind is blowing, now and later in the day, and which way and how strong the currents are flowing, now and later in the day. You must consider how winds are influenced by the shape of the land, and how currents are influenced by the shape of the waterway. You must learn how waves are made by the wind and how the shape and depth of the waterway affect its waves. Getting from one place to another in a kayak is often as much a question of the oceanography and meteorology of the area as it is a question of simple geographic navigation. This diverse but interrelated knowl-edge is best obtained by treating navigation and all it entails as part of kayaking itself, rather than something that must be learned to do kayaking.

Add a new dimension to the sport—a knowledge of the wind and the sea and the orientation skills that good navigation practice instills. Treat navigation itself as a hobby, not just the means of getting from point A to point B. Take pride in finding out where you are by different navigation methods. Practice it as a game in clear weather from a known position. Figure how long each leg of a trip should take and check your work, even when there is no need to predict the times. Predict the currents in all waters you cover and check your work. Practice listening to weather reports and watch the skies to compare surface winds with cloud patterns. Then when you need these skills, and they are not a game, you are prepared.

Keep notes of what you learn on each outing. Navigation skills progress much faster with a notebook. With good records, you can learn in one season what it takes years to learn without keeping records. On each kayak trip, a paddler is exposed to a barrage of navigational experiences and details. But it takes written records to remember more of these than you forget. Eventually local knowledge compiled from individual trips begins to jell. Lessons learned in one place can be applied to another, and the watery part of the world accessible to you begins to expand.

Kayaks are intrepid craft. They have ventured into all the waters of the globe, crossed oceans, and circumnavigated continents. It is a worthy challenge to learn the skills of seamanship and navigation that match the capabilities of the boat.

CHAPTER 2

Nautical Charts and Chart Reading

What Is a Nautical Chart?

The first step in navigation is having the proper nautical chart on board. Nautical charts are maps of waterways designed specifically for marine navigation. They show water depths, shoreline composition, extent of the tidal range on the shore, inshore rocks, navigation aids (lights, buoys, daymarks), the direction that compasses point to in the charted area, and other aids to navigation such as shoreside buildings, structures, and terrain that are visible from the water. Most mariners distinguish the name "chart" from "map" when referring to these, but this is certainly not important—it is a maritime tradition similar to calling a "rope" a "line" when it is on a boat.

Charts come in various sizes (some are big sheets, some are smaller sheets), and they are made to various scales, although U.S. issues cost the same regardless of these distinctions. Areas covered by individual charts range from single bays to entire oceans. Two charts of the same sheet size that depict areas of different sizes must have different scales. The most detailed charts cover single bays or harbors. A harbor chart scale of 1 to 10,000 (written 1:10,000) means that 10,000 inches of the harbor appears as 1 inch on the chart. It takes some trickery, however, to interpret 10,000 inches.

Considering a handspan to be just over 7 inches, chart scales can be converted to nautical miles per handspan to get a quick feeling for what they mean. A 1:10,000 scale is equivalent to 1 mile per handspan. Chart scales of 1:40,000 cover 4 miles for each handspan on the chart. To figure miles per handspan for any scale, drop the last four digits of the scale factor and what is left is the number of miles per handspan. To calibrate your handspan for this purpose, stretch your hand out along the mile scale of a 1:40,000 chart to see what fingertip is 4 miles from your thumb tip. This handspan is then the one to use to interpret all chart scales.

The terms *large scale* and *small scale* are frequently used to describe charts. As with high and low gears on a bicycle, however, the logic of the names is not apparent. Large refers to the chart scale written as a fraction—1/10,000 is larger than 1/80,000. Consequently, large-scale charts cover small areas; small-scale charts cover large areas. A specific island, for example, would appear large on a large-scale chart and small on a small-scale chart. Ocean chart scales might be as small as 1:1,200,000. The handspan trick keeps this in perspective. On this chart a handspan is 120 miles. For the purposes of kayak navigation, large-scale means 1:40,000 or larger.

Choosing Charts

Nautical charts are readily available for all navigable waters of the United States and most other parts of the world as well. Charts of American waters are prepared and distributed by the National Ocean Service (NOS), a division of the National Oceanic and Atmospheric Administration (NOAA). (See Appendix B for Internet links.) American charts of foreign and international waters are published by the National Image and Mapping Agency (NIMA), formerly called the Defense Mapping Agency. The larger NOS chart dealers will also carry the NIMA charts. Many countries have charting services of their own, which are usually coordinated by a hydrographic office. Some of these foreign charts are carried by American dealers, but most are not. See Appendix A for specific information on obtaining charts. Of special interest to North American paddlers are the excellent charts of Canadian waters produced by the Canadian Hydrographic Service.

The best way to select charts for American waters is through NOAA's *Nautical Chart Catalogs* (see fig. 2-1). These free pamphlets show maps of the cataloged region with the individual charts available outlined on it. Each chart has a specific name, number, and scale. The catalogs also list authorized chart dealers in the region. Authorized dealers are obligated to sell only the latest editions and charge only the official price. Canadian and NIMA chart catalogs are similar.

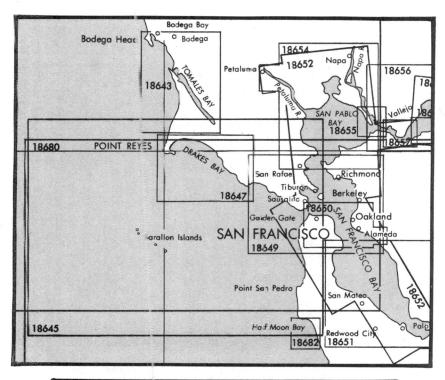

MONTEREY BAY TO CAPE MENDOCINO		
Chart Number	**Title**	**Scale**
© 18640	San Francisco to Point Arena	1:207,840
18643	Bodega and Tomales Bays	1:30,000
	Bodega Harbor	1:10,000
© 18645	Gulf of the Faralones	1:100,000
	Southeast Farallon	1:20,000
18647	Drakes Bay	1:40,000
18649	San Francisco Entrance	1:40,000
18650	San Francisco Bay—	
	Candlestick Pt. to Angel I.	1:20,000
18651	San Francisco Bay—southern part	1:40,000
	Redwood Creek	1:20,000
18652 SC FOLIO SMALL-CRAFT CHART		
	San Francisco Bay to Antioch	1:40,000; 1:80,000

2-1. *Section of a* NOAA Nautical Chart Catalog. *Each chart has a unique number, name, and scale, although some charts contain large-scale insets of specific areas, as indicated in the list of chart titles. This chart catalog is also on line; see Appendix B.*

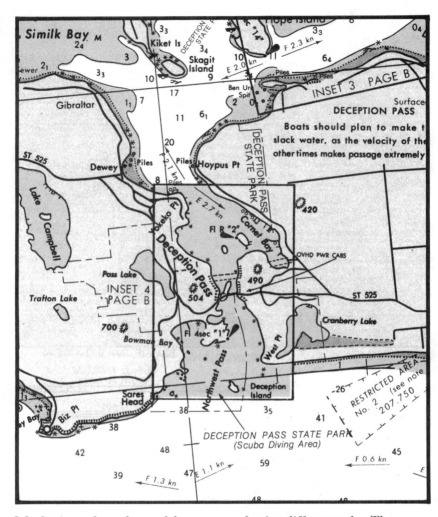

2-2. *Sections of two charts of the same area having different scales. The smaller scale is 1:80,000; the larger scale is 1:25,000. Each is from a small-craft chart that has north to the left of the page.*

Kayak navigation calls for the most detailed (largest scale) charts available. Kayakers have access to places that small-scale charts do not even show. Hazards close to the shoreline such as rocks, shoalings (that might enhance waves or currents), kelp beds, and details of the shore itself (sand or rocks, steep or flat) are not discernible from

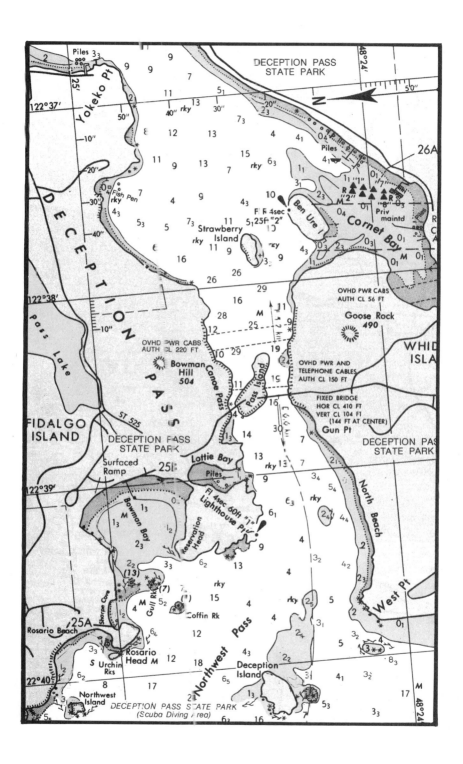

small-scale charts. Access to the shore through off-lying rocks can only be judged, if at all, from detailed charts. A small island on a large-scale chart can appear as a rock on a small-scale chart (see fig. 2-2).

For close inshore navigation, the larger the chart scale the better. As a rule, 1:40,000 is the smallest scale useful for reading features needed for landing or navigation along a rocky shoreline. One to 20,000 or larger would be even better, but they are not always available or more detailed. On the other hand, long trips call for some compromise in chart selection since a 1:20,000 chart can be just 10 miles across. The series of large-scale charts needed for a long trip makes an unwieldy stack of paper. Furthermore, long trips require at least one small-scale chart (1:80,000 or smaller) for planning the over-all route—to locate, for example, the public lands in the area. It is te-dious at best to plan long routes across several charts. Also, once underway it is difficult to identify islands on the horizon and other distant features when they are not on the same chart you are using. This is one potential disadvantage to NOAA's special folio charts, called small-craft (SC) charts, or to the commercial chart packets available for some areas.

Whenever possible, it is best to select charts by actually looking at them at the chart dealer. This way you can compare different scales of the same areas to see if the extra information provided on the large-scale charts is required for your intentions in the area. If you are only transiting a featureless shoreline, the larger-scale charts might not add significant detail to justify the extra expense and gear.

Electronic Charting

Nautical charts and topographic maps are now available in digital format, usually provided on CDs, which can be viewed and printed from a computer. Sources and related Internet references are listed in Appendix B.

Priced individually, nautical charts are more expensive digitally than on paper, but since they are printed as a complete set by region on a CD, the net price per chart ends up being much lower—if you can justify buying all the charts of a specific region.

A rudimentary viewing program is provided on the chart CDs, but for optimum use of these charts it is best to purchase one of several independent "charting software" packages (see Appendix B). These programs have very versatile display options and let you lay out and plan a trip completely on the screen. You can enter waypoints (discussed in chapter 7) with the click of a button, label them, and then have the program label the course line for each leg of the voyage with the distance and compass bearing between waypoints. The annotated chart segments of interest can then be selected, cropped, and printed out in full color for a trip. Whatever method you might use to protect your paper charts (discussed later) can be applied, including lamination, which is often very inexpensive.

Several of these programs include very convenient tide and current options, so not only can you visualize the trip on any chart scale you choose at the click of a button, you can also display and print both the tide height and current speed and direction in that region. With practice, using this type of software and digital charts is certainly the most convenient and thorough means of planning a trip, but you should still spot-check a few of its results the old-fashioned way by using paper charts and plotting tools, as discussed later in this section. And, needless to say, this computerized approach to navigation planning will not appeal to all paddlers. If it fits your lifestyle and resources, then it will be a boon; if not, you can always do this the tried and tested way that it has been done for hundreds of years with chart and pencil.

Also, bear in mind, that as with much wonderful new technology and technique, you often must go backward for a while before going forward. And this is just as true with this new electronic charting revolution. There is a learning curve to crawl up before the fun ride down the other side. It could well take longer to carefully plan a trip by computer than by hand the first couple times you do it, but if you do a lot of extended paddling that calls for navigation, then this equipment and approach to planning will prove to be very worthwhile. It could be especially valuable to schools and clubs that are providing trip planning for their members.

Larger commercial and recreational vessels use this type of electronic charting not only for planning but also underway with direct input to the computer from their GPS satellite navigation system (discussed in chapter 7). This arrangement then shows their precise position right on the nautical chart (on the computer screen) at all times and leaves a trail of dots showing where they have been. If they are drifting off course into danger it is obvious at a glance. At the click of a button they can take range and bearings to charted landmarks or compute new courses to any destination, all with a mouse click.

Looking ahead to waterproof palmtop computers with active-matrix full-color touch-screen displays, you could in principle be doing the same thing from the seat of a kayak in the next three or four years. In any event, these types of developments can indeed be hazardous to navigation, since with their availablity there is a tendency to not learn navigation . . . so let this topic go for now and get on with learning the basics that we must ultimately depend on.

Latest Editions and Corrections

The date on a chart does not always tell whether it is the latest edition of that chart. Some charts are reissued every year, some only as often as every three or four years. The decision to reissue a chart depends on the number and seriousness of the changes that must be made. The latest issue of a chart can be checked by contacting the Coast Guard or any authorized chart dealer. They in turn will refer to a quarterly NOAA publication called *List of Latest Editions*. A chart with the present year's date is probably the latest edition. One dated more than four years ago is probably outdated. The *List of Latest Editions* is online; see Appendix B.

The important things that are likely to change on new chart issues are locations of buoys and lights, flashing characteristics of lights, locations of shipping lanes, and the layout of structures on land. Much of the remainder of what charts show does not change with most new issues, but this cannot be counted on. Valuable shoreline information obtained from recent surveys might be missed if you go with outdated charts. Old charts often can be updated adequately by hand after comparing them with new ones or with lists of known chart corrections discussed below. Nighttime navigation calls for up-to-date data since it relies on proper light identification.

The latest chart data, including temporary as well as permanent chart alterations and other news of interest to marine navigation, are compiled weekly in the Coast Guard's *Local Notice to Mariners* (see fig. 2-3). These are kept on file at Coast Guard offices, marinas, chart dealers, and some libraries, and they are all online for very convenient review. A long trip into unfamiliar waters with planned nighttime paddling, or any other anticipated dependence on charted navigation aids, calls for going this extra mile in chart preparation. A quick survey of recent notices could reveal interesting information. Buoys can be dragged away by currents or collisions with ships; the only light for miles might be temporarily out of order; or an announced navy bombing run might clarify what is meant by a restricted area marked on the chart. Important notices also are broadcast daily on VHF marine-radio frequencies (discussed in chapter 10).

Once a year, all permanent chart changes that pertain to lights, buoys, and other navigation aids are compiled and printed in another Coast Guard publication called the *Light List*. If a *Light List* is newer than the latest issue of a particular chart, the data it contains supersedes that printed on the chart.

For example, suppose, early some August, you plan a trip for the end of the month. The most recent chart of the area you plan to visit is two years old. This chart claims the Cape Hazard Light flashes every six seconds and can be seen from 12 miles off. Your current *Light List*, however, states that this same light flashes every four seconds and can be seen from 10 miles off. The *Light List* supersedes the chart, so its information is what to expect and what should be written in ink on this chart next to that light. Checking the latest *Local Notice to Mariners* (dated August 2), you discover that this light is reported to be "operating at reduced intensity," meaning it cannot be seen from as far as it should. This calls for a pencil note on the chart and a check on the next several notices when available. It might even take a telephone call to the Coast Guard or a check of their Web site just before leaving to verify the status of this light. The visible range of lights and how this is determined from the *Light List* and charted light data are subjects of nighttime navigation covered in chapter 10.

As of this edition, the Canadian *Light List* is online in complete form, but the U.S. counterpart is not. It almost certainly will be available online at some point. Several of the "charting software" programs mentioned earlier include a complete digital copy of the *Light List* with options for annual updates.

This level of preparation might seem excessive when compared to navigation practice in hiking or driving. You would not, for example, call the Highway Department before a cross-country drive to verify whether the street light in Podunk was working. The difference lies in the consequence of a wrong turn. A wrong turn in Podunk will not lead to a roller coaster ride that eventually turns the car over and fills it with water. A wrong turn in a kayak can put rain on your picnic—not often, but just possibly.

U. S. COAST GUARD
LOCAL NOTICE TO MARINERS

I. SPECIAL NOTICE

SPECIAL WARNING NO. 69 - WEST COAST OF AFRICA - WESTERN SAHARA -

1. Unprovoked attacks on shipping off the coast of the Western Sahara by Polisaro front guerrillas using machine guns, grenades, and mortars continue to occur resulting in the loss of life and property. Polisario spokesmen have been quoted as stating that any vessel in Western Sahara territorial waters, which the Polisario considers to be a war zone, would be the target of attack.

II. DISCREPANCIES - DISCREPANCIES CORRECTED

The following is a list of aids to navigation that are not watching as advertised in the Light List Volume VI, Thirteenth District section:

LL #	Aid Name	Status	Chart	BNM	LNM
755/16135	Strait of Juan de Fuca Traffic Lane Separation Lighted Buoy J	Off Station	18400	0174-87	5/87
9120	Coos River Channel Light 8	Damaged/TDBN	18587	2194-85	1/86
9935	Clatsop Spit Lighted Bell Buoy 8	Missing	18521	0155-87	4/87
9970	Clatsop Spit Lighted Whistle Buoy 14	Improper characteristic	18521	0257-87	7/87
10050	Astoria Pier 3 East Light	Extinguished	18521	0222-87	6/87

III. TEMPORARY CHANGES - TEMPORARY CHANGES CORRECTED

The following is a list of aids to navigation that have been temporarily changed as advertised in the Light List Volume VI, Thirteenth District section:

LL #	Aid Name	Temporary status	Chart	BNM	LNM
None	Columbia River Entrance Test Lighted Buoy	Established	18521	1042-86	27/86
		Relocated		0130-87	4/87
9100	Coos River Entrance Light 1	Discontinued	18587	0959-86	25/86
None	Coos River Entrance Temporary Daybeacon 1T	Established	18587	0959-86	25/86

VI. ADVANCE NOTICE OF CHANGES IN AIDS TO NAVIGATION

OREGON AND WASHINGTON - COLUMBIA RIVER - HARRINGTON POINT TO CRIMS ISLAND - Aids to Navigation - Changes - Pancake Point Dike Light 59 (LLNR 10480) will be discontinued.

Pancake Point Temporary Lighted Buoy 59T, a green buoy show a flashing green light every 6 seconds with a nominal range of 4 miles, will be permanently established in approximate position 46°08'58.8"N, 123° 22'20.5"W. Chart 18523.

VIII. GENERAL

OREGON AND WASHINGTON - COLUMBIA RIVER - NAVIGATION LOCKS - Closures -
The navigation locks at Bonneville, The Dalles, John Day and McNary Dams across the Columbia River at river miles 145, 191, 216, and 292 (respectively) will be closed to navigation from 0700 local 8 March 1987 until 0800 local 22 March 1987 for annual maintenance.
Charts 18531, 18533, and 18535.
LNM CG Seattle 1, 2, 3, 4, 5, and 6 of 1987.

2-3. Sample contents of the Local Notice to Mariners. Such notices are published weekly by each U.S. Coast Guard District, and they are online at the USCG Web site (see Appendix B).

Symbols and Soundings

Chart reading takes practice. There is a wealth of information on nautical charts, much of which is presented in symbolic or abbreviated terms. Once the symbols and conventions are learned, a nautical chart becomes a wonderful resource that is easy to use. If a picture is worth a thousand words, a chart is worth a book.

The primary guide to the interpretation of chart symbols is an inexpensive booklet called *Chart No. 1* (see fig. 2-4) published jointly by

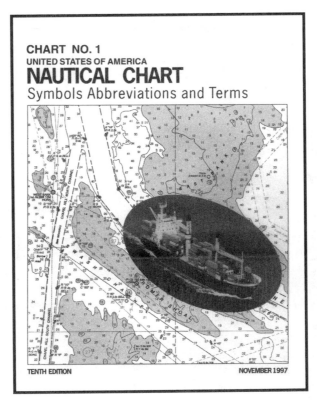

2-4. *Cover of the pamphlet called* Chart No. 1, *which lists all nautical chart symbols and abbreviations. The cover design and format of this publication change periodically, even though its contents may remain basically the same. There is also a new electronic version of this product on CD. See fig. 2-4a.*

2-4a. *Cover of the CD-ROM version of* Chart No. 1, *which is a much enhanced adaptation of the paper publication.*

NOAA and NIMA and available from most chart dealers. An enhanced CD-ROM version exists also (see fig.2-4a). It lists all chart symbols and their meanings, although quite tersely at times. Rock and shoreline symbols especially important to kayakers are explained below, but the booklet should be referred to for further details and practice. To learn the symbols, pick any chart and use *Chart No. 1* to identify symbols at random. Any marking on the chart that is not listed in *Chart No. 1* is probably an actual structure built in the shape of the mark, or the work of a passing insect. Canadian chart symbols are similar to American ones, but there are enough minor distinctions to justify having a copy of the Canadian counterpart (also called *Chart No. 1*) when using Canadian charts.

The symbols used to describe rocks—from boulders to islands—pose a special challenge in chart reading. This part of chart reading is fundamental to kayakers, as it is to all boaters. A rock the size of a room can appear on the chart as a simple asterisk "*" or tiny plus sign "+." The symbols themselves are small, and some that are only slightly different in appearance have very different meanings. All chart symbols and notations must be interpreted literally. The notation "(<u>6</u>)" beside an asterisk, as opposed to the notation "(6)," for example, can mean the difference between seeing and not seeing the same rock. An underlined number "(<u>6</u>)" means the top of the rock is 6 feet above the water whenever the tide height is precisely zero. This rock will be out of sight underwater whenever the tide height is over 6 feet. A number "($\overline{6}$)" with no underline means the top of the rock is 6 feet above the water whenever the tide height is equal to the average high-water level of the tide in that area. This rock stays in view above the surface at all times. The first notation is a drying height, the second is an elevation. In other words, the latter "rock" was an islet, too small to be distinguished as such on that chart scale. The parentheses distinguish the rock-height information from nearby water depths. Elevations are measured from the high-water level to the top of the land surface unless the elevation appears with a line over it ($\overline{6}$), in which case it is measured to the treetops on the land. Rock symbols and notations are illustrated in figures 2-5 and 2-6.

The numbers scattered across the waters on charts are actual measurements of water depths called *soundings*. The units of the soundings vary from chart to chart. They will be either feet, fathoms, or meters. One fathom is 6 feet. One meter is just over 3 feet. The international trend is to convert all charted depths and heights to meters, but NOAA is not rushing into this and there are few complaints about it. Canadian charts are in meters. Depth units on U.S. charts are noted in bold purple print on the chart border.

With one exception, the same units are used for all soundings on any one chart. The exceptions occur in the shallower depths of some charts that use fathoms. A sounding with a subscript on these charts, such as 3_2, is a mixed notation meaning 3 fathoms and 2 feet, or 20 feet. When this convention is used, the chart is labeled "SOUNDINGS IN FATHOMS (FATHOMS AND FEET TO 11 FATHOMS)." Other charts using fathoms do not follow this convention, but instead mark this same depth with a $3\frac{1}{3}$, meaning 3⅓ of a fathom. On charts using meters for soundings, the symbol 3_2 means 3.2 meters.

It is important to know what is meant by these charted depths. They cannot represent the actual depth of the water at all times, since depths change 10 or 20 feet each day in some places as the tides rise and fall. Tides are discussed in chapter 8, but details are not needed now. At any point on the chart, the tides go up and down twice a day, and books are available that tell the height of the tide at any time at that place. Tide books are made by the same agency (NOS/NOAA)

Navigation Dangers

ⓔ25 (21) ▲(4 m)	Rock which does not cover (height above MHW)
*Uncov 2 ft *(2) ⓠUncov 2 ft ⓠ(2) ⓠ ⓠDries 4 ft	Rock which covers and uncovers with height above chart sounding datum (see introduction)
⁂ ⓧ ⓠ ⓠ(0)	Rock awash at (near) level of chart sounding datum
⁂	Dotted line emphasizes danger to navigation
*	Rock awash (height unknown)
⁂	Dotted line emphasizes danger to navigation
+	Submerged rock (depth unknown)
⁂	Dotted line emphasizes danger to navigation
ⓢRk ⓨ ⓩ ⓢ ⊕B) ⓟ	Shoal sounding on isolated rock or rocks
Tide rips 〜〜〜	Overfalls or Tide rips
⌃⌃⌃⌃⌃ Symbol used only in small areas	
Eddies ↝↜↝↜ Symbol used only in small areas	Eddies
Kelp ↝↝↝	Kelp, Seaweed
Br or ⌣⌣⌣	Breakers
⌐ ⊕+++ ⃝	Limiting danger line
⌜+ rky +⌝	Limit of rocky area

2-5. *Samples of symbols from* Chart No. 1. *Photographs of examples of these dangers are shown in the electronic version of* Chart No. 1.

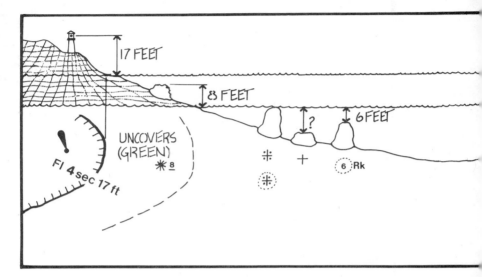

2-6. *Schematic definitions of rock symbols. Underlined numbers are drying heights relative to a zero tide level; numbers without underlines are elevations*

that makes the charts, so they use the same reference level for both, and that reference level is the one marked on charts by soundings and shoreline boundaries.

Suppose a tide book states that at noon today the tide height at Seal Rock will be 5 feet. This means the depth of the water at noon at Seal Rock will be 5 feet above the reference level printed on the chart. If charted soundings around Seal Rock all read 20 feet (meaning the sea bottom is 20 feet below the reference level), the depth to expect at noon at Seal Rock is 25 feet. The depth of the water at any point on a chart is just the charted depth plus the tide height at that time read from a tide book.

The reference level (officially called the chart datum) could be at any height above the sea bottom, but the actual level used is not chosen arbitrarily. It is always taken to represent the depth of the water at the average value of the lowest tides. In other words, charted depths represent the shallow end of the tidal range at any particular spot. This means that tide heights listed in tide books are mostly positive numbers, and the actual water depth at any point and time will most likely be greater than that printed on the chart. The only time the water will

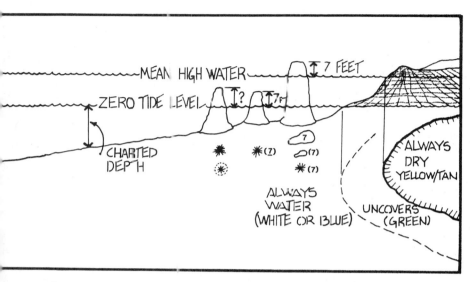

MEAN HIGH WATER — 7 FEET

ZERO TIDE LEVEL

CHARTED DEPTH

ALWAYS DRY YELLOW/TAN

ALWAYS WATER (WHITE OR BLUE)

UNCOVERS (GREEN)

relative to the mean high tide level. Elevations and drying heights are in feet on feet and fathom charts and in meters on metric charts.

be shallower than charted is during a negative tide—meaning the tide height printed in tide books is prefaced with a minus sign (-). From a practical point of view, this occurs only for a few hours each month, and even during these periods it is rare to find a tide more than 1 or 2 feet negative. Canadian tide tables use a slightly lower chart datum *(lowest normal tides)*, which results in fewer negative tides than U.S. tables.

To a chart-reading kayaker, however, the tide's effect on the exposed shore is more important than it is on the actual water depths. Since a kayak draws only 6 inches of water, a modest change in tide height can open or close water routes over low-lying lands. Areas with large tidal range can appear remarkably different from a kayak at high and low water. A broad beach can turn into a cliff; a single large island can turn into a group of small islands. This information is read from a chart by the color of the shore adjacent to the water. The foreshore—that part of the shoreline that covers and uncovers with the tides—is green on charts. Shallow water is blue on charts and dry land is yellow (tan), so it makes sense to show the mixture as green.

When the tide height is zero, land should begin where the green meets the blue. As the tide rises, the foreshore shrinks, and when the tide height reaches the average high water level for that area, land should begin where the green meets the yellow. The level of the tide must often be considered in order to identify what is in view from what is shown on the chart. See chapter 8 for information on using tide tables. See chapters 10 and 11 for discussions on the importance of tides in navigation planning. Samples of shoreline chart symbols are shown in figure 2-7.

An electronic version of Chart No. 1 (fig. 2-4a) was published in 1999 by Starpath School of Navigation (www.starpath.com). This CD-ROM product includes all of the content of the paper version plus much more. It includes annotated photographs of the various charted features, such as cliffs, buoys, rocks, and bridges to help mariners learn their identification, as well as animations of the various lighthouse flashing characteristics. There is a unique graphic search facility to help locate symbols of interest and a thorough index of all symbols and abbreviations in English and all other languages that might appear on US charts. A complete list of the hydrographic offices around the world is provided, with direct Internet links to those with web pages. This product also includes a supplementary tutorial on chart use with videos of chart-plotting techniques, including string plotters (see chapter 6) that are particularly suited to kayak navigation.

Terrain and Perspective

Wilderness canoeing and backpacking, which develop skills of interpreting the lay of the land from elevation contours on maps, are good training for nautical chart reading. This aspect of map reading is equally important in marine navigation, but with nautical charts there is a twist to the problem. On many charts, only the outline of the land is shown, with very little specific information on its height. In these circumstances, the task is to read from the chart what you should see based mostly on the horizontal extent of the land, rather than its height. Elevation information is given in many cases, but the more frequent challenge is to get by without it or to rely heavily on isolated data such as a few charted peak locations or the identification of a steep bluff here and there. An example is shown in figure 2-8.

Along a shoreline with many curves and headlands and islands or other landmasses in the background, it is often difficult to locate

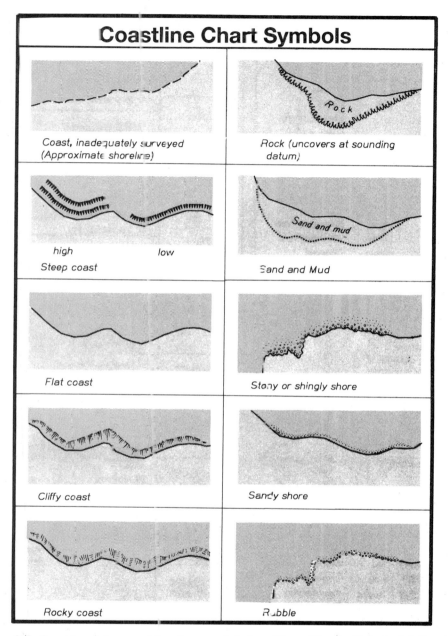

Coastline Chart Symbols

Coast, inadequately surveyed (Approximate shoreline)	Rock (uncovers at sounding datum)
high low Steep coast	Sand and Mud
Flat coast	Stony or shingly shore
Cliffy coast	Sandy shore
Rocky coast	Rubble

2-7. *Samples of shore and foreshore symbols from* Chart No. 1. *Technical definitions of stones, rubble, and the like are given in* "Choosing a Landing Site" *in chapter 10.*

2-8. *The paddler's perspective of a chart section (inset). Without local knowledge, it is often necessary to use compass bearings to identify the terrain.*

specific bays or passes when you are new to the area. In complex waterways, such as areas with many large rocks or small islands, much navigation time can be saved by keeping track of where you are as you paddle into new horizons.

Another element of chart reading that differs from backcountry map navigation—where you are free to climb to a higher elevation for a better view—is the low perspective of the land viewed from the seat of a kayak. Much of what is charted simply cannot be seen because it is blocked by the curvature of the earth. (The visible range of land is discussed in more detail in chapter 6.) A large island with two peaks might appear as two islands from some distance off, or a bluff well inland from the charted shoreline might appear as the edge of the land when viewed from a distance. In some cases, the only way to identify the various features in sight is to take compass bearings on them.

When given, the height of the land visible from the water is charted as elevation contours similar to those on topographic maps or as isolated hachure symbols that mark only the peak locations (see fig. 2-9) and their height. The hachure symbols often imply that a peak or plateau is conspicuous, although when several appear in the same direction, they must be identified from their relative heights, which can be misleading when some are farther away than others. Elevation contours must be interpreted, as illustrated in figure 2-10. In areas where the elevation contours are very complex, it is often helpful to outline a particular high contour on the chart with a colored highlight marker in order to identify peaks and valleys from various perspectives.

Latitude, Longitude, and Nautical Miles

Cities are sometimes designed with streets running north-south and avenues running east-west. An address might be the intersection of 47th Street North and 122nd Avenue West. The street-avenue grid is a convenient way to specify precise locations in a city.

Latitude and longitude designate a similar, though invisible, grid on a global scale used for specifying locations anywhere on earth. The latitude of a place tells how far it is north or south of the equator. Its longitude tells how far it is east or west of the Greenwich meridian (see fig. 2-11). Latitude and longitude are expressed in degrees and minutes because they correspond to angular distances on the globe. I am now sitting, for example, near the intersection of latitude 47°39' North and longitude 122°20' West.

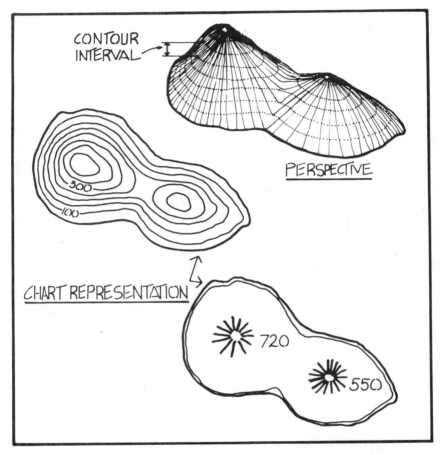

CONTOUR INTERVAL

PERSPECTIVE

CHART REPRESENTATION

500

100

720

550

2-9. *The contour and hachure representations used on nautical charts.*

Angles are subdivided just as time is: 1 degree (1°) equals 60 minutes (60') and 1 minute (1') equals 60 seconds (60"). To avoid confusion, caution is required with these units and notations. The only standard notations for angular minutes (') and seconds (") are optional notations for feet (1 ft = 1') and inches (1 in = 1"). Consequently, navigators should use only "ft" and "in" when abbreviating lengths. Also, even though one can write 30' of angle as "30 minutes" (whenever it is clear in context), it is never abbreviated 30 min, nor is 30 minutes of time ever abbreviated 30'. The same is true with seconds of angle and time.

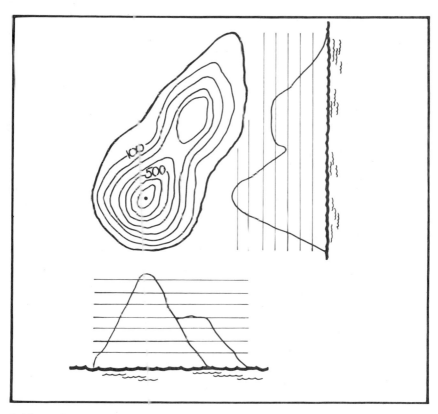

2-10. *A charted island as seen from the east and the south.*

The latitude-longitude grid is printed on all nautical charts, although there are few occasions to use it for specifying a location in typical kayak navigation unless you are using the Global Positioning System (GPS) of electronic navigation (see chapter 7). Near land, it is much better to tell and record positions relative to prominent landmarks, such as 2 miles north of Lookout Point. The only time latitude-longitude positions are used in kayak navigation is during the planning stages, when locating specific reference stations for tidal current predictions, or possibly when confirming the identity of a specific light or buoy. Nevertheless, this is reason enough to learn how this grid is printed on charts and to practice reading the latitude and longitude of some light or buoy (see fig. 2-12). Use the *Light List* to check

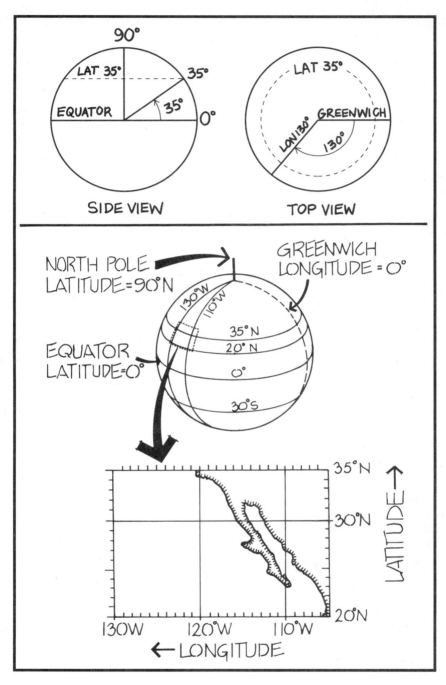

2-11. *Latitude and longitude as they appear on the globe and on nautical charts. Top section shows how latitude and longitude angles are defined.*

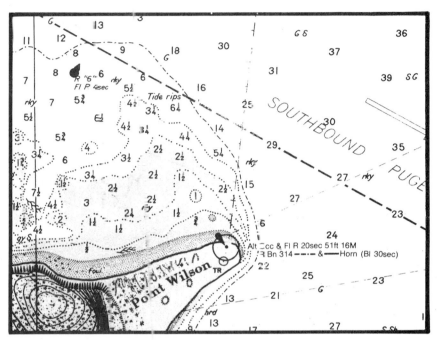

2-12. *A navigation light and buoy as represented on nautical charts. The* Light List *description of these is given in figure 2-13.*

your answer. It lists the precise latitude and longitude of all lights and buoys (see fig. 2-13).

Beyond locating positions, however, the latitude scale is useful for measuring distances between points. The north-south distance between consecutive latitude degree lines on any chart of any place on earth is always 60 nautical miles, because this is the way the nautical mile is defined. (To be formally correct, 1° of latitude is called 60 *sea miles,* but this unit does not have a fixed length; its average is 6,080 feet. A *cable* is one tenth of a sea mile. The distinction between sea miles and nautical miles is rarely made in American parlance.) One nautical mile is the distance you must travel north or south to change your latitude by 1'. A nautical mile is just over 6,000 feet, or approximately 15 percent longer than a statute mile. The official definition of a nautical mile is 1,852 meters, exactly. An official linear definition is required because the earth is not precisely spherical, so the practical definition in terms of latitude does not withstand fine scrutiny.

Nautical miles are the standard units of distance in navigation,

(1) No.	(2) Name and location	(3) Position	(4) Characteristic	(5) Height	(6) Range	(7) Structure	(8) Remarks
			WASHINGTON – Thirteenth District				
16470	*Point Wilson Lighted Buoy 6*	48 09.2 122 45.8	**Fl R 4s**		4	Red.	
	ADMIRALTY INLET AND PUGET SOUND TO SEATTLE (Chart 18441)						
	Admiralty Inlet						
16475	**Point Wilson Light**	48 08.7 122 45.2	**Oc W&Fl R 20s** 15s W fl 2.4s ec 0.2s R fl 2.4s ec	51	W 16 R 15	White octagonal tower on fog signal building.	RBN: 314 kHz Q (——•—)Il. Antenna at light tower. HORN: 1 blast ev 30s (3s bl). Emergency light Iso W 6s of lower intensity if main light is extinguished.
16480	KEYSTONE HARBOR ENTRANCE LIGHT 1	48 09.4 122 40.3	**Q W**	12		On piling.	Private aid.
16485	KEYSTONE HARBOR ENTRANCE LIGHT 2	48 09.4 122 40.2	**Fl R 4s**	13	5	TR on platform.	

2-13. *The* Light List *entry for the aids shown in figure 2-12.*

and they are also used to define the standard units of speed (knots).
A speed of 1 knot is a speed of 1 nautical mile per hour. The unit
"knots" derives from the historic sailing practice of measuring boat
speed by streaming a line (with precisely spaced knots along it) over
the stern and counting the number of knots that pass by in a particular time.

It is easy to appreciate the usefulness of the nautical mile in navigation. It makes the latitude scale on nautical charts into a miles scale
(see fig. 2-14) and helps interpret the separation of places on the

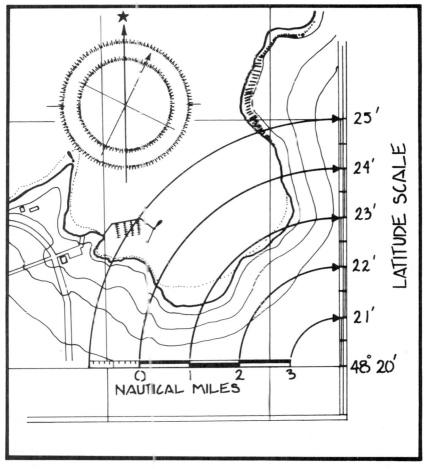

2-14. *The equivalence of latitude minutes and nautical miles (sea miles).*

basis of their latitude alone. It helps navigational thinking in general, even when not applicable to a particular kayak trip. You know immediately, for example, that Cape Flattery, Washington (at latitude 48° North), is 600 miles north of San Francisco, California (at latitude 38° North), and that Hawaii (at latitude 20° North) is 1,200 miles north of the equator. Or, that Cape Chelyuskin, Russia, the northernmost point of Asia, at 77°43' North, is just 737 miles (12°17') from the North Pole.

Bear in mind, however, that even though 1° of latitude always equals 60 nautical miles, the distance between consecutive longitude degree lines is not constant because these lines converge at the poles. Only at the equator is 1° of longitude equal to 60 nautical miles. At higher latitudes, the separation between longitude lines decreases, and the higher the latitude, the faster they converge.

Latitude north or south	Nautical miles per 1° of longitude
0°	60.0
15°	58.0
30°	52.0
45°	42.4
60°	30.0
75°	15.5

You cannot just subtract longitudes to figure the east-west separation of two places; this distance must be read from a chart. This is also the reason that the latitude-longitude grid on nautical charts is not square, but rectangular. Charts of the tropics (at low latitudes) show almost square grids, but those for Alaska (at high latitudes) are narrow rectangles, longer in the north-south direction than in the east-west (see fig. 2-15).

Reading Distances

Charts are made with all geographic features shown to scale. If two headlands are shown 4 inches apart on a 1:20,000 chart, the distance between them should be 80,000 inches, or 1.1 nautical miles (after some figuring). This method would work for any chart, but it is not practical. A simpler approach is to lay the 4 inches along the special distance scale printed somewhere on the chart, and read off the answer directly. These scales show distances in nautical miles, yards, and

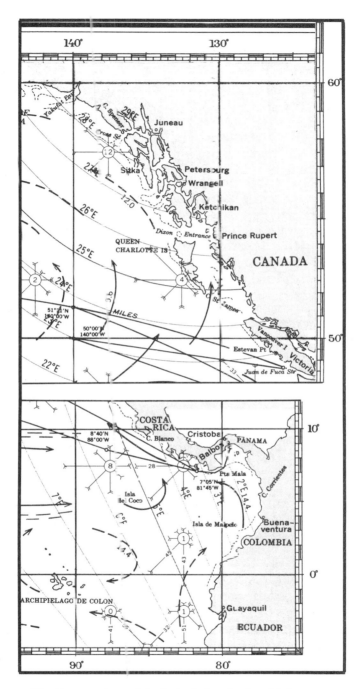

2-15. *A comparison of the latitude-longitude grid shapes at high and low latitudes.*

sometimes meters. But there is typically only one of these on each chart, and it may be under a fold in the chart when you need it.

A better and more common method is to use the latitude scale printed on the left and right border of each chart. Because 1' of latitude always equals 1 nautical mile, the latitude grid can always be used for a distance scale. To find the distance between two points using the latitude grid, measure the distance between the two points in any convenient units (inches, finger widths, or a handspan) and then transfer this length to the latitude scale. If the measured length spans 5' of latitude, the two points are 5 nautical miles apart. Latitude grids on charts with scales 1:40,000 or larger are divided into angular minutes and seconds, so this still takes a quick conversion to figure equivalent distances. For each chart used, or each exposed section of a folded chart, it is best to label some section of the latitude scale in miles or feet using the conversions given below, as shown in figure 2-16. This saves doing the arithmetic each time it is used. The following are a few convenient conversions (the values in feet are rounded off).

Latitude interval		Nautical miles		Feet
1° = 60.00'	=	60.00		
1.00' = 60"	=	1.00	=	6,000
0.25' = 15"	=	0.25	=	1,500
0.10' = 6"	=	0.10	=	600
5"	=	0.08	=	500
1"	=	0.02	=	100

The actual way a distance measurement is performed depends on where and when it is done. Reading chart distances at home when planning a trip, it is best to use a pair of dividers—a standard drafting tool with two pointed legs that are hinged so they can be set at any desired separation. The hinge is stiff enough that the dividers hold their settings as you move them from one place to another, as shown in figure 2-17. If the two locations of interest are farther apart than the dividers will extend, set the dividers to some convenient interval (like 1 nautical mile) on the latitude scale, then "walk" the dividers between the two points, and count the number of steps. The last step will be some fraction of a mile, which can be read from the labeled part of the latitude scale and added to the sum. This is also the way to measure crooked routes around land masses.

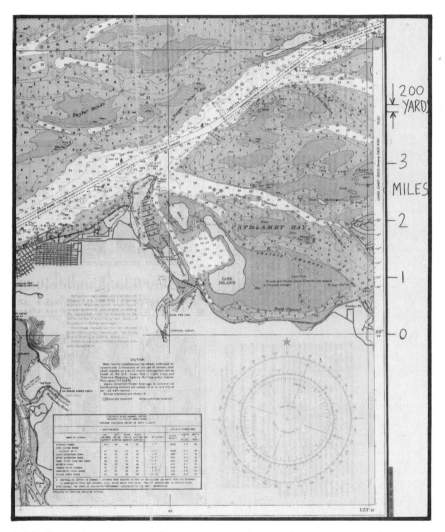

2-16. *Preparing a chart with prominent and convenient distance scales.*

Most paddlers leave their dividers at home and improvise distance measurements when underway or ashore. Two fingers used as dividers, two marks on a piece of paper, or a thumb held on a ruler's edge to mark the length will transfer a distance to the latitude scale adequately for occasional measurements. Besides, divider points are a definite hazard to any waterproof bag, and why carry something that

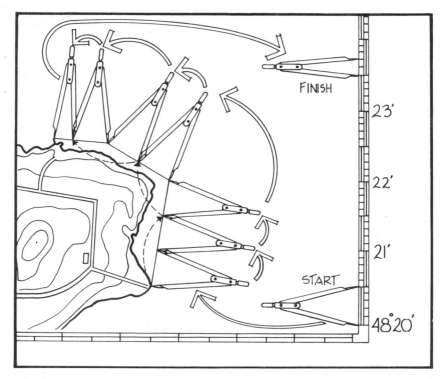

2-17. *Walking dividers across a chart to measure distance. The distance shown is 3.2 miles, measured in half-mile steps.*

can be done without? It is unlikely they would ever be used from the cockpit. A fundamental goal of kayak navigation is to navigate as much as possible by eye and hand alone, and this is best accomplished by careful planning and chart preparation before departing. This includes laying out routes and noting distances along them on the chart. With good planning, most numbers needed underway should already be noted on the chart. Examples are given in chapter 11.

When planning a long trip using a chart with a scale smaller than 1:80,000, you will notice that the special distance scale is missing, leaving no option to the latitude scale for measuring distances on these charts. Because of the mathematical way the spherical earth is projected onto the flat paper of a nautical chart, there cannot be a single distance scale that represents the entire chart of a very large region. One consequence of this projection was mentioned earlier: the rectangular latitude-longitude grid grows narrower at higher latitudes. When the chart covers a large latitude range, this grid contraction is apparent on a single chart and the length of a latitude interval is longer at the top of the sheet than it is at the bottom. It is still true that 1' of latitude equals 1 nautical mile everywhere on the chart, but because the latitude grid is expanded at the top, the number of inches per mile will be larger at the top of the chart than it is at the bottom.

To find the distance between two points at the top of a small-scale chart, use the latitude scale at the top of the chart. For points near the bottom, use the latitude scale at the bottom of the chart. Again, this is only a concern when reading distances from charts with scales smaller than 1:80,000. The absence of a separate distance scale on a chart is the sign that this procedure is required. When a distance scale is given, any part of the latitude scale can be used for any part of the chart.

Reading Directions

Nautical charts are made (mathematically projected) the way they are so that they can be used to find the direction from one point to another. To appreciate the problem on a global scale, imagine two points, A and B, marked on the skin of an orange, which you then peel and squash flat. Because north is not a unique direction on the peel, it is nearly impossible to tell from the flat peel how to get from point A to point B. It is not even easy with the peel in place on the orange. Nautical charts solve this problem, and the only price to be paid is the unusual way that distances must be measured on charts of larger areas, as mentioned earlier.

On all nautical charts, north is a unique direction everywhere on the chart, and on almost all charts this direction is straight up, toward the top of the page. The only exceptions are small-craft folio charts and river charts, which are oriented in whatever direction best matches the run of the waterway to the shape of the page.

Going back to the basics, finding the direction from some point A to some point B means finding out how many degrees to rotate away from north when standing at A, in order to face toward B. One way to read this from a chart is to draw a line straight north from point A and another line that runs from point A to point B, and then use a protractor to measure the angle between these two lines (see fig. 2-18). With this procedure you might find, for example, that point B lies 60° to the right of north. But this is more a principle than a practical method.

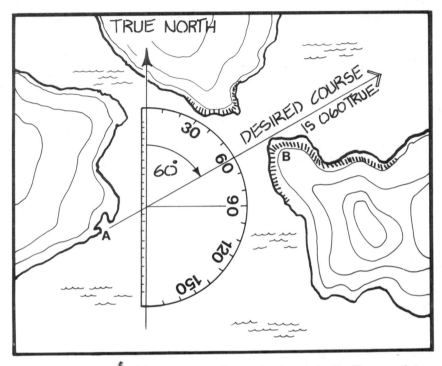

2-18. *The definition of the true course from point* A *to point* B. *True north is toward the top of the chart in all charts except some small-craft folio charts.*

Instead of taking a protractor to the line between A and B, the more traditional approach is to take the line to a protractor. Circular protractors oriented toward the north, called *compass roses,* are printed several places on each chart for this specific purpose (see fig. 2-19). As with measuring distances, the actual way the line of interest is transferred to the compass rose depends on when and where it is done.

When planning a trip at home, another special plotting tool called parallel rulers is one convenient way to transfer lines to and from the compass rose without changing their orientation. A typical application is to draw the route you intend to follow on the chart as a series of straight-line segments, and then use parallel rulers and a compass rose to determine what a compass should read when paddling along each leg of the route, as shown in figure 2-20. Details are discussed in later sections on piloting, dead reckoning, and trip planning.

Most charts have three circular scales on each compass rose. The

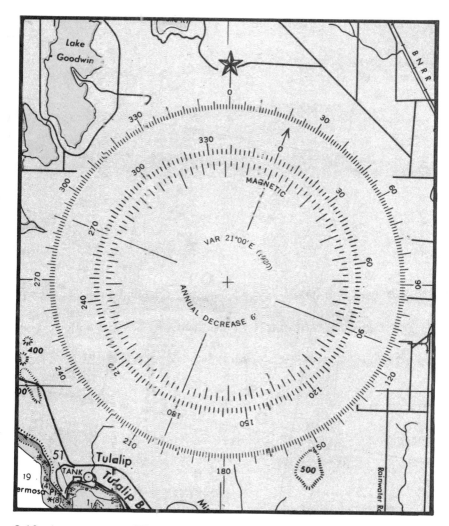

2-19. *A compass rose. The outer scale is used for true directions; the middle scale is used for magnetic compass directions; the innermost scale is a magnetic scale marked off in compass points (these are not used in modern navigation).*

outer scale is a *true scale* oriented toward geographic (true) north. The middle and inner scales are *magnetic scales* oriented toward magnetic north. The middle scale is the one used almost exclusively, because it is the one that shows what compasses should read. There is little call if any for the true direction given by the outer scale, because

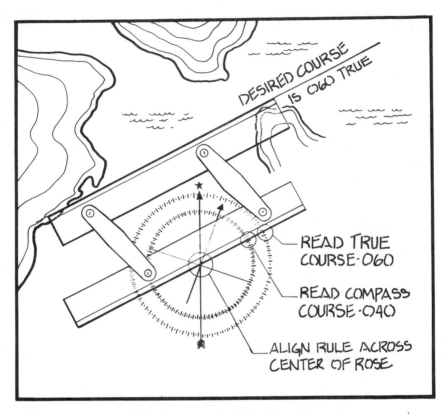

DESIRED COURSE IS 060 TRUE

READ TRUE
COURSE·060

READ COMPASS
COURSE·040

ALIGN RULE ACROSS
CENTER OF ROSE

2-20. *The use of parallel rulers to read the direction of a compass course. A pencil rolled from the course line to the compass rose is a makeshift alternative method. The use of various plotting tools is covered in chapter 6.*

a kayaker's only practical reference is the compass.

The innermost scale is also on the magnetic orientation, but it is divided into *compass points,* not degrees. Compass points mark the cardinal and intercardinal directions such as (for the northeast quadrant) north, north by east, north-northeast, northeast by north, and northeast. This scale remains on charts mostly for the sake of maritime tradition. Each compass point is 11.25°. The salty phrase "Ship ho!, two points on the starboard bow," means "Look, a ship is in sight, about 22.5° to the right of the front of the boat."

When dealing with chart and compass directions in navigation—of kayaks or ships—it is best to use specific numerical angles on a 0-360° scale, rather than relative angles or descriptive labels. When asked the direction to paddle, the answer "340" is less likely to cause confusion than "north-northwest" or "20° west of north." Furthermore, isolated phrases like "due east" or "north-northwest" always imply true directions unless otherwise specified. Another valuable custom is to preface directions that are numerically less than 100° with a zero. When telling the direction to paddle, say 075 (zero seven five or "oh" seven five), rather than just 75 (seventy-five). These customs minimize confusion in communications and record keeping.

Strangely enough, of all the directions used in navigation, none is called a "direction." Standard navigation practice calls for the following distinctions in names:

Direction name	Meaning
Heading	Direction the boat is pointed
Course	Direction you want to go
Bearing	Direction to some landmark
Course over ground	Direction you are actually moving
Course made good	Direction from where you started to where you ended up

As a kayaker paddles the compass *course* 050, the *heading* might oscillate between 040 and 060 with passing waves, but the *bearing* to Lookout Point remains 135 magnetic. "They were paddling course 060 according to the chart, but the current was strong and their actual *course over ground* was about 080, so the Inlet was not in sight when they got across." "We paddled course 030 from 7 A.M. till 10 A.M. and then turned to paddle 050 until noon, and when the fog lifted, we were right at Seal Inlet, so our *course made good* was 060 as planned." There are other directions in navigation with special names, but these are the fundamentals that others are based upon (see fig. 2-21 and further discussion in Chapter 7).

Aids to Navigation

In marine navigation there is a distinction between *navigational aids* and *aids to navigation*. Anything used on board to assist navigation is called a navigational aid. Examples include charts, books, compasses and other instruments, plotting tools, binoculars, and even special procedures. Things external to a vessel that assist with navigation are called aids to navigation. These include lights, buoys, daymarks,

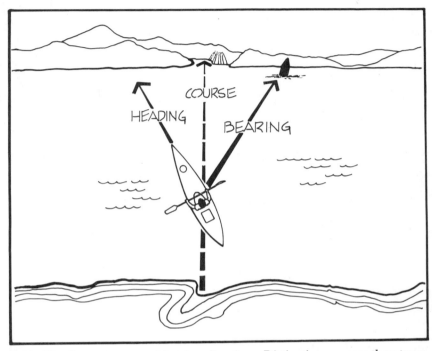

2-21. *Heading, course, and bearing directions. Distinctions among these terms are important in navigation. Course over ground (COG) and course made good (CMG) are illustrated in Chapter 7.*

foghorns, and various radio transmissions. The distinction in terminology often clarifies the context of American writings on navigation, although this distinction is not made in British usage.

All aids to navigation are listed in the Coast Guard's annual publication *Light List*. The terms *lights* or *lighted aids* mean those specifically placed along a waterway as aids to navigation. Their positions and descriptions are included on charts and in the *Light List*. Most are maintained by the Coast Guard but others are "private aids" maintained by other organizations to aid local boating or commercial operations. In contrast to lighted aids, the lights carried on vessels to identify their type and motion are in a separate category with separate definitions and rules. Vessel lights (see chapter 10) are not discussed in the *Light List;* they are covered in the Coast Guard's *Navigation Rules.*

Lights

The size and brightness of lighted aids vary from a simple bulb on the end of a post, barely visible from 1 mile off, to giant structures housing the brightest lights in the world, some of which can be seen from more than 25 miles off. The brightest lights are located in conspicuous places such as a point of land or a prominent place along a cliff. They are valuable landmarks even when they are not lighted, so it is important to be able to identify them from their charted or tabulated descriptions. Lights are on from sunset to sunrise, although most are operated automatically by light-sensitive switches so they do come on during daylight hours in the reduced visibility of fog and rain. Unfortunately, a bulb on a post and a giant lighthouse or tower have the same chart symbol: a small purple teardrop (meant to represent a light flash) emanating from a black dot placed at the precise location of the light (see fig. 2-22).

The prominence of the structure housing the light is best determined from its *Light List* description, although it can often be judged from the light's characteristic noted on the chart beside its symbol. Simple lights without prominent structures have charted labels such as:

Label	Meaning
F	White light, always on
F R 25ft	Red light, always on, positioned 25 feet above the high-water tide line
Qk Fl	White light, flashes on once a second
Fl 4sec	White light, flashes on once every 4 seconds
Fl G 6s "3"	Green light, flashes on once every 6 seconds with the number "3" on the structure
Iso 6sec 80ft	White light, on 3 seconds and off 3 seconds, positioned 80 feet above the high-water tide line

The abbreviations used to describe lights and their meanings are given in the *Light List* (see figs. 2-13 and 2-23); they are discussed further in chapter 10 (notice that "seconds" might be abbreviated "s" or "sec" in light labels). These and similar notations next to the teardrop imply the light has a simple mounting: on a post, on the end of a pier

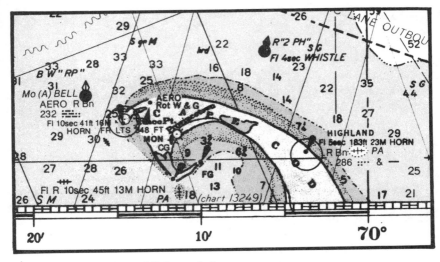

2-22. *Samples of charted light symbols.*

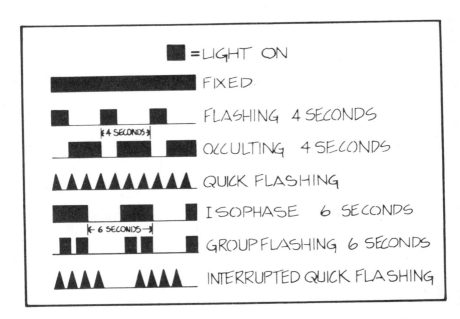

■ = LIGHT ON

FIXED

FLASHING 4 SECONDS

OCCULTING 4 SECONDS

QUICK FLASHING

ISOPHASE 6 SECONDS

GROUP FLASHING 6 SECONDS

INTERRUPTED QUICK FLASHING

2-23. *Samples of light patterns used on aids to navigation. A complete list is in the introduction to the* Light List.

or breakwater, or on some relatively plain concrete, steel, or wooden structure on shore or in the water. The only part of this notation that might help identify the light as a landmark is the height of the light when given. When not given on the chart, the height is usually given in the *Light List.* These notations do not represent lighthouses, but they must be fixed to land as opposed to a buoy or other floating structure—lighted buoys do not use the teardrop symbol, and their charted notations are in italics, as are the descriptions of all floating aids. Although these labels do not represent bright lights, the actual brightness of these lights cannot be deduced from their labels or symbols, nor can their range of visibility from a kayak be deduced from these data alone. The visible range of these lights must be figured from the brightness and height of the light given in the *Light List,* as explained in chapter 10.

When the structure of the light must be guessed from a chart without a *Light List* available, the charted clue that a light might be a lighthouse or conspicuous tower is an additional notation of its brightness following the other characteristics of the light. A light's brightness is specified by its *nominal range* (in nautical miles) with a notation such as "10M" following the other data on the light. The nominal range of a light is how far it can be seen in clear weather when the observer's view of the light is not limited by the curvature of the earth. It is important to remember, however, that this charted range is not how far you are able to see the light from a kayak; it is just a measure of the brightness of the light and a clue to the type of structure you might look for to use the light as an unlit landmark in daylight. From a kayak's low perspective, the curvature of the earth limits the range of visibility, so it is usually the height of the light that determines how far it can be seen, not the actual brightness of the light.

As a rule of thumb, any light listed with the nominal range of 14 miles or more is probably a lighthouse or other large tower, often painted in a conspicuous pattern.

Not prominent structures	Lighthouse or tower
Fl 6sec 27ft 10M	Gp Fl (2) 6sec 40ft 14M
I Qk Fl 15ft 6M	Fl 5s 39ft 15M
Fl 6sec 21ft 11M "1"	Alt Fl W & R 10sec 27ft 16M
Iso 6s 30ft 6M	Gp Fl (3) 10 sec 27ft 19M

The nominal range, however, is only a guideline to the type of structure; a few simple flashing lights that are very bright are on quite plain structures. A light in Hawaii, for example, labeled "Fl W 15sec 169ft 24M" is on a plain skeleton tower 20 feet tall.

A complex flashing pattern is another clue to a prominent structure because these patterns require large rotating lenses that need large structures to house them. With a *Light List*, however, you need not guess the form of the structure from its charted label; the structure type of each light is included in the light's description. The Coast Guard further classifies each aid in the *Light List* by type style.

Primary seacoast lights are in upper case in boldface:
NORTH HEAD LIGHT Gp Fl W 30s 194ft 26M.

Secondary lights and large navigational buoys are upper and lower case in boldface:
Point Bonita Light Occ W 4s 124ft 18M.

River, harbor, and other lights are all upper case:
ANITA ROCK LIGHT Qk Fl W 20ft 6M.

Lighted buoys are in italics:
Blossom Rock Lighted Bell Buoy BR I Qk Fl 6M.

Unlighted fixed aids and unlighted buoys are in upper and lower case:
Village Rock Daybeacon 12.
Deep River Channel Buoy 8.

Whenever lights are numbered, the numbering follows the same sequence used for neighboring buoys described below.

Buoys

Buoys are used to mark waterways much as street signs are used along highways. Buoys, however, convey their information with their shape, color, sound, and numbering rather than with the use of words and arrows. It is rarely necessary for a kayaker to know the fine details of the various buoyage systems used throughout the world, because the purposes of buoys are usually clear from their charted locations. Kayakers might, in some special areas, follow buoys as they would street signs, but they are far more commonly used for reference marks in piloting rather than guides to the proper route.

Remember, however, that buoys might not be precisely where the chart shows them to be. They are fixed to the bottom only with an anchor, and the anchor can be dragged in strong current or wind (or from collisions with vessels that pull them off station). Those susceptible to drag are also occasionally repositioned in search of more stable locations, and these changes might not be shown on the latest chart edition. Piloting with buoys must be done with caution. Some buoys at river bars and other inlets are used to mark shifting sandbars. These are often not even charted because their positions change frequently. Buoys also are used to mark dangerous shoalings—of interest to kayakers because of the influence of shallow water on current flow and sea state. Yellow or yellow-and-white buoys are used for special purposes such as marking temporary dangers and restricted areas.

The meanings of specific buoys and conventions of the various buoyage systems used in specific areas and countries are explained with diagrams in the backs of the *Light List* and *Chart No. 1*. The primary use of buoys is to mark the safe boundaries of channels or other waterways, although safety in this sense is relative to the size of the vessel. If a shoaling, for example, extends out to near the middle of a waterway, the end of it would be marked with a buoy. In this situation, the waterway viewed from a vessel might look much the same on either side of the buoy, so a mariner approaching this buoy must either look at the chart (to see what the buoy marks and from this know which side to pass it on) or be able to "read" this instruction from the buoy itself.

Buoys that mark channel boundaries are red on one side of a channel and green on the other side. The most common rule for interpreting buoys in *U.S. and Canadian waters* is "red right returning." The rule is a reminder that vessels traveling toward more inland waters ("proceeding from seaward") should pass buoys in such a way as to keep red ones on their right (starboard) side and green ones on their left (port) side. When headed toward the sea, the reverse is true: A vessel approaching a red buoy anywhere within a waterway that leads toward the sea should steer right of the buoy, so the buoy passes on the left side of the boat. If it were a green buoy, the vessel would steer to the left of it, leaving the buoy to the right. For kayakers, this rule is valuable for predicting the routes of larger vessels seen approaching buoys, so that they can keep clear of them. Along coastal routes or on inland waters where the "returning" direction is uncertain, the conventions illustrated in figure 2-24 are used to define this

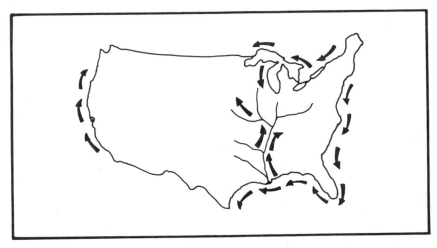

2-24. *U.S. conventions on the "returning" direction for coastal waters. Buoy and daymark numbers increase in the directions shown.*

direction for the purpose of buoy placement and numbering.

Besides the color of the buoy, which might not be discernible in twilight or when viewed toward the sun, shape, number, and sound signals also are used to distinguish buoys:

In the returning direction

Left-side buoys
Solid color
Green
Can shape
Odd numbers
White or green lights

Right-side buoys
Solid color
Red
Nun shape
Even numbers
White or red lights

Midchannel or junction buoys

Striped two-colors
Various shapes
Letters without numbers
Red, green, or white lights

When the color of a buoy is uncertain, its shape might identify its type. The can shapes and the truncated cone shapes called "nuns" are

2-25. *Buoys and daymarks along a channel. Associated chart symbols are shown next to each aid. Complete definitions are in* Chart No. 1.

illustrated in figure 2-25. The whistles, bells, and gongs placed on some buoys are activated by wind and waves. The bell and gong sounds are similar if heard separately, although bells are higher pitched. Bells can be distinguished from gongs because each device has several clappers. The several bells all have the same tone, whereas the several gongs have different tones. If a buoy heard in the fog makes different tones, it is a gong buoy. If it makes all the same tone, it is a bell buoy. There is no consistent convention for which sound signal is used on which buoy. Relatively few buoys have sound signals; buoys with sound signals are usually lighted.

Buoys are numbered sequentially with the numbers increasing in the returning direction, toward more inland waters—usually, but not always, the direction of the tidal flood. New sequences begin at new channels and at the intersections of waterways. Occasionally the numbers are out of order or a number is skipped (permanently or temporarily, during repairs), but they will always be odd on the left side and even on the right side. Buoys marking the sides of channels are solid colors (green or red) and all are numbered. A few have numbers and letters such as 2D or 8A.

(Solid color buoys in Canada, on the other hand, do have numbers and letters. The letters are area designators as defined in the Canadian *Light List*. The odd-even numbering convention, increasing toward more inland waters, is the same, however. Details on all Canadian aids and conventions are listed in *The Canadian Aids to Navigation Systems,* Canadian Coast Guard Publication TP 968E.)

Buoys marking the entrances, middles, or junctions of channels are painted two colors (white with orange or red; or red and green). These buoys are lettered rather than numbered. The letters are often chosen from the initials of the name of the buoy: Blossom Rock Buoy is lettered BR, the Yaquina Bay entrance buoy is labeled Y. Sequential letters are used on sequences of buoys: the sequence of midchannel buoys that leads south to Seattle, Washington, along Puget Sound is labeled SA, SB, SC, and so on. Proceeding farther south, they switch to a Tacoma sequence: TA, TB, TC. Some buoy lettering, however, has no apparent significance.

There are numerous chart symbols for buoys, but the most common is a diamond extending from a dot that marks the location of the buoy. The diamond color matches the buoy color. A lighted buoy has an additional purple dot overlaying the position dot and part of the triangle. Notations next to a buoy symbol include its light characteristic, letters or numbers that name the buoy (those actually painted on

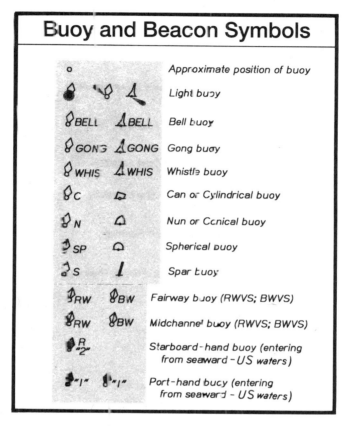

Buoy and Beacon Symbols

o	Approximate position of buoy
	Light buoy
BELL, BELL	Bell buoy
GONG, GONG	Gong buoy
WHIS, WHIS	Whistle buoy
C	Can or Cylindrical buoy
N	Nun or Conical buoy
SP	Spherical buoy
S	Spar buoy
RW, BW	Fairway buoy (RWVS; BWVS)
RW, BW	Midchannel buoy (RWVS; BWVS)
R "2"	Starboard-hand buoy (entering from seaward – US waters)
"1", "1"	Port-hand buoy (entering from seaward – US waters)

2-26. *Samples of buoy symbols from* Chart No. 1. *Photographs of each type of buoy are shown in the electronic version of* Chart No. 1.

the buoy are inside quotation marks), and sometimes letters to specify the shape and color of the buoy. Examples are shown in figure 2-26.

To prepare for buoy identification when planning a kayak trip, it is best to check the *Light List*, using *Chart No. 1* as a guide. In foreign waters, check the local equivalent of these publications when available, or refer to the International Association of Lighthouse Authorities (IALA) Maritime Buoyage Systems A and B explained in the *Light List* and in *Chart No. 1*. The "red right returning" rule, used in the United States and Canada, for example, is part of the IALA-B system; most other countries use the IALA-A system, where the rule is "red left returning."

Daymarks

In shallow inland waters, daymarks (also called daybeacons) are used much as buoys are to mark the waterway. They are unlighted signs on posts or other structures in the water or on shore. Their chart symbols are small triangles or squares corresponding to their actual shape. Letters beside the chart symbols for daymarks are coded to give the purpose, color, and shape of the mark. The code is given in the *Light List* and in *Chart No. 1*. Daymarks are named with numbers and letters similar to the way buoys are. Examples are shown in figure 2-25. Daymarks usually have reflective borders, which might help in locating them with a bright flashlight at night.

CHAPTER 3

Other Navigation Aids

Nautical charts are the primary source of navigation data for kayak trips, but they do not contain all of the pertinent navigation information you will need. In addition to tide and current references (discussed in chapter 7), several other sources should be consulted when planning a trip. This preparation takes time and effort, but it is worthwhile. Other than kayak tour guides, these additional references are not specifically intended for kayakers, so it takes time to ferret out the relevant parts: isolated notes on winds and currents, hazards and havens, or other bits of "local knowledge" (the mariner's catchall phrase for any information that aids navigation in a specific area).

Once you get there, local knowledge accumulates in the usual way, by direct experience. Good navigators, however, obtain as much of this knowledge as possible ahead of time. They know the sources and do the work to check them—which takes some running around because these references are rarely found in the same store or library.

Topographic Maps

Topographic quadrangle maps produced by the U.S. Geological Survey are used by hikers to find their way around the backcountry. They show detailed elevation contours and the locations of towns and roads. They are made in three scales, named by the latitude extent of the map. The two of interest to kayaking are the 7.5' series (scale of 1:24,000) and the 15' series (scale of 1:62,500). As with nautical charts, dividing the scale factor by 10,000 gives the number of nautical miles per handspan on topographic maps, although distance scales and mile markers along major rivers are given in statute miles on these maps. Similar maps from other countries use different scales. As with charts, scales larger than 1:40,000 or so are of most value to kayak navigation.

Topographic maps are always valuable to kayakers for locating campsites underway or access to put-ins at the start of a trip. Locations of roads, streams, swamps, houses and other structures, hiking trails, and the shape of the terrain near shore are presented much more thoroughly on topographic maps than on nautical charts. River expeditions usually call for topographic maps, as nautical charts are only available for large rivers that are accessible to large vessels. For coastal trips, topographic maps show more clearly than charts how to get back to civilization by land in the event of an emergency—or how to be reached from land after reporting an emergency by marine radio.

Because topographic maps always show terrain contours clearly (whereas nautical charts vary significantly in this aspect), they are often a better guide to shelter from wind near shore. A topographic map might help locate adequate shelter for a kayak downwind of a small hill on a spit, which would not be discernible from a nautical chart. And because wind is usually focused and accelerated in valleys, wind flow on inshore waters (or over a campsite at night) can often be more readily predicted from maps than from charts.

For actual navigation on inshore waters, topographic maps will not often be the primary reference, but there are exceptions. For some remote coastal regions, topographic maps show more detail along shore than their nautical counterparts (see fig. 3-1). The same is true in a few cases on inland waters. Some quadrangle maps (then called topographic-bathymetric maps) are made in conjunction with NOS/NOAA and consequently show depth contours and inshore rocks in some detail. But even in these special cases where quadrangle maps add much to navigation preparation, they do not replace nautical charts as required equipment. Topographic maps do not show navigation lights and buoys, they are not dependable for soundings or inshore rock locations, they do not warn of tide rips and other hazards, and very few can match the foreshore information given on large-scale nautical charts. Do check these maps when planning a trip, but compare them carefully with nautical charts of the same area before deciding they alone might be adequate. Topographic maps do not show compass roses, so marine compass navigation with them is not as simple as it is with charts. Sources for U.S. Geological Survey maps and several commercial versions are listed in Appendix A. Electronic versions on CD-ROM are also available along with special software for viewing them (See Appendix B for the Web site address).

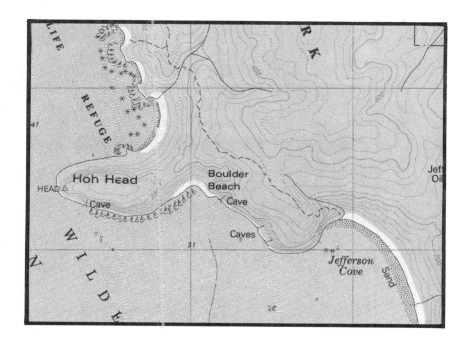

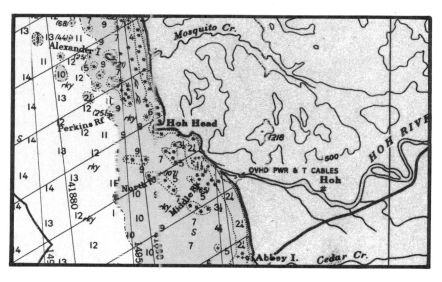

3-1. *Sections of a 7.5' topographic map (top) and the only nautical chart available (1:76,253) for the region (bottom). In isolated coastal examples, such as this one, topographic maps might provide more information on the waters and shoreline. Notice that these two sources do not agree on the positions of coastal rocks, as is often the case. Figure 3-4 contains the* Coast Pilot *description of this region. Jefferson Cove beach is 0.5 mile long.*

When planning a side trip up a coastal river, use a topographic map; it might provide an estimate of the river speed. River paddlers are accustomed to using topographic maps this way, because they show all rivers and streams. The drop rate of a river determines its speed, and this can be read from the elevation contours that cross the river. To figure the drop rate, subtract the elevation at the take-out site from that of the put-in site and divide by the length of the river between the two sites. Since rivers meander, the length measurement must be done with dividers set to a small separation. A string or light chain laid along the river is one way to get an accurate length. An average drop rate of over 30 feet per mile usually means fast water with rapids, although average drops can be deceiving. Sudden drops are not apparent in an average value found this way, and these might be difficult to discern from the maps. Books that discuss this use of topographic maps are listed in Further Reading, at the end of this book.

Coast Pilot and Sailing Directions

Pilots, *Coast Pilot*, and *Sailing Directions* are titles that various government agencies use for similar publications. They include the same types of information, in the same format. "Pilot" means guide, and these are guidebooks to the waterways they cover. Beyond this, the titles are misleading. *Coast Pilots* cover inland waters as well as coastal, and *Sailing Directions* have very little to do with sailing these days.

These publications are required reading for larger vessels because they include specific rules and regulations on shipping as well as navigation, weather, and current data. *Coast Pilots*, for example, show where shipping lanes must be followed in certain areas, or where international right-of-way rules change to inland right-of-way rules. They are required reading for kayakers as well, because these books include the bulk of navigational information not presented on charts. Again, much of their content is not pertinent to kayaking, but certain parts are essential to all mariners, in any craft. The *U.S. Coast Pilot* (see fig. 3-2) will be used as an example of these references; the content and use of others listed below are similar. (Sources are listed in the Further Reading section of this book.)

Publication	Source	Waters covered
U.S. Coast Pilot	USA (NOS/NOAA)	American
Sailing Directions	USA (NIMA)	foreign
Sailing Directions	Canada	Canadian
Admiralty Pilots	British	worldwide

United States Coast Pilot 8

**Pacific Coast Alaska:
Dixon Entrance to
Cape Spencer**

Seventeenth Edition

**U.S. DEPARTMENT OF COMMERCE
National Oceanic and Atmospheric Administration
National Ocean Service**

3-2. *Cover of a* U.S. Coast Pilot. *The appendix to each* Coast Pilot *contains a complete listing of addresses and telephone numbers of all agencies that provide navigational and related information for mariners.*

The *U.S. Coast Pilots* cover all U.S. waters in nine volumes, including inland waters such as the Great Lakes (volume 6), Puget Sound (volume 7, chapter 13), and San Francisco Bay and connecting waters (volume 7, chapter 7). Each volume has an introductory chapter on general information that applies to the waters of the entire volume. These are general discussions of navigation (specialized to specific areas) that should be read as a supplement to this book. The introduction is followed by chapters that divide the region into sections. Each section lists the pertinent chart, and then proceeds, point to point, along the shoreline on that chart discussing the areas. A map at the front of each volume shows the chapter sections outlined in it.

The appendix to each volume is an extensive list of all relevant navigation publications and where they can be obtained, as well as the addresses of relevant agencies including all Coast Guard and National Weather Service offices in the region covered. It also lists shore stations that provide medical advice by marine radio on request. The appendix is followed by a set of tables that include extensive marine weather statistics and various conversion tables.

Coast Pilots are published annually, but unlike tide and current tables or the *Light List,* an outdated *Coast Pilot* is still valuable. Piloting information relevant to kayaking does not change from year to year. Kayakers should check these volumes for weather, current, local hazards, and prominent landmarks in the area. Facilities for boaters also are listed, but this information is sparse and may be outdated.

Weather data are listed in three places in each volume of the *Coast Pilot:* the tables section at the back of the book, the separate introductions to each chapter, and in each section of each chapter covering specific areas. All three should be checked. The tables list climatic statistics that help plan the time of a trip and tell what wind, sea state, and water temperature to expect during each month. A sample is shown in figure 3-3. Text sections warn of local weather such as unusual storm patterns, hazardous afternoon sea breezes, and the probability of fog. Sections on the Hawaiian Islands, for example, might warn that the windward side of an island has frequent rain (often obscuring visibility), whereas the leeward side is dry. Individual sections also tell where to find shelter from certain winds, although a kayak might find shelter other places as well.

Information on currents in the individual sections is mostly a reminder of what you will find by checking the current tables or current charts, but in a significant number of other cases this *Coast Pilot* information is unique. Often enough, you will find current information here that does not appear in any other reference: rough rules on when currents turn relative to tides, the locations of large consistent eddies, the likelihood of tide rips, the average current speed at headlands or secondary passes not listed in current tables, as well as other details such as wind-driven currents or tidal current flow that are not predictable from current tables. Maximum currents in major channels reported in the *Coast Pilot* are sometimes significantly larger than those predicted in current tables. This apparent discrepancy—an important note for kayakers—can occur whenever the precise location of the reference station used in the current tables is not at the narrowest part of the channel. (These points are discussed further in chapter 8.)

Coast Pilots also list other matters of interest to kayakers. These

METEOROLOGICAL TABLE FOR COASTAL AREA OFF NORTH BEND
Boundaries: Between 42°N., and 44°N., and from 127°W., eastward to coast

Weather elements	Jan.	Feb.	Mar.	Apr.	May	June	July	Aug.	Sep.	Oct.	Nov.	Dec.	Annual
Wind ≥ 34 knots (1)	6.9	3.9	2.8	1.8	1.3	3.5	2.8	1.0	2.2	2.3	5.0	4.3	3.1
Wave height ≥ 10 feet (1)	28.0	25.6	31.2	6.4	15.7	11.6	10.2	1.4	3.5	15.0	20.4	20.0	10.1
Visibility < 2 naut. mi. (1)	3.4	4.1	1.6	4.4	1.0	2.9	5.3	9.9	6.9	5.7	6.4	4.7	4.5
Precipitation (1)	18.6	17.6	15.8	7.4	7.8	5.0	3.9	4.3	3.1	8.4	20.3	16.3	10.5
Temperature ≥ 85°F (1)	0	0	0	0	0	0	0	0	0	0	0	0	0
Mean Temperature (°F)	49.1	49.6	49.6	50.8	53.1	56.7	58.6	59.7	59.0	56.6	54.2	51.3	54.1
Temperature ≤ 32°F (1)	0	0	0	0	0	0	0	0	0	0	0	0	0
Mean relative humidity (%)	82	82	81	81	82	84	86	87	85	85	85	81	83
Sky overcast or obscured (1)	40.7	45.6	32.6	36.7	31.4	32.7	32.6	30.9	27.7	29.3	45.0	33.0	34.8
Mean cloud cover (eighths)	5.5	5.7	5.3	5.3	5.0	5.0	4.7	4.3	4.0	4.4	5.6	5.3	5.0
Mean sea-level pressure (2)	1018	1019	1017	1019	1019	1018	1018	1018	1017	1018	1017	1017	1018
Extreme max. sea-level pressure (2)	1036	1037	1034	1032	1031	1027	1038	1028	1033	1033	1034	1039	1039
Extreme min. sea-level pressure (2)	988	988	994	994	1000	1002	1000	1008	1004	979	984	984	984
Prevailing wind direction	S	S	S	N	N	N	N	N	N	*	S	S	N
Thunder and lightning (1)	0	0	0	0	0	0	*	0	*	*	*	0	*

(1) Percentage frequency.
(2) Millibars.
∗ 0.0-0.5%

These data are based upon observations made by ships in passage. Such ships tend to avoid bad weather when possible, thus biasing the data toward good weather samples.

3-3. Sample of the weather statistics from a U.S. Coast Pilot.

include the likelihood of deadheads (nearly submerged logs floating vertically), locations of kelp beds, commercial fishing practices in the area, locations and descriptions of public shoreline lands, restrictions near wildlife preserves, and customs procedures at the Canadian and Mexican borders. There is also extensive discussion of passageways into harbors or temporary shelters. When the *Coast Pilot* describes a passageway as hazardous to small craft, they are referring to vessels up to 65 feet in length. Kayaks can sometimes negotiate such passes more readily than larger vessels, but nevertheless, these warnings should be noted. Study the chart and current tables carefully to decide whether specific *Coast Pilot* warnings apply to kayaks as well. If there is shallow water along the edges, it can usually be used to avoid strong currents and rips; but if the edges are steep and rocky, they may be even more dangerous than midstream.

An equally important part of the *Coast Pilot*'s data is its tips on fair-weather navigation. Often it is difficult to identify peaks and valleys from charted elevation contours alone, especially from an uncertain position. Much of the *Coast Pilot*'s text is devoted to descriptions of the land as seen from the water (see fig. 3-4). It points out prominent landmarks useful for piloting fixes, and it warns of features that are deceiving when viewed from the water, such as one island that appears as two from certain perspectives, or a peak on a headland that appears as a separated island. Pictures and drawings of the coastline are included. It also tells the colors of hills and which structures near towns are conspicuous, in addition to other pieces of local knowledge that cannot be read from chart symbols.

Pilots and *Sailing Directions* for the same area (but produced by different agencies) could have more or less detail of interest to kayakers. The only way to know is to check all sources. When planning a trip to British Columbia, for example, the *U.S. Coast Pilots* would not be applicable because their coverage stops at the border. The *U.S. Sailing Directions* (No. 154) covers this area and it is these that should be read along with the *Canadian Sailing Directions,* the primary reference in this case. Paddling along the west coast of Mexico, the *U.S. Sailing Directions* (No. 80) and the British *Pilots* would be the primary references.

Coast Pilots are big books, and it is neither practical nor necessary to carry them on board. Pertinent notes can be made directly on the charts to be used, or photocopies of the pertinent sections can be carried along instead of the volume. Quick-print shops can drill holes in a *Coast Pilot* or a *Canadian Sailing Directions* and then cut off the binding so it can be ring-bound in selected parts. *U.S. Sailing Directions,* origi-

Chart 18480. For 5.5 miles from Destruction Island to Hoh Head, the coast trends in a general NW direction. The cliffs are 50 to 100 feet high, and many rocks and ledges extend 1.2 miles offshore in some places.

Abbey Islet, 3.5 miles NE of Destruction Island, is over 100 feet high and covered with trees. It is 200 yards off the cliffs. Many rocks are close S of it the most distant of which is **South Rock,** 46 feet high, 1 mile S, and 0.5 miles offshore.

At the mouth of **Hoh River,** 2 miles SE of Hoh Head, is a broad sand beach; the absence of cliffs for 0.5 mile is noticeable for a considerable distance offshore. In smooth weather the river can be entered by canoes, but the channel shifts. An Indian village is on the S bank at its mouth.

Hoh Head 200 feet high, is a bright yellow cliff covered with a dense forest. It projects a little over 0.5 mile from the general trend of the coast. A large cluster of rocks is off the S cliff of the head and covered rocks extend to about 1.6 miles offshore between the head and North Rock. A rock covered 2¼ fathoms lies 1.8 miles WNW of Hoh Head.

Middle Rock, North Rock, and **Perkins Reef** are other dangers within 1.5 miles off Hoh Head. Middle Rock, 65 feet high and black with vertical sides, is 0.8 mile off the mouth of Hoh River. North Rock, a mile S of Hoh Head, s 107 feet high and grayish in color, with steep sides; in the afternoon sun this rock shows white, which makes it a very distinct landmark. Perkins Reef is a long, bold, and jagged islet, 1.1 miles W of Hoh Head. This area has numerous other rocks, covered and bare.

The coast continues rugged and rocky from Hoh Head to La Push, 11 miles to the NW. The cliffs are 100 to 120 feet high, broken here and there by small streams. Several rocky islets, 25 to 120 feet high, and covered ledges extend in some places as much as 2 miles offshore.

Alexander Island, 121 feet high, is 2 miles NNW of Hoh Head and a mile offshore. It is covered with low vegetation and is flat-topped with steep sides. The island is prominent in hazy or smoky weather. A covered rock, 1.8 miles WNW of Alexander Island, is the outermost known danger in this vicinity.

3-4. *Sample text from the* Coast Pilot *that describes the region shown in figure 3-1.*

nally printed in loose leaf, are now also in bound volumes. Do not avoid doing this research for a second trip even if nothing relevant was found when you looked for an earlier trip to another location. Some remote places that kayakers go to are not mentioned at all in pilots, and some descriptions of other areas do not suit kayakers. In the long run, however, time spent going through these books will improve your navigation—even in those cases when it does not aid particular trips.

As of January 1999, U.S. *Coast Pilots* are not online, but chances are they will be in the future. Several volumes of the NIMA (National Imagery and Mapping Agency) *Sailing Directions* are online, and they clearly show what a wonderful resource this can be—although these are only for foreign waters. See Appendix B for link information.

The *Light List*

The Coast Guard publication called the *Light List* (see fig. 3-5) was mentioned in chapter 1 as an annual source of corrections to charted light and buoy data. But it is more than that. It includes information about lights and buoys that is not on charts, and the general information section of the *Light List* is comparable to that of *Coast Pilots*. At

3-5. *Cover of the* Light List.

some point it should be read as a supplement to this book for details of navigation by lights and buoys. It includes all definitions and conventions used in navigation by lights, as well as practical guidelines and technical details that are often crucial to understanding notes in other sources. (Kayak navigation at night is covered in chapter 10.)

The bulk of the *Light List* text consists of details on each light, buoy, and daymark in the region covered by the volume at hand. A sample section is shown in figure 2-13. Each lighted aid has a unique *Light List* number. All are listed, although those located near intersections of major waterways may take longer to locate in the book because of the way it is organized. It breaks the covered region up into separate sections for seacoasts, rivers and harbors, and secondary channels, and then lists the lights sequentially along each subsection. A light at the mouth of a river might be listed in both the seacoast section and the river section, or it could be in just one of these sections. Sometimes both must be checked to find it. The same search might be required for lights at the mouth of a secondary channel onto a river.

The *Light List* is most important for navigation at night or in the fog, because it provides uncharted information on the visible range of lights and the bearings from which they are obscured, as explained in chapter 10. For daytime navigation, it tells of privately maintained aids (both lights and buoys) that are sometimes not shown on charts. It also describes locations and mounting structures of daymarks, which help with their identification.

When planning a trip, the *Light List* should be checked to verify charted aids and to find uncharted ones to add. Once in the right section of the book, it is easy to run down the list to make chart notes as the tabulation follows the shoreline in each section. Again, notes or copies are all that are needed on a trip, not the book itself. If there is a bright light in the region, it usually can be found in the index from the name of its location. The index gives the *Light List* number of the light (not a page reference), from which the light can be located in the book. If no such light exists, the names of prominent points or capes in the area might be found in the index, and they can guide you to the proper place in the book.

Tour Guides and Other References

The best source of local knowledge for kayaking is other kayakers who have been to where you want to go. The Further Reading section lists several kayak tour books that cover specific regions along with more general kayaking books that also discuss experiences in various areas. These should be checked for information about a planned kayak trip. It pays to follow a few known routes that such books describe before breaking new ground on your own, but try not to rely on any single reference when it comes to predicting conditions at a particular area. Whenever possible, check several references to a particular area and note the dates of the trips. Then check the weather statistics in the *Coast Pilot* to see if the writers' experiences were typical for the season and to learn what conditions could be present at the time you plan to go. Idyllic coastal coves in calm air can be hellholes when exposed to strong winds and big seas.

Magazines such as *Sea Kayaker, Canoe & Kayak, Paddler, Wavelength,* and *Atlantic Coastal Kayaker* are excellent sources of local knowledge. *Sea Kayaker* also lists the names and addresses of newsletters from kayak clubs and similar organizations on their excellent Web site. Memberships typically cost no more than the price of a book, and they provide access to a wealth of knowledge from experienced paddlers. Internet web addresses for these magazines and clubs are listed in Appendix B.

Sailor's travelogs or cruising guides are another potential source of local knowledge for nearly all waters of the globe. There are far too many of these to list in the Further Reading section; the best bet is to look through a good nautical bookstore once you have planned a trip to a specific place. Some of these books are very informative, especially with regard to shoreside attractions (or distractions), prominent landmarks, and occasionally with winds and sea states. Sailing magazines are another source. Regional magazines often include detailed cruising guides to waters in their area. Most paddling and sailing magazines are not carried by most libraries or even included in the *Reader's Guide to Periodical Literature,* so you must skim through compilations from friends or clubs to find articles of interest. You may also contact the magazine editors directly.

For broader preparation, look for specialized books whose very topics are local knowledge, such as Richard Thomson's wonderful book *Oceanography of the British Columbia Coast* and Environment Canada's excellent book *Wind, Weather, and Waves,* among others listed in Further Reading.

CHAPTER 4

Compass Use

Every kayaker on an extended trip will eventually need a compass of some kind. But even when it is not essential, a good marine compass—mounted on deck so it is always in view—is a valuable aid for many aspects of kayak navigation, and this value increases with usage. Although it is quite possible to paddle many safe and happy miles with little more than an occasional glance at an inexpensive hiker's compass, getting by without much compass use should not distract from the benefits of practiced compass use. Good navigation calls for frequent use of a good compass.

Compasses are used for steering, finding position, identifying landmarks, and monitoring the effects of wind and current. Within each of these broad categories are numerous specific applications. The primary use of a compass is to tell which way to go when it is not apparent from just looking around. When circumnavigating a large island, for example, a paddler faces new horizons at every corner. Often there are so many bays, headlands, and other islands in the background that the course to the pass around the next corner is uncertain (see fig. 4-1). To solve this common problem, locate your position on the chart and read the compass bearing from there to the pass using the chart's compass rose, as illustrated in chapter 2, figures 2-16 and 2-20. Point the boat in that direction using a compass, and the target should be dead ahead. From then on, you could paddle toward the target and not rely on the compass, although it still pays to keep an eye on the compass. After paddling toward the target for some time you might discover that the boat's compass heading has changed, even though the target has not left the bow. This means that

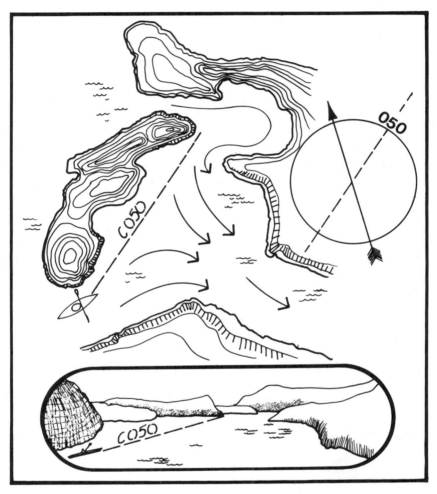

4-1. *Use of a compass to identify landmarks.*

current is pushing the boat off the original line to the target (as shown in fig. 4-2), which is another example of compass use: Compass readings have told you something about your position and motion, independent of its use as a steering guide.

Compass use in clear weather and daylight is often more a matter of efficiency than safety. In rare cases, a mistaken target could lead to dangerous waters, but such errors usually only lead to more work, not danger. Eventually the mistake becomes apparent, as does the extra distance that must be paddled to correct it. But if you are caught off-

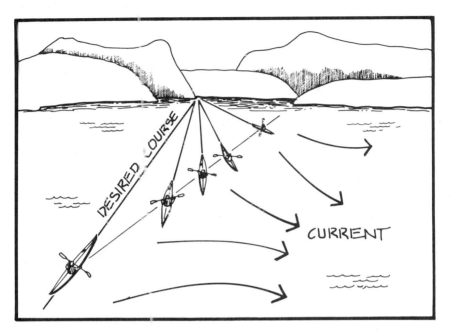

4-2. *A boat set off course by current with bow kept on a constant heading toward the target.*

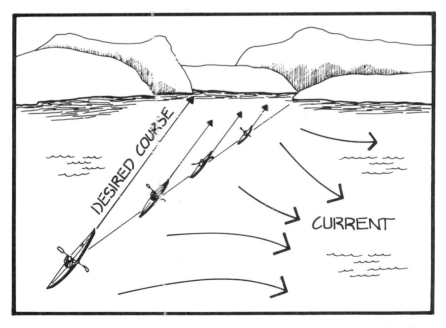

4-3. *A boat set off course by current with bow kept on a constant compass heading.*

shore when darkness or fog is setting in, it is essential to take a compass bearing to your destination while it is still visible. That bearing is the only way to get to your destination after landmarks fade away. As pointed out in the last example, it is equally important to know of any currents in the area and how to adjust the compass course to compensate for their effects (see chapter 9). Without the target in view, the effect of current on your course line will not be detectable (see fig. 4-3).

A compass is frequently required on long crossings. In some areas, for example, large open waters can be hazardous on summer afternoons when thermal winds (sea breezes) build to 25 knots or more. Such waters are usually calm in early morning, which makes this a good time to cross. But in the early hours of daylight, radiation fog that builds up overnight may not have burned off. A paddler might face a choice between paddling a compass course in calm water and fog, or waiting for clear weather and risk being caught on open water as the wind builds.

When relying on a compass, it is important to know what it reads, what affects the reading, and how to check the reading. A compass error of 6° causes a boat to slip sideways off its intended course line by 10 percent of the distance paddled (see fig. 4-4). Paddling at 3 knots, this compass error would take a boat off course by 0.3 mile each hour. Such a large compass error, however, would have an even worse effect on locating a position or judging current flow from compass bearings.

It is also fundamental to remember that the compass heading of a boat tells which way the boat is pointed, *not which way the boat is moving*. In the example of a paddler headed for the corner of an island (fig. 4-2), the paddler kept the boat headed toward the pass, and the compass course changed as current pushed the boat off the original course line. Had the pass been obscured by fog as the paddler maintained a constant compass (fig. 4-3), he or she would not have noticed that the pass moved off the bow as the current pushed the boat off course and thus would not have gotten there on that heading.

How a Compass Works

The earth's magnetic field flows northward like a prevailing wind, and compass needles align with this field as wind vanes align with the wind. The direction of magnetic field flow at any location is called *magnetic*

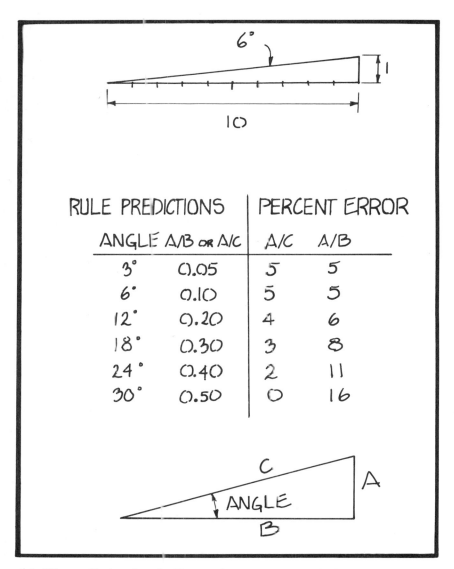

4-4. *The small-triangle rule. To a good approximation, the height of an angle of 6° is one tenth of the length of either side. The rule can be extended as shown to larger or smaller angels using multiples of 6°.*

north, but the name is misleading. This is not a unique direction world-wide. The field flow meanders around the magnetic terrain of the earth as it moves northward. In New England, magnetic north is toward a true direction of 340; in the Pacific Northwest is to toward 020.

The difference between magnetic north and true north at any location is called the magnetic *variation* of the place—in contrast to navigation on land where the same thing is called *declination.* Magnetic variation is labeled east (E) or west (W) depending on whether magnetic north lies to the east or west of true north. Magnetic variation along the Pacific coast of North American is easterly, decreasing from 27° E at Anchorage, Alaska, to 10° E at Cabo San Lucas, Baja Mexico. Along the Atlantic coast it is westerly, decreasing from 27° W at the Island of Newfoundland to 2° W at Miami, Florida. The line of zero variation runs northward along the gulf coast of Florida. Magnetic variation is given on all nautical charts, in the center of each compass rose (see fig. 4-5), along with the year it was measured. The additional note telling how it changes with time, such as "annual decrease 6'," is of no practical interest to kayaking. It takes many years for the variation to change a full degree. By the time this correction reaches a degree or two, the chart would be far outdated.

A standard marine compass is a magnetized needle attached to a circular card graduated in degrees. The north-seeking end of the needle is attached at the 000 position on the card. The card is balanced on a jeweled pivot within a dampening liquid. The 000 point on the card stays oriented toward magnetic north as the boat turns under it. The compass heading of the boat is read directly from the compass card using an index mark on the compass housing attached to the boat. The line drawn through the index mark and the pivot point is called the *lubber's line.* To read the proper compass heading, it must be parallel to the boat's centerline (bow to stern).

When a boat's compass heading is 050, the boat is pointed 50° to the right of magnetic north. If magnetic north in the area lies 20° to the right of true north (variation 20° E), the boat is pointed 70° to the right of true north. With this magnetic variation, a compass heading of 050 means a true heading of 070. The general rule for finding true directions from compass directions is to add the variation to the compass reading when the variation is east, or subtract the variation from the compass reading when it is west. "Correcting add east" is the standard reminder of this rule.

This correction of compass directions to get true directions, however, is rarely required in a kayak. Nautical charts show magnetic directions explicitly on the magnetic scales of compass roses, so there is no need for true directions. All inshore navigation can and should be

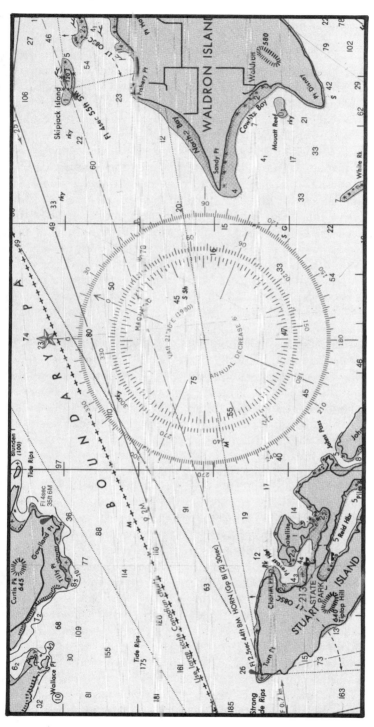

4-5. *A compass rose can be used for converting true to magnetic directions or vice versa. The line showing the boundary of the obscured sector of Turn Point Light has a true bearing of 260 and a magnetic bearing of 238. Accidentally, this line passes through the center of the compass rose on this chart.*

done with compass directions alone. If conversions between compass and true directions must be made, they can be read from a compass rose without knowing the rules, as shown in figure 4-5. Tidal current flow and the directions from which lighthouses are obscured are given in reference books as true directions. These can be converted to magnetic directions with a compass rose.

To read proper magnetic directions, however, the compass needle (000 on the compass card) must always point toward magnetic north, which means the earth's magnetic field at the compass site must not be disturbed by magnetic objects packed in the boat. Consider the wind vane analogy: If a wind vane is aligned with the natural wind and a fan is directed toward it, the vane will shift off the natural wind direction and point to whatever direction the true wind and fan wind add up to. A compass needle behaves the same way when equipment on the boat produces a disturbing magnetic field at the compass site. If a compass needle does not point to magnetic north, the compass is said to have *deviation* (see fig. 4-6).

When a compass has deviation, the compass heading it shows is not the proper magnetic heading of the boat. Nautical charts show magnetic directions; compasses show compass directions. With no deviation, these directions are identical, which is what every kayaker wants. With deviation, they are different, which is bad news for navigation. Furthermore, because a magnetic disturbance is from something in the boat, when the boat turns, the direction of the net magnetic field turns, which means the needle orientation depends on the boat orientation (see fig. 4-7). Consequently, a compass with deviation error on one heading will have different errors on other headings. A compass that reads 15° low when headed north could read 10° high when headed east. These errors cannot be predicted; they must be measured for each heading. Compass deviation is a nuisance to any navigator, but it is especially troublesome for kayakers because whatever causes it will likely change the next time the boat is packed. Compass errors measured for one packing will not be useful for the next.

Fortunately, it is easy to determine what will influence the compass, so the boat can be packed in such a manner that the compass is not disturbed. The primary troublemakers are metal objects containing iron. Potential sources of iron that pose a problem to a deck-mounted kayak compass are steel ammunition boxes (popular for waterproof and crashproof stowage of cameras and radios); large knives, axes, and stoves for camping; steel battery casings in flashlights; tin cans (which are actually made of steel); magnets in radio

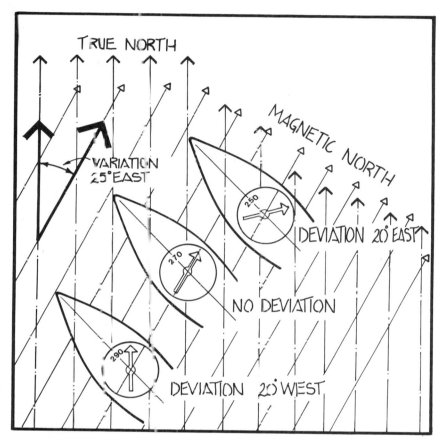

4-6. *Compass heading versus true and magnetic headings. When a compass has deviation, the compass needle does not point to magnetic north as it should.*

speakers; or guns; or portable freon air horns (an effective way to attract attention in traffic). A more subtle problem is the metal nickel, often used in metal plating as a base substrate. Chrome-plated brass (both nonmagnetic) might contain a thin layer of nickel, which could disturb a compass. Most stainless steels, on the other hand, do not cause magnetic disturbances, even though they contain both iron and nickel. The alloy structure alters its magnetic properties.

To test any object for magnetic disturbance, bring it up to the compass while closely watching the compass needle. If the needle does not move with the object touching the compass, the object is not a problem. If an object is a magnetic disturbance, like a weather

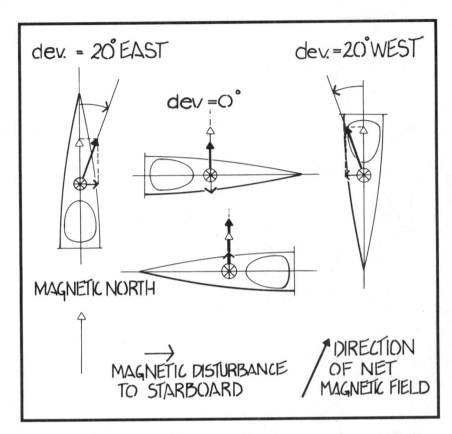

4-7. *How deviation changes with boat heading. The boat has a magnetic disturbance to starboard, which rotates relative to the earth's magnetic field as the boat turns. Compass needles point in the direction of the net magnetic field.*

radio, this test should show that the object must be kept at least three or four times its bulk dimension away from the compass to avoid shifting its reading. When checking a compass indoors with steel folding chairs nearby, the chairs should be moved three or four times the size of the chair away from the compass.

To learn the terms of compass use, muse about the analogy that God makes variation and man makes deviation.

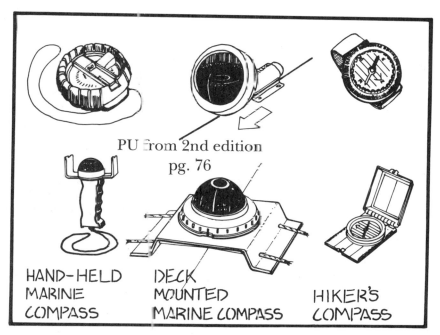

4-8. *Types of compasses: hand-held marine compass, deck-mounted marine compass, and hiker's compass.*

Types of Compasses

Compasses commonly used on kayaks include deck-mounted marine compasses, hand-bearing marine compasses, and hand-bearing hiker's compasses (see fig. 4-8). Marine compasses are designed for boats, so they work better for kayaking than hiker's models. Nevertheless, hiker's compasses are used in kayaking, so they are discussed here as well.

An important distinction between hiking and marine compasses is the way they are read. Marine compasses have the circular scale of numerical directions attached to the needle; hiking compasses have this scale attached to the compass housing—on a ring that can be rotated around the needle. When a marine compass turns (attached to a boat or held by hand), the numbers remain stationary, and the index mark on the housing circles the numbers to mark the compass direction. On hiking compasses, the numbers turn with the compass, so they must be rotated into alignment with the needle by hand be-

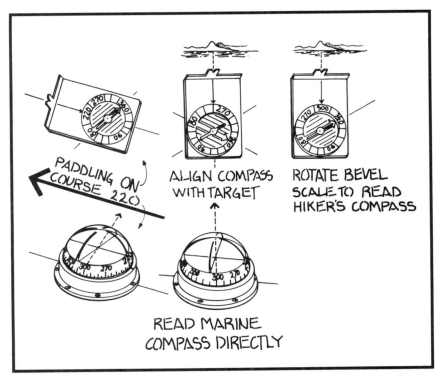

4-9. *The operation of a hiker's compass compared to a marine compass. Marine compasses can be read directly; hiker's compasses must be adjusted and then read.*

fore a compass direction can be read (see fig. 4-9).

Marine compasses are dome shaped, so the card can be read at large tilt angles as the boat rolls and pitches in a seaway, whereas thin, flat, hiking compasses tend to stick when tilted. A deck-mounted marine compass can be read in a seaway without touching the compass. To read a hiking compass, it must be kept level by hand as the numbers ring is rotated to align 000 with the needle position. Hiking compasses often have an adjustment to offset the 000 position for the local magnetic variation, so true directions can be read directly from the compass. This is convenient for land navigation using topographic maps, but it is not an asset to marine navigation using nautical charts. Marine compasses never have an adjustment for magnetic variation.

There are also significant differences among marine compasses. Larger well-damped deck compasses can be read to within a few degrees in calm water; smaller ones swing back and forth through many degrees in the best conditions. Larger models have the further advantage that they can be read when mounted farther forward, leaving more room for charts on the foredeck. In most cockpits, however, charts must be carried on the spray skirt to be read, so this is not a problem. The use of charts underway is discussed under Preparation in chapter 11. Do not mount your compass out of reach, however; in waves or rain, water drops must be wiped off occasionally in order to read it. Some compasses are mounted on a bracket above the deck; others require a hole to mount flush with the deck. One quality model of the detachable type is nicely designed to work equally well as a steering compass or a hand-bearing compass. Compass mounts are discussed further in chapter 11.

Deck compasses are meant primarily for steering. They are always in view, so paddling need not be interrupted to read a compass heading. This type is much preferable to a hand-bearing compass whenever a compass course must be followed with no landmarks in sight. Bearings to landmarks can be taken with deck-mounted compasses by pointing the boat at the mark. Hand-bearing compasses are stowed on the boat or paddler and only removed for occasional sights, either to choose a course or take bearings for a position fix. To use these in a single kayak, the boat must be stopped. Hand-bearing compasses have limited value in rough conditions that require continuous paddling or frequent bracing. Beware of small flat compasses used for dinghy racing. These are no more than hikers' compasses that mount on the boat. This style usually has a compass face marked off in quadrants of alternating colors. These are not intended for steering or taking bearings. They are just a questionable means of recording relative wind directions when racing small sailboats.

Hand-bearing compasses differ as much as steering compasses do. Some can be read to within one half of a degree, others to within only five degrees. Some have good dampening, others do not. There are two basic types. One is held by a handle at arm's length; the other is held up to the eye as the bearing is read through a lens and mirror from an internal scale. The latter style is more accurate and compact. Nighttime bearing sights require models with internal lights. Some hand-bearing compass lights are battery operated; others include a cell of radioactive gas that emits electrons onto a phosphor that lights up as a TV screen does. (Procedures for taking bearings are covered in chapter 6.)

High-quality deck-mounted compasses include internal magnets that can be adjusted to cancel out any deviation that might be present. These adjustments are important for large boats but have no practical value for kayaks. On the contrary, they can cause trouble if not set to zero—effectively adding deviation to an otherwise accurate compass. If your compass has these adjustments, the first step is to check that they are set to their neutral position, and if not, to do so.

The adjustment screw on the fore-and-aft axis of the compass (sometimes extending through the housing and accessible from either end) usually controls east-west errors; the one perpendicular to it on the side of the compass controls north-south errors. To check their adjustment, set the compass on a table, well away from magnetic materials, and draw a line on the table oriented toward 000 according to the compass. Then turn the compass around facing the other direction on the line. If the north-south adjustment is set to neutral, the compass should now read 180. If not, turn the north-south screw one eighth of a turn and make the check again, repeating the process until opposite readings are achieved. Then do the same on a 090-270 line using the other screw. Then double-check the north-south line again. The neutral position of the adjustment screw usually corresponds to vertical or horizontal alignment of the screw slots.

Paddling a Compass Course

When circumstances require you to follow a particular compass course that is read from a chart or chosen by other means, you must paddle the boat in such a way that the compass always reads this particular value. This is called "steering by the compass," but the name is misleading and it makes learning to do it well more difficult. In practice, when steering by the compass you rarely look at the compass, but instead concentrate on various reference marks on the horizon in front of the boat. These references could be landmarks, distant cloud formations, stars, or just a slight change in the shading of the sky.

The procedure is to bring the bow in line with the desired compass heading and note what reference mark lies dead ahead or just to one side of the bow. Then paddle to keep that reference mark at the same place on the bow. When a wave or passing through leads you off course, you will detect it by noting that your reference mark is no longer where it was, relative to the bow. Steer the boat toward the mark, and when your mark is in place, the compass will read properly. You need only check the compass occasionally to verify that the mark is still a good one for the course, or whether its proper place on the bow should be adjusted. All such marks must be considered temporary when following a compass course—some might last hours, others only a few minutes. When one mark is no longer useful, choose another that is on line, and steer toward it.

On the other hand, if you try to follow the compass card itself, or compass needle with a hiker's compass in view on the deck, your heading will swing erratically, and could pose control problems in a seaway. Even in waves where the course must be altered temporarily at each wave, you turn back to your mark to set up for the next wave, and only then check the compass. If you rely on the compass reading when course adjustments must be fast, you might turn the wrong way; the card might have overshot the mark on the last swing and be way off at the time you look at it.

Bearing these cautions in mind, whenever your mark is lost in the waves or the fog is too thick to see anything at all, there is no choice but to steer directly by the compass card. In these circumstances, a good marine compass is worth its weight in gold. On these compasses you see the full face of a well-damped card and your "steering mark" is the course number on the card. If the number is to the right of the index pin, turn right to come back to course. If your compass is a dome or disk with the numbers on its side, the opposite will be true. Think of your course number as the bow, and steer it toward the index pin. In one case you bring the bow to the number; in the other, you bring the number to the bow. After practicing with the same compass, it becomes automatic. At night the compass must be illuminated as discussed in chapter 10.

To steer by a hiker's compass without reference marks is more work but still possible in moderate conditions. Set the bevel ring of compass directions to your desired course, align the compass with the centerline, and fix it so it stays there—either with tape, under elastic cord, or tucked into a transparent chart bag. Then come onto the course that aligns the north end of the needle with the north end of the north-south line marked on the compass. With this arrangement, the north-south line can be viewed as the centerline, which you must steer toward the needle whenever you fall off course. The principle is easier than its practice, however, because the line is sometimes difficult to see, the needle is not well damped, and it sticks frequently with the motion of the boat. If you end up steering this way very often, you will think of ways to improve the hiker's compass for this application, and eventually you will invent the marine compass.

Checking a Compass

Hand-bearing compasses (marine or hiker's) never include internal adjustment magnets, and they are typically not influenced by external disturbances because they are held far from these when used. Generally, it is safe to assume they read properly. Deck-mounted compasses, however, have more frequent and varied uses in kayak navigation, and these are susceptible to error and must be checked by one of the following methods. If doubts do arise about a hand-bearing compass, it could be tested with these same methods.

Since a compass with deviation error on one heading will have different errors on other headings, the only way to know if the compass works right is to check it on all headings. In practice, this reduces to checking it on the four cardinal headings, because a typical kayak compass that works right on these headings should work right on others.

Before checking for deviation, however, it pays to check the compass card's pivot point. With the boat stable or on land, note the precise compass heading, then briefly place a radio speaker or other magnetic object near the compass to purposefully move the card off its rest position. Then watch its motion as it returns to rest when the disturbance is removed. The card should swing back smoothly, slightly overshooting its original position, and return to where it started. If it does not, or if its motion is jerky, the pivot jewel is probably worn, and the compass may not be dependable. Expensive compasses can be repaired; inexpensive ones must be replaced.

Next check that the lubber's line of the compass is parallel to the boat's centerline. This usually can be done by eye alone to within an accuracy of a few degrees using the axis of the compass housing or its mounting holes as a guide. If the lubber's line is skewed 3° off the centerline, the compass will read 3° too high or too low on all headings, depending on the misalignment direction. Although this is generally not a serious problem—the compass can be read to the left or right of the index pin to correct for this—it is still best to mount the compass as straight as possible because the most versatile method of checking a kayak compass will not reveal this error. The mounting should be secured solidly so the alignment cannot change under way.

The quickest way to check the steering compass on a loaded kayak is to compare its reading with another compass that is not in doubt. Orient the loaded boat on the beach toward north magnetic (000) according to the deck compass and stand behind the boat with a hand-bearing compass to check the heading of the bow. Then repeat the check with the boat headed 180, 090, and 270. If the hand-bearing compass confirms the deck compass on these headings, the deck compass is probably okay. It is unlikely that the hand-bearing compass will be off. The only things that might affect it are steel in eyeglass frames, a flashlight held too close to it at night, or possibly wristwatch batteries. This method also works underway if a second compass is available.

If you know fairly precisely where you are, another quick method is to read the magnetic bearing to a distant landmark from a chart and then point the boat toward it to see if the boat's compass agrees. This can be done on land or water, but because it requires a prominent landmark (2 or 3 miles off) to be both in view and on the same chart you are on, the method is not always possible.

Closer landmarks can be used if two are in sight that form a line from your perspective. Such lines are called *natural ranges*. They are extremely valuable to piloting (discussed in chapter 6) because it is easy to tell when you are on the line. You might, for example, paddle between two charted rocks, keeping one on the bow and the other on the stern, or paddle along the extension of the line between two rocks, which lie ahead or astern of the boat. Then compare the compass heading when on the line to the magnetic bearing between rocks read from a chart (see fig. 4-10). The same can be done paddling along a breakwater or straight toward a charted street visible from the water. Charted buoys are not dependable for this application because they could be far enough off station to give false range bearings.

When using any of these methods, it is important to compare the compass heading to the charted magnetic bearing headed in both directions, toward the mark (or up the line) and away from the mark (or down the line). If the compass checks out on both directions, it is right on those two headings. If the compass reads high (or low) by the same amount on both directions, then either the lubber's line is skewed off the centerline by the difference found, or the charted bearing was read improperly by this amount. In either case, the loading of the kayak is not the problem.

If the compass reads high when headed in one direction and low *by the same amount* when headed in the opposite direction, then the compass has deviation, and the way the kayak is loaded is likely to be the problem. Check the packing near the compass by testing each questionable item as it is removed. If the compass has internal adjustment magnets, these may be the source of the problem, not

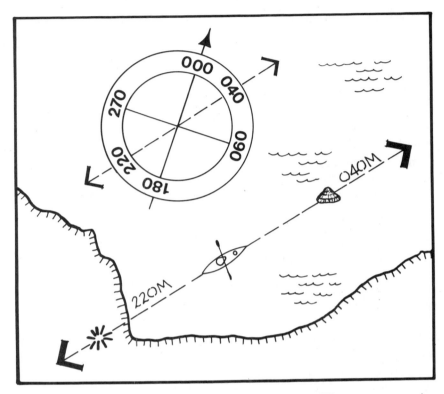

4-10. *Checking a compass by paddling a natural range. The compass error is the difference between the compass reading when on the range and the proper magnetic direction between the rock and peak, which is measured from the magnetic scale of the compass rose.*

the packing. They should be adjusted to neutral as explained earlier. If compass errors are found, but they are neither equal nor equal and opposite on reversed headings, then you have a combination of the above problems. Empty the boat and do the compass checks again.

The above ways to check a compass require a second compass or a chart and special circumstances. When neither of these conditions is met, a compass can still be checked using the fundamental principle of compass errors: they should be equal and opposite on reciprocal headings, as illustrated in figure 4-7. This method requires no special aids and it can be used on land or water. It is prudent to know how to do it. To apply this method, pick some reference direction

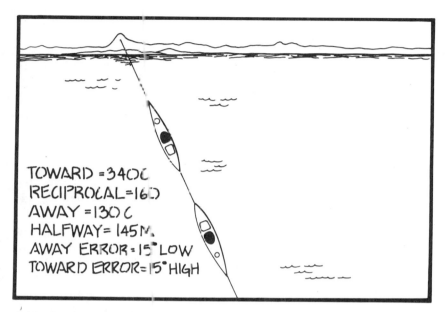

TOWARD =340C
RECIPROCAL=160
AWAY =130 C
HALFWAY= 145 M,
AWAY ERROR=15° LOW
TOWARD ERROR=15° HIGH

4-11. *Checking a compass on reciprocal headings. Point toward a distant object or along a range and read the compass; then point away from the object and read the compass. The compass error is half the difference between the compass reading on the away course and the reciprocal of the compass reading on the toward course, or vice versa. No chart is required for this method.*

that you can align the boat with, put the boat on that line, and read the compass (see fig. 4-11). On land this can be a line between two sticks in the sand; on the water it must be a natural range or the direction to a distant landmark. After you have done this, swing the boat around and head the opposite direction on the line. The compass should read exactly 180° different. If it does, the compass is right on both those headings. Next, check it the same way in a direction perpendicular to the one just used. If it also checks on this heading, it is likely to be right on all others. If the toward and away readings are not exactly 180° different, the compass has deviation. On land, rearrange things until the reciprocal headings check out.

If this test is made underway, as a second thought, repacking may not be possible. It will be necessary to figure the actual compass error, and then use the corrected reading until it is convenient to repack. To do this, choose a distant landmark in the direction you want to go, head for it, and read the compass. As an example (fig. 4-11) say it reads 340. Turn to head directly away from the landmark and read the compass again. Now suppose it reads 130. If the compass had no error on this heading, it should have read 340 minus 180, which is 160, but it reads 130, so there is deviation error on both headings. The actual error can be found from the equal-and-opposite principle of deviation errors: On opposite headings, the errors should be opposite. This principle implies—after some thinking about it—that the correct magnetic heading away from the mark is always halfway between what you get and what you expect.

In this example you got 130 and expected 160; and halfway between these two is 145. Since 145 is correct and you read 130, the compass reading away from the mark was 15° too low. The equal-and-opposite principle tells us that the reading toward the mark must be 15° too high. When the compass read 340, the correct reading was 325. All compass readings on headings near 340 will be too high by 15°. On different headings, however, the error will be different, and the test must be repeated.

Taking the back bearing without tipping over takes coordination and care in some boats. When alone, you can sight along your paddle held parallel to the centerline for an accurate orientation, without turning all the way around. A companion in another boat can help check your alignment on the away course.

When paddling in a group into areas that might require compass steering, such as coastal routes exposed to sea fog, it is prudent to check the compass on each boat. This can be done by checking one of them carefully and using it as a standard for the others, or by aligning all the boats to spot the ones that might be in error. Once a compass has been checked, you can count on it. A typical marine compass is a rugged and reliable instrument. If it worked right once, and nothing near the compass has been changed, it is safe to assume it still works right. When questions rise about where you are or what you see, believe your compass. It should be the last thing to blame for discrepancies in navigation.

CHAPTER 5

Dead Reckoning

Navigation is called both art and science. To the extent that this is true, it applies more to kayaks than to ships. Science is learned through principles; art is learned through practice. The art part of kayak navigation is knowing how fast you are going—assuming you don't have a GPS (Global Positioning System, see chapter 7) tied to the deck! The rest is science. Ships have speedometers (called knot-meters) to tell their speed; kayakers must judge their speed by how hard they are working, the "feel" of the boat, and the knowledge of how wind and waves affect their speed.

Knowledge of boat speed is fundamental to safe and efficient kayak navigation because it is required to predict the time it will take to cover a given distance (the passage time) or to predict how far you might go in a given time period (such as from now until sunset or high water). Predicting and then checking passage times along your route is the only way to monitor progress and learn about paddling speed in various conditions. Deciding whether to turn back or carry on along some particular route is a crucial decision that can arise in various circumstances of kayak navigation. Regardless of other factors (weather, fatigue, or the time of tides or sunset) that might determine the final decision, the predicted passage times in both directions remain essential to the choice. If the question of turning back came up at all, something went wrong, and more wrong predictions at this point could make things worse.

Recall from chapter 1 that dead reckoning means navigation without the aid of landmarks. You determine where you are or where you are going to be purely from a compass course and distance, using an estimated paddling speed and time under way. The basic problems in dead reckoning are to find speed when time and distance are known, to find time when speed and distance are known, or to find distance when speed and time are known. These problems can be solved with actual calculations or with tricks. The calculations are most easily done using formulas adapted for specific recurring questions. The adaptations mostly relate to keeping the hours, minutes, and seconds part of the time in order.

One of the first questions that arises when planning a trip is how long it will take. The distance of the trip is read from a chart, the anticipated speed of the boat can be estimated from the several factors discussed below, and from these two, the passage time can be calculated:

$$\text{Time (hours)} = \frac{\text{Distance (nautical miles)}}{\text{Speed (knots)}}.$$

In marine navigation, speeds are always expressed in knots (1 knot equals 1 nautical mile per hour), and distances used in dead reckoning are always expressed in nautical miles. (The units are often abbreviated to "miles" in conversation and text. In this book, *miles* means nautical miles unless otherwise specified.) If you are paddling at 3 knots, a trip of 13 miles should take 13 divided by 3, or 4.3 hours. If doubts arise about the application of the formula or the results, they can be quickly checked by multiplication, usually without pencil and paper:

$$\text{Distance (nautical miles)} = \text{Speed (knots)} \times \text{Time (hours)}$$

Checking the last example: 3 miles per hour times 4 hours is 12 miles, so 4.3 hours is probably right for 13 miles. Both formulas derive from the definition of speed:

$$\text{Speed (knots)} = \frac{\text{Distance (nautical miles)}}{\text{Time (hours)}}.$$

If you traveled 8 miles in 2 hours, your average speed was 4 knots.

Actual speed along any route depends on how fast you are paddling through the water (paddling speed), and how fast the water itself is moving (current speed). Paddling speed depends on muscle power, wind power, and "wave power"; current speed depends on the location and time of day. The simple question of how long it will take is not always so simple to answer. Many factors affect how fast you will proceed (called your "speed over ground" at any one moment or "speed made good" when averaged over some time period).

One approach is to assume a paddling speed of 3 knots for all applications. This is a reasonable average for many paddlers. At 3 knots, each mile takes twenty minutes. A 5-mile run would take one hundred minutes, or one hour and forty minutes. But anyone who can paddle at an average speed of 3 knots also can paddle at 4 knots for some period of time, or slow to 2 knots with frequent breaks. Paddling speed can vary significantly over a single run, and it takes practice to judge average speed in various conditions. Granted, it is not often that speed must be known precisely, but these are usually the same times that navigation itself is not a concern. When you must navigate, it is important to know your speed. And in some circumstances, 3 knots, plus or minus 1 knot, is not adequate.

Knowing your speed is not merely an academic concern. Experienced paddlers have gotten in trouble (and back out again, because they were experienced) by overestimating their progress against head winds along a foggy coastline. After heading in toward a planned landing site at the corner of a beach, they found waves breaking over rocks instead of a beach. The beach was another mile or more down the coast. On a leeward shore in strong winds, this is a dangerous situation to be in.

But safety is not the only motivation for keeping track of speed. If navigation is to be a hobby—an attitude that ultimately does make kayaking safer—then knowing boat speed in various conditions is just part of the sport. Powerboaters who do predicted-log racing provide a good analogy. Log racing is pure navigation. The winner is the one who has done the best job of predicting the time required for each leg of the course, accounting for current, wind, and boat speed. They use compasses (and knowledge of their boats) but no other navigation instruments. Predicted-log racers receive reduced insurance rates because they have fewer accidents than most boaters. Their hobby makes them safer boaters.

Finding Boat Speed

To learn your paddling speed, begin by choosing a place out of the wind and current. From a chart, figure the length of a straight run between two landmarks, approximately one half mile apart, then use a stopwatch to measure the time it takes to paddle the distance at a steady, comfortable rate. Do this several times, in both directions, noting the wind direction if any. Then average the times. Suppose the run was 0.45 mile long, and it took an average of 8 minutes and 20 seconds. Convert this time to decimal minutes by converting the seconds to minutes: 20 seconds = (20/60) minute = 0.33 minute. The average time was 8.33 minutes. Then calculate the paddling speed from the following variation of the earlier speed formula, adapted to time in minutes:

$$\text{Speed (knots)} = \frac{\text{Distance (nautical miles)} \times 60}{\text{Time (minutes)}}$$

$$= \frac{0.45 \times 60}{8.33} = 3.24 \text{ knots.}$$

This speed is your benchmark to work from. Record it in a notebook with other details, such as the boat and paddle used, the loading of the boat, wind and water conditions, and whether you were tired at the beginning or the end of the tests. Then do this again, whenever the chance arises, both fresh and tired, loaded and empty, and on windy days to check the effect of wind on speed.

It also pays to measure your sprinting speed in this way when there is no wind to see how fast you can go if need be. These records will help monitor training and preferred equipment, as well as improve navigation preparation. Knowledge of your maximum speed and how long you can paddle that fast will help when planning current crossings. It also will give indirect insight into the effect of head winds on your cruising speed, because the work required to paddle at one speed against the wind can be compared to the work required to paddle at a higher speed in calm air. The analogy helps with the planning of windward routes.

Training sessions such as these are the starting point. Once under way on a trip, the process should be repeated at each opportunity. When paddling with a loaded boat, or in a group, it is likely that your average speed will be different from that of a training session. The more often speed is checked, the more you learn about your paddling and the water you paddle through. To prepare for these checks, measure the distances between prominent points along the intended route, figure the times each leg should take at 2, 3, and 4 knots (explained below), and note these times on the chart next to each course line. With this preparation, a common wristwatch lap timer is all it takes to monitor speed. If you notice, for example, that as the day progresses you are going faster and faster, even though you are not paddling as hard, then the wristwatch also has served to detect an increase in favorable current—current flowing in the same direction you are going.

When paddling with the current, the current speed adds to your paddling speed (see fig. 5-1). Paddling at 3 knots with a favorable current of 1 knot, you will progress along the shoreline (speed over ground) at a rate of 4 knots. Paddling at 3 knots against a current of 2 knots, you will be creeping along at 1 knot while working just as hard as you were when making 4 knots in favorable current. Current is clearly a major concern.

More examples of finding boat speed under way to learn about currents are given in chapter 9. Chapter 7 discusses the use of GPS electronic navigation. With a GPS you can accurately determine the distance between any two points, which might serve as a convenient

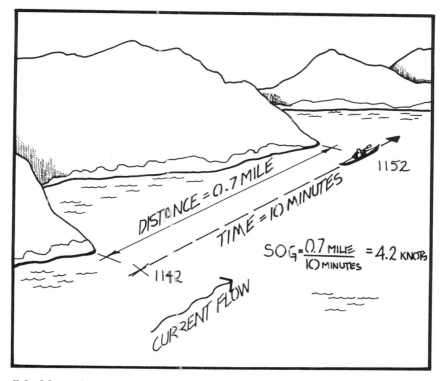

5-1. *Measuring speed overground (SOG) by timing the run along a known distance. If the answer is faster than you know you are paddling, you are in favorable current, and vice versa.*

place to check paddling speed.

Another way to check speed on an uncharted lake or under way well off of landmarks is to use a long light line with a float attached. Measure off at least 50 feet of line, tie one end to the boat and the other to a float (i.e., a small plastic bottle, partially filled with water). Without a tape measure, it is convenient to know the span of your outstretched arms, fingertip to fingertip. This is the original fathom measurement used by fishermen to measure line lengths, but individual spans will vary from exactly 6 feet (when I draw out 10 fathoms this way, I get 56 feet). Toss the faked-out line and marker forward of the boat, paddle toward it, start timing when you pass the float, and stop timing when you first tow the float.

Paddling speed in knots is then 0.6 times the line length (in feet) divided by the number of seconds it took to extend the line. The simple formula derives from the approximation that 1 knot is 100 feet per minute, which is equivalent to calling a nautical mile exactly 6,000 feet. If the line is 50 feet long and it takes 10 seconds to tow it, your paddling speed is 0.6 times 50 divided by 10, or 3.0 knots. Individual results are not as accurate as those measured for longer runs, but the average of several provides a useful gauge of paddling speed. This trick takes practice. The first attempt can put more knots into your string than you can get out of your boat.

The Effect of Wind on Boat Speed

Wind speed and direction sometimes affect kayak speed more than current does. Even modest winds of 8 to 10 knots have significant effect on paddling speed over a long run. Paddling into the wind is hard; paddling with the wind is easy. Wind exerts force on the boat, the paddler, and the paddle, and this force increases as the square of the wind speed. Assuming a 10-knot wind exerts a force of approximately one pound on the front or back of a stationary boat and paddler (a crude estimate of a complex interaction), this force would double to two pounds if the wind increased to just 14 knots (see fig. 5-2).

When paddling at 3 knots into a 14-knot wind, the apparent wind on the boat and paddler increases to 17 knots. With 17 knots of wind on the boat, its force increases to three pounds. Two or three pounds may not seem like much force, but this much wind resistance is approximately equal (another crude estimate) to the water resistance a paddler must overcome to make the boat go 3 knots in calm air and

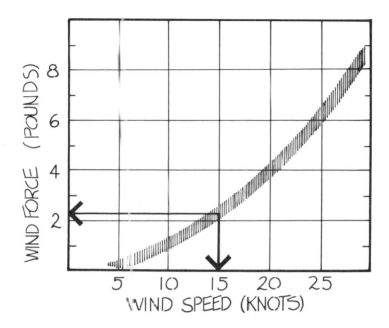

5-2. *The force of the wind on 2 square feet of flat surface perpendicular to the wind. The curve approximates the force on a paddler and boat, but it probably overestimates the true average force on a paddler in waves at higher wind speeds.*

flat water (see fig. 5-3). Either the paddler works twice as hard or, more likely, the boat slows down. It is not often possible or prudent to paddle long distances working much harder than usual.

Figure 5-4 shows a practical summary of this effect adapted from John Dowd's book, *Sea Kayaking—A Manual for Long-Distance Touring*. The data are for average calm-air paddling speeds of 3 to 4 knots, but the same trend can be expected for other average speeds. The key here is to know the trend and then get a few strong wind benchmarks of your own to scale the curve with. It is difficult to be more specific since many factors are involved: the precise wind direction on the boat, the sea state, the style and weight of the boat, and the experience and fitness of the paddler.

Paddling just off the wind is usually more difficult than going straight into the wind, and boats of some designs are easier than others to keep headed into the wind. Loaded boats of all designs are usually easier to control in wind than are empty ones. The data also assume limited wave height, either in new wind or in sheltered

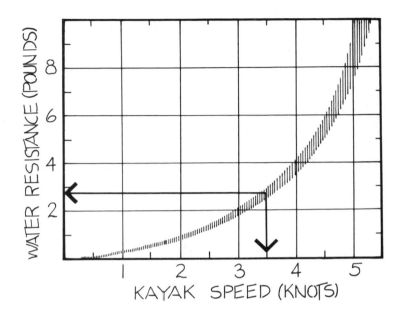

5-3. *Water resistance that must be overcome by the paddler to propel the boat at various speeds. The values shown are adapted from actual measurements made at the British Columbia Research Ocean Engineering Centre (presented in* Sea Kayaker *magazine, fall and spring 1986, by John Dawson). To paddle at 3.5 knots, the paddler must apply an average force of approximately three pounds to the boat. The values represent paddling in calm water; the studies show that the resistance could be as much as twice as large when paddling in waves that match the boat length.*

regions with limited fetch. If a 25-knot wind, for example, blows for two days over 600 miles of fetch, 5 percent of the waves will be over 18 feet high. The data obviously do not apply to these conditions. Such conditions do occasionally occur just a few miles off the California coast in the summertime, but they are clearly reported on NOAA marine weather radio broadcasts as they develop.

To make guidelines on windward paddling speed requires guidelines on judging wind speed, assuming a hand-held anemometer (such as the Turbometer from Davis Instruments) is not available for measuring it. Actual wave heights do not help with this, even if they could be estimated accurately, which is unlikely. It is better to use the general appearance of the water as described by the Beaufort Wind

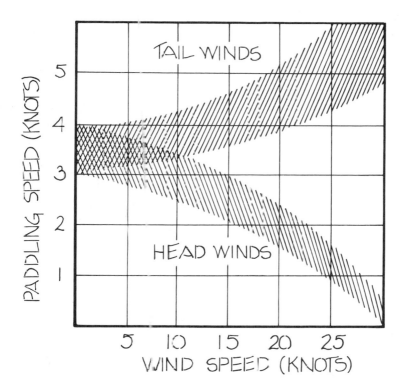

5-4. *Typical paddling speeds in various wind conditions. The curves are adapted from data presented in* Sea Kayaking—A Manual for Long-Distance Touring *by John Dowd, with additional information from several paddlers. These practical estimates are fairly consistent with the data of figures 5-2 and 5-3. Actual values in particular circumstances depend on the paddler, boat, loading, and sea state.*

Scale in figure 5–5. Wind speed can be read from the water this way to within 5 knots or better, after practicing with an anemometer to check the guesses.

A wind speed of approximately 10 knots is the easiest to read from the water, which is fortunate because this is the wind speed at which kayakers must definitely start considering the wind's effect on progress. With no current flowing, the appearance of the first few isolated whitecaps means the wind speed is approximately 10 knots. At this wind speed, search the surface to detect these few whitecaps that

Beau-fort number	Wind speed		Estimating wind speed	
	Knots	Seaman's term	Effects observed at sea	Effects observed on land
0	Under 1	Calm	Sea like a mirror.	Calm; smoke rises vertically.
1	1-3	Light air	Ripples with appearance of scales; no foam crests.	Smoke drift indicates wind direction; vanes do not move.
2	4-6	Light breeze	Small wavelets; crests of glassy appearance, not breaking.	Wind felt on face; leaves rustle; vanes do not move.
3	7-10	Gentle breeze	Large wavelets; crests begin to break; scattered whitecaps.	Leaves, small twigs in constant motion; light flags extended.
4	11-16	Moderate breeze	Small waves, becoming larger; numerous whitecaps.	Dust, leaves and loose paper raised up; small branches move.
5	17-21	Fresh breeze	Moderate waves, taking longer form; many whitecaps; some spray.	Small trees in leaf begin to sway.
6	22-27	Strong breeze	Larger waves forming; whitecaps everywhere; more spray.	Larger branches of trees in motion; whistling heard in wires.
7	28-33	Moderate gale	Sea heaps up; white foam from breaking waves begins to be blown in streaks.	Whole trees in motion; resistance felt in walking against wind.
8	34-40	Fresh gale	Moderately high waves of greater length; edges of crests begin to break into spindrift; foam is blown in well-marked streaks.	Twigs and small branches broken off trees; progress generally impeded.
9	41-47	Strong gale	High waves; sea begins to roll; dense streaks of foam; spray may reduce visibility.	Slight structural damage occurs; slate blown from roof.
10	48-55	Whole gale	Very high waves with overhanging crests; sea takes white appearance as foam is blown in very dense streaks; rolling is heavy and visibility is reduced.	Seldom experienced on land; considerable structural damage occurs.

5-5. *The Beaufort Wind Scale, which relates sea state to wind speed.*

look like scattered bits of popcorn on the water. Current flowing into the wind steepens the waves, so they break making whitecaps more easily. With a current of 1 or 2 knots flowing into the wind, the "popcorn" will appear sooner, at approximately 8 knots of wind. Current flowing with the wind stretches out the waves, so the wind speed must build to 12 knots or so before any specks of white are seen.

At an honest, sustained wind of 20 knots, the popcorn is the first thing that catches the eye. Individual whitecaps are bigger, and there are many more of them. During the first few hours of wind, before the seas build, the water looks like a speckled quilt of whitecaps, but there is little if any spray. Nearby wave surfaces, however, will show prominent streaks of cat's paws (ripples that look like fish scales), which show very clearly the instantaneous wind direction. Conspicuous spray blown off the crests of whitecaps and streaks of foam are the signs of 30 knots of wind. This, however, is very strong wind, indeed. There are not many places close to land where such winds last more than an hour, and even in these places, if this wind persists for over an hour it must be associated with a large weather system that would have been well forecasted. A sustained wind of 30 knots will likely contain gusts to 40 knots or more. To appreciate the forces involved, imagine holding your paddle blade out of a car window when traveling at 40 miles per hour (35 knots).

Just for reference, at the low end of the spectrum, 4 knots of wind is the threshold for feeling the wind on your face or neck. This is not a particularly significant observation for kayakers, but it is a fairly accurate measure. Weaker winds can be seen to move smoke but are not felt. If you can definitely feel the wind on your face, it is more than 4 knots.

Figure 5-6 shows another way to think about paddling into the wind, which should help you plan windward progress. Once you know from training sessions how fast you can paddle and how much work it takes to do so, you can estimate from this curve how hard you must work to paddle against winds of various speeds. To paddle at 2 knots into a wind of 15 knots, for example, you must work approximately as hard as you did to paddle at 4 knots in calm air. These are crude estimates, but they should serve as guidelines as you accumulate more specific personal data.

Paddling downwind, the wind has just the opposite effect. The wind pushes you along, so you go faster with less effort. Because of the change in *apparent* wind speed when headed downwind versus upwind, however, a moderate wind does not help as much when

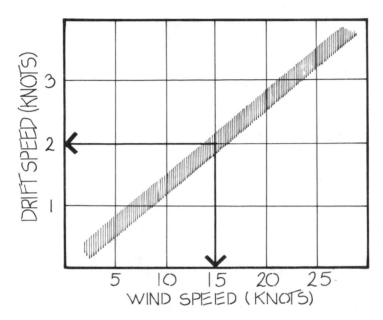

5-6. *Estimates of typical "drift" speeds based on figures 5-2 to 5-4. These are semi-empirical guesses that might be used for rough estimates of the effect of wind on boat speed when planning routes. To use the curve, assume you must paddle as hard as shown just to hold your own against the wind. Against 15 knots of wind, the prediction is 2 knots, which means to make good 1 knot you must paddle about as hard as you do to go 3 knots in calm air. Likewise, paddling about as hard as you do to go 2 knots in calm air, you would go about 4 knots downwind in 15 knots of wind. These are crude estimates, but the limits and the implied work required at various speeds should be fairly close for many paddlers.*

paddling downwind as it hinders when paddling upwind. Paddling at 3 knots in 10 knots of wind, the apparent wind is 13 knots upwind and 7 knots downwind. Because the wind force is proportional to the square of the apparent wind speed, the favorable downwind push is only 30 percent of the adverse upwind push. As downwind speed increases, however, the boat begins to surf on the waves, which greatly reduces the water's resistance. Wave power in these conditions is as important as muscle power and wind power for making speed. Gravity and wave motion propel the boat forward, and this additional boost in speed more than compensates for the loss of apparent wind, although boats that tend to broach more easily require extra paddling attention to take advantage of this speed.

Consequently, it is reasonable to assume that the amount of speed to be gained when headed downwind is about the same as would be lost when headed upwind in the same wind, at all wind speeds. Compiled speeds in figure 5-4 support this approximation, but the same uncertainties of wind direction, boat type, and paddler experience that modify the upwind predictions also apply to the downwind predictions. Nevertheless, all paddlers in all boats go faster downwind than they do in calm air, and the amount by which they go faster should be studied to improve dead reckoning navigation.

Another factor to consider when predicting boat speed is the depth of the water. If you paddle for some hours at a steady, fast pace in deep water and then suddenly enter very shallow water, you will notice that it takes much more work to keep the boat moving at the same speed. The origin of the extra drag is a subtle interaction of the boat's turbulence and bow wave with the bottom of the waterway. The effect is most important when trying to paddle fast in very shallow water—in which case the effect is not as subtle as the theory behind it.

It would be prudent, for example, to predict a cruising speed of one half of your usual speed when planning long runs in 1 or 2 feet of water. Such occasions might arise when paddling close to the shore to avoid adverse current, or when taking advantage of a high-water passage across a wide delta or similar mud flat. This effect on speed is important to think about when paddling *into* an area at high water that must be paddled *out* of at low water. Many popular kayaking waters of the Florida Keys and Everglades include miles of beautiful, but very shallow water. The effect can occasionally be felt in water as deep as 3 or 4 feet, but the extent to which these depths impede speed depends on how fast you are going. It is something to watch for and to test for yourself.

Figure 5-7 shows theoretical predictions of this effect on a hypothetical hull with a draft of 6 inches. The results imply that when paddling at 3.5 knots in 1 foot of water, the bottom drag increases the resistance you must overcome when paddling by 90 percent, which means you must work about twice as hard to maintain this speed. The numerical results are only guidelines to real conditions; the trends in speed and water-depth dependence are possibly more pertinent.

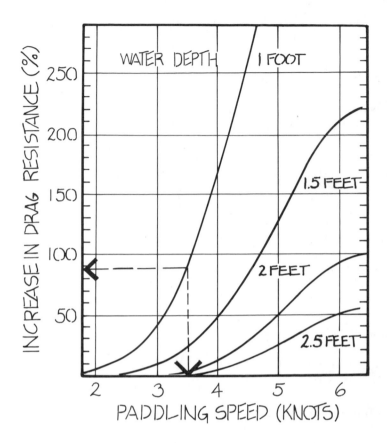

5-7. *Estimates of the increase in water resistance in shallow water as a function of paddling speed and water depth. Paddling at 3.5 knots in 1 foot of water, the resistance increases by nearly 100 percent, meaning it would be about twice as hard to paddle at 3.5 knots in 1 foot of water as in deep water. These estimates assume a draft of 6 inches.*

Figuring Passage Times

To figure the length of a trip, first estimate paddling speed for each leg of the trip, taking into account wind and waves and water depth if necessary. Then estimate how long you might want to rest for each hour of paddling. Rest periods slow progress dramatically, so they must be figured into the itinerary. If you paddle for only fifty minutes out of each hour, for example, your average speed is reduced by a factor of fifty divided by sixty. When paddling in current, the rest periods are likely to be in the current as well, so this motion also should be included. Your *speed made good* in current and with rest periods can be figured from the sum of your average paddling speed, which depends on the length of the rest periods, and the current speed:

Speed made good = Average paddling speed + Current speed

with

$$\text{Average paddling speed} = \frac{\text{Minutes paddled per hour}}{\text{Sixty minutes}} \times \text{Paddling speed.}$$

For convenience, average paddling speeds for various rest periods are listed in table 5-1. If you plan to paddle at 4 knots with ten-minute rest periods each hour, your average speed will be 3.3 knots. If you do this in an adverse current of 0.5 knot, your speed made good will be 3.3 minus 0.5, or 2.8 knots.

As another example, suppose you plan to paddle at 3.0 knots, resting a total of fifteen minutes each hour, but you are traversing a waterway with increasingly favorable current. Your average paddling speed will be 2.3 knots for the run (see table 5-1), but the current will progressively help you along. In a current that is predicted to be 0.5 knot during the first hour, 1.1 knots during the second, and 1.8 knots during the third, you would expect to make good 2.8 miles in the first hour, 3.4 miles in the second, and 4.1 miles in the third. In strong currents that vary significantly with position along the waterway as well as with time, this estimate of progress must be done step by step because the speed of the current where you start determines where you will be after an hour, and only after figuring that can you predict what the current will be for the following hour.

For steady or insignificant current, progress is easier to determine. When the distances are known, but the use of a chart is not convenient, passage times are most easily determined by thinking of your average speed in minutes per mile. The conversion from knots to minutes per mile can be made by inverting the definition of speed, and replacing one hour with sixty minutes. This reduces to dividing sixty by the boat speed:

Speed in knots	Minutes per mile
1.0	60
2.0	30
3.0	20
4.0	15
5.0	12
6.0	10

Table 5-1. *Average Paddling Speeds for Various Rest Periods.*

Rest period in minutes per hour						
0	5	10	15	20	25	30
2.0	1.8	1.7	1.5	1.3	1.2	1.0
2.5	2.3	2.1	1.9	1.7	1.5	1.3
3.0	2.8	2.5	2.3	2.0	1.8	1.5
3.5	3.2	2.9	2.6	2.3	2.0	1.8
4.0	3.7	3.3	3.0	2.7	2.3	2.0
4.5	4.1	3.8	3.4	3.0	2.6	2.3
5.0	4.6	4.2	3.8	3.3	2.9	2.5
5.5	5.0	4.6	4.1	3.7	3.2	2.8
6.0	5.5	5.0	4.5	4.0	3.5	3.0

If in favorable wind and current or an energetic mood, a speed of 5 knots is anticipated, then a 3-mile run should take three times twelve, or thirty-six minutes. Paddling in adverse conditions at 2 knots, the speed would be thirty minutes per mile, and this same run would take three times thirty, or ninety minutes.

Unless you are unusually adept at division in your head, problems such as figuring the time at 3.5 knots for a twenty-seven-mile run are much easier to solve with a chart. With a chart showing the full route in front of you, it is not even necessary to measure the distance first. Just set dividers (or fingers) to a separation in nautical miles equal to the boat speed in knots, using the chart's distance or latitude scale, and count the steps it takes to walk the route across the chart. With the dividers set this way, each step is one hour. Fractional steps at the end can be estimated.

The itinerary of a trip can be recorded on the chart by noting the times you expect to be at various checkpoints along the way. Then a glance at a watch and a quick note on the chart of the actual time at the point is all that it takes to monitor progress. Average speeds can be figured later on to help plan the next day or the next trip.

Basic dead reckoning navigation from speed, time, distance, and compass course is fundamental to all navigation, of kayaks or of ships.

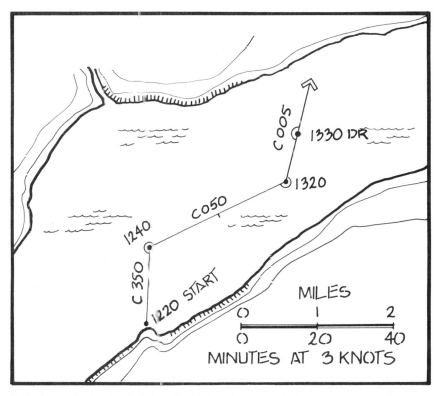

5-8. *A simple dead reckoning (DR) plot showing a DR position at 1330. Knowing your average speed in minutes per mile, your position can be estimated by tracing out your path on the chart as shown. This plot assumes there is no current present.*

And the reason is the same for kayaks and for ships: Sooner or later, it may be all there is to go by. According to Murphy's law, this will happen just when good navigation is most important. Figure 5-8 shows a course line and the resulting position figured from dead reckoning as it might be recorded on a chart during a long run in the fog. Figure 10-11 in chapter 10 shows a similar example, with corrections applied to the course and speed to account for current. The philosophy and accuracy of dead reckoning in the fog is discussed in chapter 10.

CHAPTER 6

Piloting

It is not often that a kayaker must resort to pure dead reckoning for navigation, as it is not common to paddle without landmarks in sight. But some degree of dead reckoning enters into all kayaking, even with landmarks in sight. The simple act of figuring you should be halfway across a 3-mile-wide bay in thirty minutes when paddling at 3 knots is dead reckoning. The navigation becomes piloting once you notice that after thirty minutes of paddling you are not halfway across, but closer to one side than the other.

It is also fortunate that pure dead reckoning is not often required, because it provides only a deduced position, not a true position fix as piloting does. Dead reckoning can be wrong. If you assume you are paddling at 3 knots but are in fact paddling at 3.5 knots, then the dead reckoning position goes wrong by 0.5 mile each hour. In two hours you would be 1 mile farther along your route than figured from dead reckoning alone. This is where piloting comes in. To know where you truly are you must take a position fix using some piloting method. Most kayak navigation underway is done by frequent position checks from landmarks with very little actual dead reckoning.

It is usually a surprise to all boaters when they first discover how rapidly surroundings become unfamiliar on the water. Just turning the first corner away from a bay you have paddled in for years is all it takes. Every corner you round provides new horizons. It is not like on land, where streets provide some continuity for orientation into strange surroundings. Looking back after paddling around a corner shows what to look for on the return, but the back view is just another new perspective on where you have been. It helps little to tell where you are at the time. Most shoreline terrain in a given area is similar. It is difficult to tell a bump in the shoreline from a major headland. You might think you are halfway across a bay, when only halfway to the bump.

Practice in chart reading helps with the identification of shoreline terrain, but even so, keeping track of position in unfamiliar waters is rarely a casual matter and certainly never becomes instinctive. Since a paddler cannot see around corners or bumps on the shoreline, the lay of the land must be judged from the perspective of a bug on an imaginary chart that has all the printed shoreside elevation contours raised to the proper scale as discussed under Terrain and Perspective in chapter 2. But even this fails when the chart in use does not have adequate elevation contours to identify the curves and hills and headlands seen from the water. Furthermore, close to shore, the shape of nearby terrain is not apparent, and the shape that is seen farther off is often that of the treetops and not the land.

Things only get worse if you postpone the task and let your position become more uncertain. Without knowing where you are on the chart, it is often impossible to make useful judgments of what should be seen from an approximate position. Consequently, good navigation into unfamiliar waters, as when first rounding a corner, must be done with frequent reference to the chart—at least until you are quite convinced of what you see and where you are.

Identifying what you see does not tell where you are. Scenery must be viewed not with a sightseer's eye but with a navigator's eye. This type of looking—to see where you are—is called piloting. On clear days on inland waters there are many things to see, and piloting is easy. But when only one light shines through the fog or only one point or one peak can be identified on the horizon, piloting is more challenging, and only those who have practiced navigation will know where they are. A good navigator should be prepared to use whatever can be seen to find position. Piloting by natural ranges and compass bearings is fundamental to kayak navigation and will be used many times on any trip. Other methods are crucial only in special circumstances; they can rest deeper in the navigator's bag of tricks.

Needless to say, we are talking here of position navigation without GPS. An obvious value of GPS is its ability to tell your position to within a few yards from a simple glance at the dial. A remarkable convenience, but also one that you could easily get used to and eventually take for granted. Once this happens, and the batteries die or you lose it overboard, you will be glad to have learned these fundamentals of the traditional methods of piloting.

Natural Ranges

If you are paddling along shore and notice that you happen to be directly in line with a long, straight street running down toward the shoreline, then you have done some very precise piloting as soon as you can identify that street on the chart. The street is a straight line on the land part of the chart that can be extended with a pencil onto the water part. If you are looking straight up the street, you must be located somewhere on that extended line. The extended line on the chart is called a *range,* and the fact that you know you are somewhere on that line makes that range a *line of position,* or LOP. It is called a line of position because you know you are on the line, but you do not know where you are on the line. A boat anywhere on that line would have the same perspective on the street, but only those who are on that line would get the "runway view" straight up the street. Viewing in that direction from other locations, you might not see the street at all, or would see it partly obscured.

Range, in navigation, is a general term meaning the alignment of any two objects, or the ends of one long feature such as a street or breakwater, used to find a LOP. In British usage, ranges are called transits, but this latter term is reserved for land navigation in American parlance. A range is only one example of a LOP; a compass-bearing line is another. But a range is an especially valuable LOP, because it is quick to take and easy to locate and plot on the chart, besides being more accurate than a typical compass-bearing line. A LOP from a range requires no instruments other than eyes, and eyes are very precise instruments for judging the alignment of two objects.

A range can be found from the alignment of two objects in front of the boat or in back of the boat, or from objects on opposite sides or opposite ends of the boat. (Examples are shown in figure 6-1.) For objects on opposite sides of the boat, it is best to use the paddle as a sighting line to determine precisely when you cross the range. This is especially important when crossing a range diagonally, meaning the objects do not appear on the beam when crossing the range.

Ranges of opportunity, drawn between various natural and man-made charted features, are called *natural ranges* to distinguish them from *navigational ranges,* which are those specifically set up by the Coast Guard for navigation. Navigational ranges are two well-separated vertical markers (usually lighted), with the mark closest to

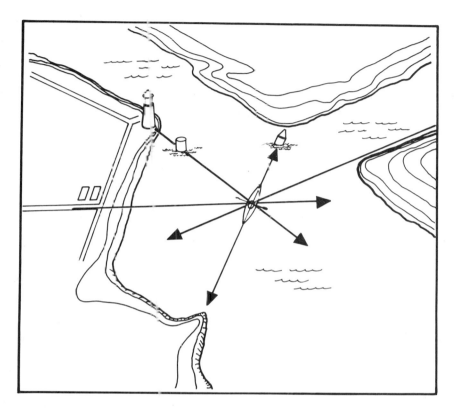

6-1. *Samples of natural ranges. Any two charted objects that appear in line from your perspective can be used to locate a line of position on the chart.*

the water set at a lower elevation than the more inland mark. These ranges guide vessels onto the preferred channel of a harbor or waterway. By noting whether the top light is to the right or left of the bottom light, navigators can tell at a glance if they are to the right or left of the range, as shown in figure 6-2. Navigational ranges are important aids to larger vessels because the presence of range markers means it is hazardous to be very far off the range. If you see a large vessel approaching a harbor marked with an entrance range, you can count on it heading toward the buoy that is usually in place marking the outer end of the range, at which point it will turn onto the range itself. Knowing this you can negotiate your route through the area accordingly.

The white running lights of large vessels (over 50 meters long) are positioned on the deck like a navigational range: The forward one is lower than the aft one. These lights alone tell which way the vessel is moving and provide the first warning that it might be turning toward you. A ship's "range lights" are visible long before its red or green sidelights are. This point is discussed further in later sections on navigation at night and in traffic.

Figure 6-3 shows a special type of natural range that offers frequent opportunities for accurate LOPs in many areas. When the chart shows that an island, obscured behind a headland from your present perspective, will come into view shortly if you remain on your present course, prepare for a quick and accurate piece of navigation. The moment the island first peeks around the corner, you can draw

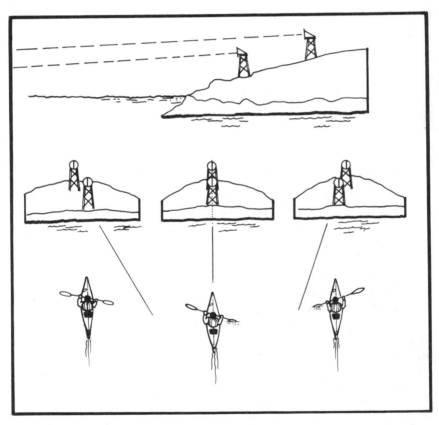

6-2. *A navigation range. Larger vessels will follow these ranges closely in confined waterways.*

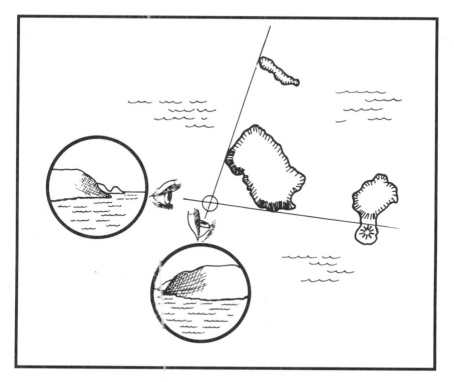

6-3. *Natural ranges along the tangents to islands. When one landmark first appears around the corner of another, their range on the chart is your line of position.*

an accurate LOP on the chart. The line of sight tangent to the head-land must be drawn carefully, however, keeping in mind the elevation contours shown on the chart. The bluff that blocked the island could be well inland of the actual shoreline shown on the chart.

One range gives one line of position. A precise location on that line—a position fix—can be found from the point where a second range line, made from two other objects, crosses the first. This is the standard way that all piloting is done. A position fix is the intersection of two or more LOPs. To find position this way, the objects used for the ranges must be shown on the chart, or the lines cannot be drawn.

Note that from a kayaker's perspective, another virtue of a range for navigation is that you can plot the LOP on the chart with a simple ruler. It is just a single, straight line, drawn right where it is observed. In contrast, you will see shortly that other types of LOPs can require more complicated plotting—using other improvised tools, or moving lines from one place to another on the chart. Piloting by ranges is accurate, versatile, and easy to record.

Natural ranges made up from uncharted features also are still extremely valuable even though they do not provide a position fix or a LOP. A natural range can be made from any two things in sight that happen to line up, such as a treetop on the shore you paddle toward and a distant mountain peak in its background. Neither of these will be on the chart, but the line is still there in front of the boat, and it can serve as a dependable guide.

You can, for example, use an uncharted range of this type to tell what the current is doing as you paddle along the range. If the tree at the end of the range is more than a mile or so away, the compass heading to it is not a sensitive measure of where you are, which is what you need to know to judge the effect of current. Recalling the rule of thumb for small-triangle dimensions (see fig. 4-4), and keeping sight of a tree that is 1 mile off, the current must push you 0.1 mile off course to the side before the compass would show a 6° change in heading. In choppy waters with the compass card swinging around, this is approximately how large the shift must be to detect it.

Let's say you are paddling across a channel that has a current of 0.5 knots (water moves 1 mile every 120 minutes). If you kept the boat pointed straight across the channel as you proceeded to cross, it would take twelve minutes for this current to drift you off course by the 0.1 miles needed to cause a detectable bearing shift of about 6°. Depending on how fast you are paddling, however, you would be well underway in crossing the channel during these twelve minutes. The closer you get, the faster the bearing shift will occur, but in any event, noticing such a shift in an average-bearing angle will always be much slower than detecting the misalignment of a natural range. We can easily see fractions of a degree in misalignment with the human eye, which would translate in this example to seeing the effect of the current in a minute or two rather than twelve minutes. For example, note that a treetop and mountain peak dead ahead align exactly as you start across, and watch that they remain that way as you proceed—or conclude from which way they shift how you must adjust your course. This important method of crossing currents is covered in chapter 9.

During daylight hours on inland waters, look around long enough and you can usually find two LOPs from natural ranges that will tell you where you are. Sometimes the lines must be drawn on the chart to locate the intersection, other times an adequate position can be found by tracing the lines with a finger. But even if lines are not required, it is still good practice to make a note on the chart of the position found and label it with the time. It could turn out to be your last good fix from which subsequent positions must be found by dead reckoning. Put another way, it is poor practice to anticipate that conditions will remain favorable for good fixes and therefore not bother writing anything on the chart. The farther back any dead reckoning must be carried to find present position, the more uncertain the results will be.

Indeed, this last point cannot be overemphasized. We often call it "the most important rule in navigation," namely: mark your position on the chart and label it with the time frequently, as shown in figure 6-4. It does not matter how you arrived at the position; it could be from just passing close abeam of a buoy, or from a GPS reading, or from the intersection of two natural ranges. Regardless of how you get a position determination, find that position on the chart and label with the time, such as 1206, or 1423 for P.M. times. And what is meant by "frequently"? That depends on the circumstances; it could be every hour or so, or even more frequently. In some cases, though, it won't be needed so often, and every couple hours might do—and in some cases we do not need to navigate at all. But when we do navigate, this becomes Rule No. 1. This procedure alone tells most of what you need to know in a hurry, and it is the one procedure that will prevent most navigation problems underway. See notes in the caption for figure 6-4.

Compass Bearing Fixes

Although in most daylight conditions on inland waters natural ranges are available for position fixing, it can sometimes take a while to find them. When ranges cannot be found in a reasonable time, compass bearings are the next best alternative. At night, natural ranges are not visible, so there is no alternative but compass bearings for finding position.

The bearings can be taken with a hand-bearing compass or with a deck-mounted compass. Good hand-bearing compasses give more precise bearings than deck compasses do, and they can be used without changing headings. Their disadvantages are that the boat must be stopped to take the sight, and they are redundant equipment when a good compass is mounted on deck for steering. A good deck compass will give adequate bearings, but the boat must be pointed at the

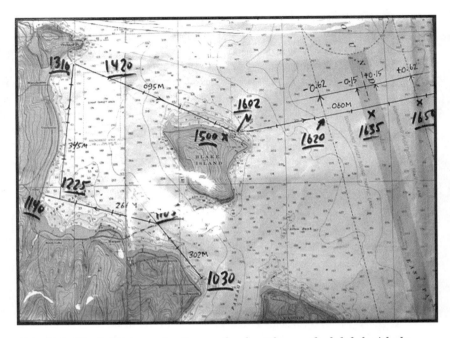

6-4. *Rule No. 1: Plot your postion on the chart frequently, labeled with the time. Here we show a route planned out on the chart before departure with compass headings and tick marks every .5 mile along the track. Once underway, we used a grease pencil (china marker) to write the time we passed various waypoints along the planned track. Also shown are the borders for a vessel traffic lane and the associated cross-track errors that we might read from a GPS using the trick covered in Chapter 10 (see fig. 10-4). In this passage it took about thirty minutes to cross the lanes.*

object to take the sight. This is awkward in strong winds and waves, but the hand-bearing compass is no better in these conditions since the paddle must be set aside to do the sights. If turning is difficult, it is probably important to keep the paddle in hand. Double kayaks might have the best of both, with the aft paddler using a hand-held compass for bearings and the forward paddler watching a deck-mounted compass for steering—or vice versa.

With either type of compass, the procedure for obtaining bearing lines is the same (see fig. 6-5). The compass is aimed at the sighted object and then watched for a few seconds. The compass card will swing around, even in fairly calm conditions, so the observer must choose the best average reading. In less favorable conditions, this

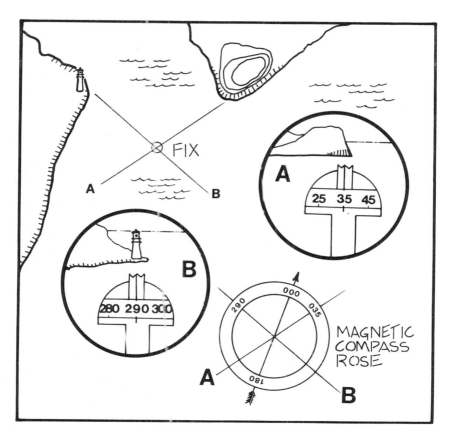

6-5. *A bearing fix from the intersection of two bearing lines.*

might take a minute or so. Once an average bearing is decided upon, the bearing line must be drawn on the chart—an imaginary line traced with a finger will not do for this application. The principle of the position line is easy: If a lighthouse is seen from the boat at bearing 290, the lighthouse attendant would see the boat in the opposite direction at a compass bearing of 290 minus 180, which equals a magnetic bearing of 110. The LOP on the chart is a line emanating from the lighthouse in direction 110, and this direction can be read from the magnetic scale of the chart's compass rose.

On larger vessels, bearing lines are drawn on the chart with the aid of parallel rulers. The rulers are first aligned in the proper magnetic orientation across the center of the compass rose nearest to the lighthouse symbol (magnetic directions are shown on the middle scale of the compass rose). The alignment of the rulers on the compass rose can be done using the observed bearing, without figuring its reciprocal (used above to explain the principle), because the line from the center to the observed bearing will automatically pass through its reciprocal. After alignment on the compass rose, the rulers are then stepped over to the lighthouse, and the line is drawn. This way the proper direction read from the compass rose is transferred to the lighthouse (see fig. 6-6).

Parallel rulers are useful for preparing charts for a kayak trip, but they are not practical for this application on the deck of a kayak. When underway in a kayak, this job must be improvised, and simpler tools are called for. Charts must be protected in a kayak, either with simple coatings or in transparent plastic bags. Options are discussed later, but for any method of protection, a grease pencil (china marker) is often the best way to write on the surface of the chart cover. The simplest approach to drawing bearing lines is to sketch a line across the compass rose in the proper orientation and then draw another line—that is parallel to the one at the compass rose—pointed toward the lighthouse.

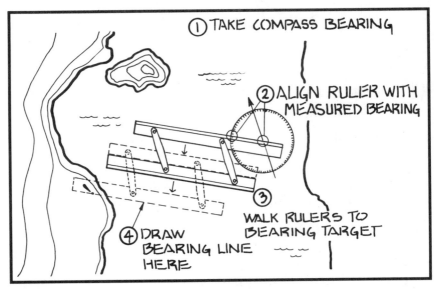

6-6. *Using parallel rulers to plot a bearing line. Parallel rulers are not practical under way, but they can be used in planning a trip. See also fig. 2-20.*

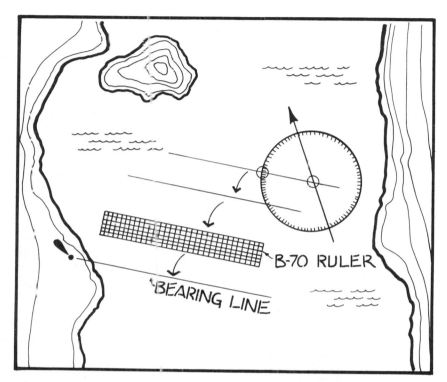

6-7. *Using a large flat ruler to draw a bearing line while under way.*

These lines are adequate for many applications, but if more precision is required, the line can be drawn with a wide ruler that is moved to the lighthouse from the compass rose one ruler width at a time (see fig. 6-7). Navigation supply stores carry one popular ruler style that is 4 inches wide and 12 inches long with a grid of lines drawn across it parallel to the long edge. The grid facilitates the last step, which will be some fraction of a ruler width. A less expensive and still convenient alternative is the C-Thru brand ruler (model B-70) that has a uniform grid over a 2-inch-by-12-inch ruler. The other extreme is a clear, gridded template approximately 12 inches on a side. Several brands are available. These will often span the distance from compass rose to sighted object without requiring steps. One edge of the template is kept on the object as the template is rotated until a grid line crosses the center of the rose at the proper orientation. The grid is then held in place as the line is drawn along the edge of the template in line with the object.

A special chart tool developed by and for kayakers called the "Small Crafts Nav Aid" is a convenient way to measure bearings and course lines. It is a simple 360° protractor printed on a square grid with a string attached to the center. Align the base or one of the grid lines with the chart for proper orientation, and then pull the string out in the direction to be measured. Read the true bearing where the string crosses the protractor, as shown in fig. 6-8. The device is small, lightweight, inexpensive, and essentially indestructible. The original commercial version is available in kayak stores or by mail order. It is easy to improvise one from standard materials if necessary.

Bearing lines need not extend all the way to the sighted object but should just cross the water region of your approximate location.

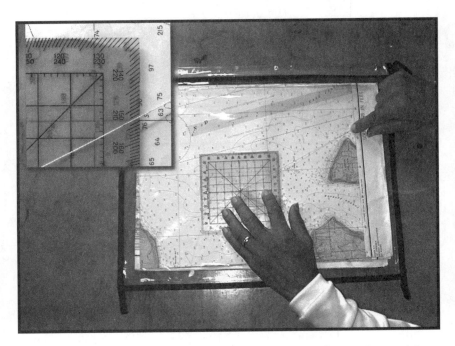

6-8. *An improvised string plotter used to measure a course line. This model was made from a 5-inch square protractor. Read the true course from where the string crosses the protractor. Sometimes using the protractor alone without the string is a more convenient way to measure course headings. The waterproof chart pack shown is a super-durable model from Mariner Kayaks.*

The more optimistic you are about knowing your position, the shorter the lines can be. A position fix will be found from the intersection of a second bearing line with this first one, and if the second bearing line does not cross the first because it is too short, it can be extended as needed. A general goal of chart work is to make the minimum amount of marks on the chart required for neat, consistent, unambiguous notation.

When doing a position fix by compass bearings there are several points to keep in mind that will optimize the accuracy of the fix. When using just two bearings, the two objects should be well separated on the horizon. Ideally they would be 90° apart, but as long as they are more than 30° apart the fix should be good. Sights of nearby objects (less than 10° apart, for example) give narrow intersection angles when the LOPs are plotted, and with narrow intersection angles, small errors in compass reading or in plotting the bearings result in a large error in the fix. This geometric enhancement of the errors diminishes rapidly for intersection angles over 30°. Fixes from intersection angles of 60° or so are essentially as good as those for perpendicular LOPs. With one arm pointed to one object and the other held at 90° to it, it is easy to judge where 45° would be, and from there to pick well-placed targets. A look at the chart from your approximate position helps identify good targets for bearing fixes. Reference to the chart before bearing fixes is often necessary anyway, since potential targets must be located on the chart if they are to be used.

It is also important to use the closest of two potential candidates for sights when you have a choice. Accuracy is again the reason. Small angular errors in compass reading or plotting cause large intersection errors when the object sighted is a long distance from your position on the chart. Think of the extreme cases: With an arm around a buoy, it does not matter if the bearing to it is completely wrong, you still know where you are. Whereas the bearing to a distant mountain peak remains the same even after traveling several miles. Knowing the bearing to a very distant object does not help locate your position.

Permanent landmarks like lighthouses and peaks are better targets for bearing fixes than buoys. Although anchored, buoys have large scope, so their positions when used as close marks are not reliable or, worse still, they could have been moved from the charted location or dragged off station by currents. Tangents to bluffs and hills are frequently good for bearings, but as with their use in ranges, the lines must be drawn carefully by matching charted elevation contours with what was actually sighted (see fig. 6-9).

The uncertainty in a position found from compass bearings can be tested by taking bearings to more than two objects. Two bearing lines intersect at only one place, but three bearing lines will normally intersect each other at three places. Only if all three sights and lines are exactly right will the three intersect at a single point. Consequently, the spread of the three intersections is an approximate measure of the accuracy of the fix, as illustrated in figure 6-10. This is not a rigorous test of accuracy when the lines do not agree, but it is certainly reassurance of the fix when they do nearly agree. After some practice, two lines taken carefully yield as good a fix as three lines do, provided you are certain of the location of the objects sighted. If the identify of a peak

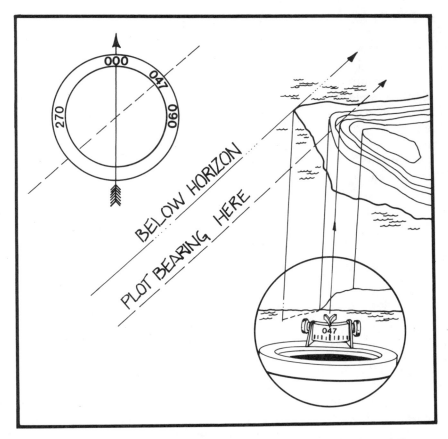

6-9. *In some cases, charted elevation contours must be considered carefully when drawing bearing lines.*

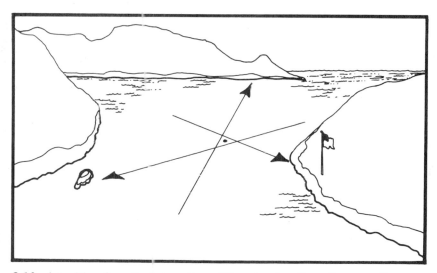

6-10. *A position from the intersection of three bearing lines. Because of unavoidable small errors in each individual measurement, the lines will not intersect in a single point. The size of the triangle is a rough measure of the uncertainty in your position fix.*

or light is in doubt, then three sights are necessary to remove the uncertainty.

Taking multiple sights from a known position is a good way to practice the method. This is the only practical way to learn how the precision of the compass reading and plotting affects the final position location. Practice also is required to develop your own preferred method of plotting the lines underway. Practice with different types of compasses also will show why some cost much more than others.

A graphic way to study the accuracy of bearing fixes at home with a chart and parallel rulers is simply to pick a location on the chart and two objects that might be used for sights from that position. Then measure the bearings from that location to the objects using parallel rulers, and assume these were the average readings obtained. The chart work is just the opposite of plotting bearing lines. Align the rulers with the lines from the chosen location to the chosen object and then step them over to the compass rose to measure the bearing. Then, considering that each of these average values has an uncertainty of, say, plus or minus 3°, plot the two extremes. If the average was 050, plot bearing lines at 047 and 053. This will yield a region of uncertainty, as illustrated in figure 6-11, that shows how the fix

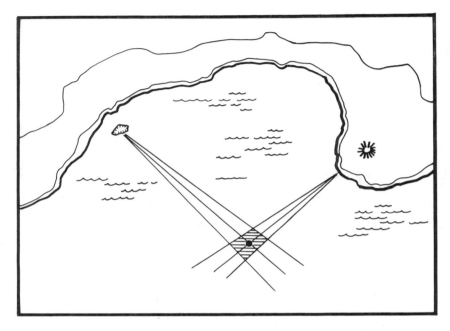

6-11. *The uncertainty of a position fix found from two lines. The width of the shaded area is approximately 200 yards per mile off the bearing target in typical measurements made underway.*

depends on the precision of the measurement.

If you do the same with close objects and far objects, you quickly learn why close objects are better targets for bearing sights. With an uncertainty of plus or minus 3°, the bearing-angle spread will be 6°, and the distance across the end of this triangle that represents your position uncertainty will be 10 percent of the distance to the sighted object (the small-triangle rule). Using two objects, each approximately 0.5 miles (1,000 yards) away, the full width of the uncertainty for sights accurate to within 3° would be 100 yards, so your position by bearing fix would be accurate to within plus or minus 50 yards—in principle. In the real world of a kayak seat, however, twice this uncertainty is closer to the truth. To be safe, assume that bearing fixes made underway are only accurate to within plus or minus 10 percent of the distance to the farthest object sighted, which translates into an uncertainty of 200 yards per mile off. With practice, a quality compass, and good conditions, you should be able to reduce this significantly.

Finding Position from Water Depth

Kayakers do not often take advantage of electronic depth sounders for navigation, but that does not detract from their concern for or use of water depth for navigation (small hand-held units are available these day for those who might want one for research or navigation). In many parts of the world, water is clear enough to see the bottom, even in deep water. In less clear waters, whenever the bottom can be seen at all it is at least known that the water is not deep.

When the slope of the bottom is gradual these observations are not of much value, but in many waterways around the world there are sudden drop-offs or shelves along the shoreline, and in some of these cases it is possible to tell from a kayak when you are on or off the shelf. These shelves are marked on charts by an abrupt change in depth contours, so whenever you notice you are crossing a shelf, you have found a crooked line of position—the charted contour of the shelf. A compass bearing to a landmark on shore then locates your position at the intersection of the bearing line and the shelf contour (see fig. 6-12).

When such shelves exist, it is usually important to know where you are relative to them in order to find favorable current. When the shelf cannot be detected from the boat, natural ranges or bearing fixes should be used to find out where it is. Current speed and direction often change at the edge of a shelf. Riding with the current, you want to be in the deep water off the shelf; paddling against the current usually calls for being in the shallow water on the shelf. Buoys often mark the corners of a shelf wherever waterways turn and thus provide useful range markers for orientation relative to shelves too deep to detect.

For more general position finding, remember that vast areas of shallow water might contain patches of deeper water. Detectable shoalings on banks can rise from very deep water indeed, as very shallow spits can extend a mile or more off the end of a headland. Shoalings that might be useful for navigation are usually shaded blue on charts. Often an extensive kelp bed signals the presence of a bank below it, even when the water is far too deep to see through. When such depth anomalies are shown on the chart, they should be anticipated for use with navigation. And whenever you notice or suspect the depth has changed, check the chart to see if it might tell something about where you are. Marking such potential aids on the chart

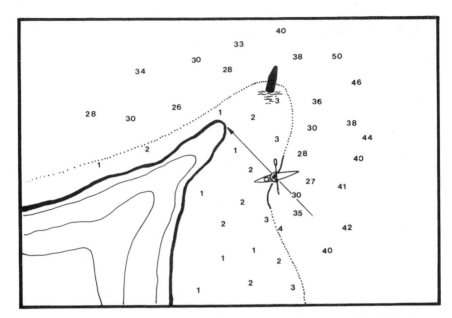

6-12. *A position fix from a bearing line and an underwater shelf visible from the boat. The shelf is effectively a crooked line of position on the chart.*

before the trip is part of navigation planning. In clear tropical waters, charted coral heads over 30 feet deep can still be seen when the sun is high and can be used for piloting offshore. Polarized sunglasses are a big help with these observations.

The sea state also can signal the presence of shallow water. Currents accelerate when flowing over banks, and when this current is against the wind, the waves steepen and break more frequently. Sometimes the outline of a bank can be detected from the pattern of whitecaps on it—or along it, when strong current flows around it but not over it. Banks exposed to strong, deep current also can be detected by a fog boundary. The upwelling at the edge of the bank brings cold water to the surface, which cools the air to the dew point and forms fog. If a bank or other shoaling can be detected this way, it can help with orientation even though it is some distance off.

For close inshore paddling, remember that waves break to form whitecaps on a beach or spit when the water depth diminishes to roughly 1.3 times the wave height (although at a river bar or other waters with opposing current, they will break in deeper water). In moderate winds, you can often detect long spits ahead before seeing them from an extension of the surf or from whitecaps. Once you locate the spit this way and identify it on the chart, you have more information on your present position.

Visible Range of Land and Other Things

Everyone is familiar with the image of a ship sailing over the horizon. As the ship sails away, less and less of it can be seen because the curvature of the earth limits the line of sight to the ship. The last thing you see with binoculars is the tip of the mast. The taller the ship, the farther off it can be seen; likewise, the higher you are when looking, the farther you can see. From the seat of a kayak, you can easily see a freighter 5 miles off, but you cannot see a kayaker paddling beside it. Knowing how to estimate the actual visible range of other vessels, rocks, peaks and islands, and elevated lights is fundamental to marine navigation. It is important for navigation, and it is important for safety.

During daylight in clear weather and flat water, the visible range of an object is called its *geographic range*. It is determined by the curvature of the earth and the heights of the object and the observer. The proper mathematical solution to the geometry problem is presented in tabular form in the *Light List*. The table gives geographic ranges for various heights of objects and observers. These results, however, are needed more often than the *Light List* is, so it pays to know how to figure geographic range without a table. In clear weather and flat water, geographic range in miles can be figured from:

$$\text{Geographic range} = \sqrt{\text{Land height}} + \sqrt{\text{Eye height}}.$$

where both heights are in feet above the water (see fig. 6-13).

Eye height in a kayak is about 2 feet, so its square root adds approximately 1.5 miles. It is adequate to assume that this is constant, and that the geographic range of an object viewed from a kayak is the square root of the object's elevation (in feet) plus 1.5 miles:

$$\text{Geographic range} = \sqrt{\text{Land height}} + 1.5 \text{ miles}.$$

If an island is 49 feet tall, the top of it would be first discernible on the horizon at 7 plus 1.5, or 8.5 miles off. The square roots of less convenient heights can be approximated by squaring a few guesses—

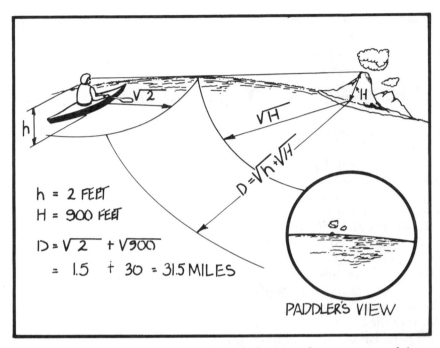

6-13. *A landmark will first appear above the horizon when you approach it to within the geographic range* (D), *provided the atmospheric visibility is at least as large as that geographic range. The paddler's eye height* (h) *and the height of the land* (H) *are in feet above the water.*

higher precision is not required because even the best theories of what this range should be are only accurate in practice to within 10 percent or so. Likewise, beyond 8.5 miles off a 49-foot-high island could not be seen, even if it had a bright light on it (at ground level) and you looked with binoculars. The elevations of shoreline cliffs, peaks, and inshore rocks that are needed to figure their geographic ranges are charted or listed in *Coast Pilots*.

Results of the simple square-root formula for geographic range are 15 percent smaller than the "proper" theoretical values in the *Light List*. Nevertheless, the formula results are more dependable in practice. A slight chop on the water or haze in the air will reduce this range by more than 15 percent when looking for low features. Even the square-root predictions should be considered optimistic predictions that apply best when using binoculars in clear weather and flat water. These predictions are naturally limited by the prevailing atmospheric visibility. If the visibility is 15 miles—a relatively clear day—you could not see a peak 2,500 feet high until you were within 15 miles of it, even though the tip of it is over the horizon at 50 miles off. This is, in effect, the definition of *atmospheric visibility*.

The formula can be used not only to predict when an island or peak should first be seen (depending on atmospheric visibility), but it also can be used to tell how close you must be to it if you do see it. If a bright navigational light, for example, is charted as 25 feet high, whenever you can see the light at all, you must be within 5 plus 1.5, or 6.5 miles of the light, although you do not know the actual distance off by just seeing the light. On the other hand, when you *first see the light*, you can assume you are approximately 6.5 miles off.

Predictions of the geographic-range formula are also of interest to safety. A ship that is about 81 feet high would be seen first (looking carefully in best conditions) at a distance of 9 plus 1.5, or about 10 or 11 miles off. Two kayakers will lose complete sight of each other at a separation of about 3 miles in flat water. In rough seas or swells, however, they would have only intermittent sights of each other at much closer distances, when one or both happen to be on a wave crest. In big waves, you can lose sight of each other when only a few boat lengths apart. In the case of an emergency at night, it is clearly important to carry flares that can be shot into the air when paddling in rough waters. For routine paddling in even moderate seas, there is some virtue in carrying a steady light (like a chemical light) in addition to a personal strobe light. In some conditions, the steady light would be a better way to keep in touch. Strobes can be seen from farther off and are definitely superior for attracting attention, but it is very difficult to judge distance off a bright flashing light. Consequently they are less valuable as aids for keeping a group together. They also are likely to be out of phase with the waves, unlike a steady light.

In fog, rain, or snow the visible range of unlighted land is more complicated to determine. First, you must be within the geographic range of the land or you will not see it; this limit does not depend on the atmosphere, only on the curvature of the earth. When well within the geographic range, the visible range of unlighted land is simply called the *visibility* or atmospheric visibility. It is not something you can calculate; it must be measured by reading from a chart the distance to the farthest objects you can barely see. One trick that helps estimate this range when no visible features are present is to note whether you can discern the sea horizon—a line between sky and water or distant land and water. From the geographic-range formula, you know that if you can see the horizon, the visibility must be at least 1.5 miles (the answer corresponds to putting the height of your target equal to zero feet). The section on navigation at night in chapter 10 discusses the visible range of lights in reduced visibility.

Finding Distance Off

In rough water, strong wind, or fast current, a kayaker's hands must be kept on the paddle. Consequently, kayak piloting is at its best when it can be done without the use of hands, as when using natural ranges or noticing a sudden change in water depth. The next best methods are the ones that use the hands the least. Finding position from intersecting compass bearings is accurate and versatile, but it occupies the hands some time to plot the fix. A convenient compromise is a single compass bearing to an object that you can estimate the distance to. If you know you are 1 mile away from a lighthouse in direction 215, then you can point to your position on the chart. With a deck-mounted compass to take the bearing, this measurement might require hands for only a few seconds. With well-prepared charts, it might take just one hand a few seconds, or no hands at all.

The other virtue of this approach is it takes only one identified feature to find position. Natural ranges take four (two features per range, two ranges for a fix); bearing fixes take two. Whenever only one charted feature can be identified, estimates of distance off become essential to finding position. Furthermore, a position fix can be found from the distances to two separate features without the aid of a compass, which could prove useful if the compass was lost on an extended trip. There are several ways to find distance off—some take more hands than others, and some take more practice than others. These measurements are a challenging and rewarding part of the sport of navigation. They will be convenient more often than crucial, but are well worth the practice and could save your boat (so to speak) some day.

Guessing

Guessing distance is a cultivated skill. Some boaters do it well; others, like myself, might be fair at 25 yards (the length of a swimming pool) and 100 yards (the length of a football field) but must admit very shaky results for unaided guesses of miles. But regardless of skill level, sea state and time of day also affect the result. This method is mentioned only for the sake of those who might potentially do it well—something that can be discovered only by practice from known positions in different conditions.

Many of those who get useful results from guessing use various tricks to get some modicum of measurement into the guess. "Don't shoot until you see the whites of their eyes" is such a rule for short distances. Obviously, distance judged this way depends on your eyes, as well as the eyes of the target. The same uncertainties inhibit the accuracy of these common guidelines:

Approximate distance	Typically visible to naked eye
5 miles	Large houses, towers, ships
2 miles	Large trees, chimneys— can count windows
1 mile	Large sea buoys, tree trunks, branches—can count trees
½ mile	Small buoys—people appear as dots or posts
¼ mile	Hands, arms, paddle blades, outboard motors
⅛ mile	Faces, clothing, deck gear, buoy shapes, numbers, or letters

To be of value, these guidelines must be adjusted to individuals and to the scenery. You may find that a rule that works in one area will not work in another, or you may find other useful guidelines for specific places or scenery. It is something to try, and then decide how useful it is for you. It is possible, for example, to be in the middle of a bay, 3 miles across, and be able to see individual trees on the west side but not on the east side. All such rules are approximate at best.

Commercially available range finders are not much better than guessing. These are optical instruments that read distance off similar to the way the focus adjustment on a camera does. Large, expensive ones used on artillery do the job, but the small, expensive ones designed for marine navigation typically do not. Specific brands have limited ranges over which they work reasonably well, but they are generally not dependable. Furthermore, even if they did work, they are redundant, since accurate distances off can be measured with fingers. The same applies to the range finders built into some expensive binoculars.

Estimating distance off relative to the width of a channel or bay, such as one half or one third of the way across, can be a more quantitative form of guessing. With practice this is a useful technique. A variation is to estimate that your distance off a point is about equal to the distance between two features on shore, (i.e., you might estimate that your distance off a point to the northwest of you is about equal to the width of the cove that follows it around the point). You can then locate your approximate position on the chart without even measuring any distances from the chart, as shown in figure 6-14.

You can reverse this last generic process to make a very specific piloting procedure that is well suited to kayak navigation in many circumstances. To discover your distance off a given charted feature on a more-or-less straight shoreline, look straight toward the shoreline at that feature and then look 45° to the right or left. If you happen to see at one of those locations another identifiable charted feature, then you can immediately know that your distance offshore is equal

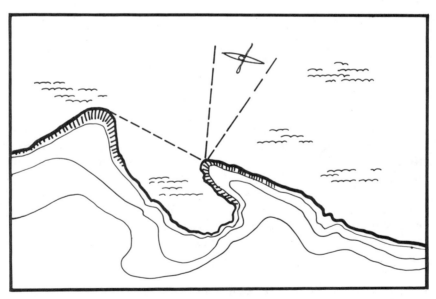

6-14. *A position fix from a relative bearing and distance off. This paddler knows he is oriented parallel to the coast, with the headland near his beam, and at a distance off that is about equal to the width of the bay. With these observations, a position can be noted on the chart.*

to the distance between these two features on the chart. This is a very good trick that takes little practice to master. There will not always be some convenient reference feature right where you want it, but you can sometimes estimate what you want, such as "my 45° mark is halfway between that church and that road," etc. Notice that since you know you are a given distance straight off the shoreline from a particular point, you have here not just a distance off but an actual position fix. This method relies on the simple property that the sides of a 45° triangle are equal (see fig.6-15).

Horizontal Angle

To get precise distance off, you must know the actual dimensions of what you are looking at. The width of a bay, the width of a big rock or island, or the distance between two rocks or two peaks are typical horizontal dimensions that can be read from a chart and used for figuring the distance to them. The procedure requires a measurement of the angle that this known distance subtends from your perspective. This measured angle emanating from your eye, along with the known base width of the charted feature, defines a unique triangle whose height is your distance off the base. For small triangles—meaning the distance off is much larger than the width of the target—this distance can be figured easily by scaling known triangle proportions.

The small-triangle rule is the simplest way to scale the result, since it states that the ratio of the sides of a 6° triangle is 1:10—for small angles it is not important to distinguish between sides and heights. Suppose the chart shows that the entrance to a bay lying dead ahead is 0.3 mile across, and an accurate compass shows that the bearing to one side of it is 050 and to the other side is 056. The bay subtends an angle of 6° from your perspective. The short side of the triangle is 0.3 mile across, so the long side of the triangle (distance to the entrance) must be ten times as long, or 3 miles off.

That is the principle of how the method works but not a practical way to do it. Only the best bearing compasses used in ideal conditions can provide bearings precise enough for this application. The more practical approach is to measure the subtended angle directly, without individual bearings to its edges. On larger vessels, these angle measurements are made with a sextant, but sextants, even small plastic ones, are not practical for routine use in a kayak. Furthermore, small angles can be measured to a precision adequate for this application without a sextant.

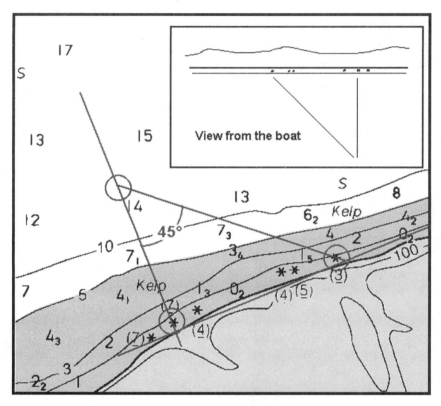

6-15. *Piloting trick for estimating position without the use of the hands. When looking straight onto a shoreline, notice what charted feature lies straight ahead and then what charted feature lies to the right or left by 45°. Your distance offshore is then equal to the distance between the two landmarks sighted. Diagonals drawn at 45° on the deck in front of you or on your transparent chart protector cover could be used to locate the relative bearing of 45°.*

The angle measurements are made by scaling a similar triangle whose base is held at arm's length, and whose height is the length of the arm. The proportions are shown in figure 6-16, but each of the several ways to improvise the measurement must be calibrated to the individual. One method is to use finger widths for the base dimensions. The average finger width at the average arm's length subtends an angle of approximately 2°. The bay in the last example would have been three fingers across.

Accurate measurements, independent of arm and finger sizes,

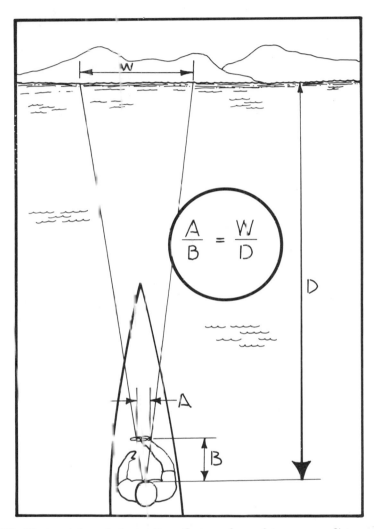

$$\frac{A}{B} = \frac{W}{D}$$

6-16. *Horizontal angle proportions that can be used to measure distance off a landmark. A hand width (A) at arm's length (B) covers a width (W) at the shoreline at a distance (D) away.*

can be made with a simple instrument called a *kamal*. It is just a graduated base plate attached to a string that keeps the eye-to-plate distance constant. For a string 57 centimeters long, each centimeter along the edge of the plate subtends exactly 1°. This is a convenient length to hold forward in a comfortable position. A common 15-

centimeter plastic ruler makes a convenient graduated plate, which can be attached to the string by a bridle to keep it from tilting, as shown in figure 6-17. A knot at the end of the string is held in the teeth, which frees one hand and keeps the measurements consistent. Measured with a kamal, the bay in the last example would have been 6 centimeters across.

A kamal is easy to make and easy to use, costs and weighs nearly nothing, and is extremely valuable for the vertical-angle method discussed later in this section. It is named after an ancient Arabic device of similar design used to measure the height of the North Star for dhow navigation along the Arabian Gulf and east coast of Africa.

The small-triangle rule can be converted into a formula for dis-

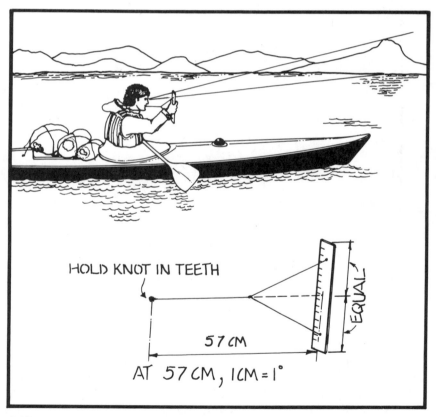

HOLD KNOT IN TEETH

57 CM

AT 57 CM, 1 CM = 1°

EQUAL

6-17. *The construction and use of a kamal for measuring vertical angles.*

tance off that can be used for this type of small-angle measurement (angles less than 30°).

$$\text{Distance off (in miles)} = 60 \times \frac{\text{Target width (in miles)}}{\text{Target angle (in degrees)}}.$$

A bay 0.3 mile across that appears 5° wide (or 5 centimeters on a kamal) must be 60 times 0.3 divided by 5, or 3.6 miles off. This is the distance to the center of the bay at the point on the chart where its width was measured. If the two sides of the bay are not equally distant from you, the width of the bay must be estimated as it would be seen from your perspective. The direction of your perspective can be determined from a compass bearing. If two inland peaks are used for a target, the same consideration of perspective and measurement point applies (see fig. 6-18).

For narrow features viewed from closer distances, the distance formula can be modified to:

$$\text{Distance off (in miles)} = \frac{\text{Target width (in feet)}}{100 \times \text{target angle (in degrees)}}.$$

This formula is equivalent to dividing the target width, expressed in hundreds of feet, by the angle in degrees. Two prominent rocks separated by 300 feet that appear 2° apart must be 3 divided by 2, or 1.5 miles off.

The calibration of a kamal can be tested by measuring the angles between stars. The Pointers on the cup end of the Big Dipper are 5.4° apart, and the equivalent two stars of the Little Dipper (called the Guards) are 3.2° apart. In southern latitudes, use the Southern Cross Pointers, which are 4.4° apart. The three stars of Orion's belt, visible from north or south latitudes in the winter, form a short line that is 2.7° across. When the stars are high, the head should be tilted back to keep the eye-to-kamal distance the same as it is when looking forward. Star pairs also can be used to estimate the angular widths of fingers, but this might be better done by just assuming a width of 2° and then adjusting this assumption until the formula reproduces the proper distance off of a known position.

A convenient variation of this method that works well with practice is to put graduation marks for angle measurements directly onto the paddle shaft, as shown in figure 6-19. Then only the paddle need be raised to make a distance measurement. The proper spacing for 1° intervals depends on arm length, but it should be within a few

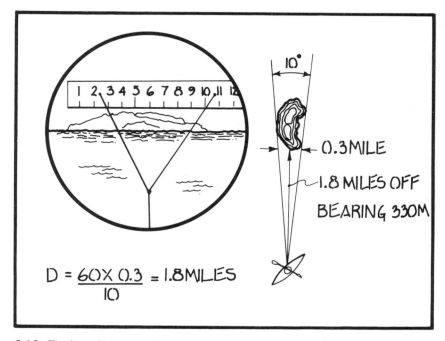

6-18. *Finding distance off by horizontal angle.*

millimeters of 1 centimeter. One way to test it is to tape a photocopy of a centimeter ruler on the shaft and then use it to measure the widths of several features at varying distances from a known position. If each of the distances figured from the formula (assuming 1 centimeter is right) turn out to be 20 percent too large, then reduce the factor of 60 in the formula by 20 percent, i.e., use 48 instead of 60 for future measurements. Raised graduations work better than a taped-on scale, if some variety store product can be found that does the job.

Winking

A clever variation of the horizontal-angle method employs the distance between the eyes as the base reference for the angle measurement. The average ratio of eye separation to arm length is approximately 1:10, which means a finger held at arm's length will shift 6° across its background when viewed with alternate eyes. In the bay example used above, if the finger were aligned with one edge of the bay viewed with the right eye closed, it would align with the other edge of the bay

6-19. *A makeshift kamal on a paddle shaft.*

with the left eye closed. By noticing that the finger shifted one bay width, you know the bay is 6° across, and therefore must be 10 times the width of the bay away from you.

With this method, it is not actually necessary to go through the intermediate step of figuring the angle. You can just figure distance off is 10 times the distance that your finger shifted along the horizon (see fig. 6-20). If your finger had only shifted halfway across the bay when you winked (the finger moved 0.15 mile), then your distance off would be 10 times 0.15, or 1.5 miles. Had your finger shifted past the other edge of the bay by half again the width of the bay, the distance off would be 10 times 0.45, or 4.5 miles.

This method is more approximate than the use of a kamal or graduated paddle shaft because you must judge by eye alone the fractional shift of the finger relative to the size of the target. But it is quick and much better than an unaided guess. It can be improved by fine tuning the factor of 10. To do this, measure the distance from eye to finger and then divide it by the distance between your eyes. Eye separation can be found by adjusting binoculars to fit and then measuring the separation of eye pieces, center to center. The result should be somewhere between 9 and 11, and it is this ratio that should be used in place of 10 when figuring distance off by winking.

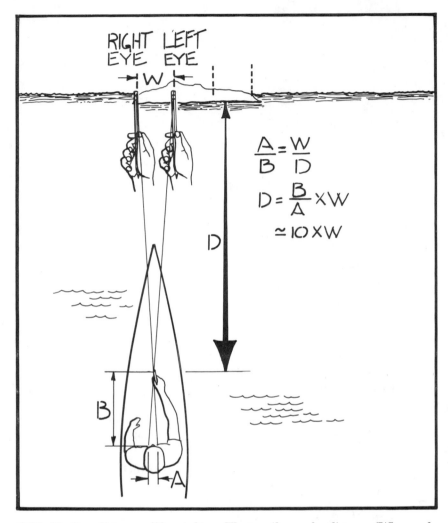

RIGHT LEFT
EYE EYE

$$\frac{A}{B} = \frac{W}{D}$$

$$D = \frac{B}{A} \times W$$

$$\approx 10 \times W$$

6-20. *Finding distance off by winking. The pencil moved a distance* (W) *equal to one third of the width of the islet that is located a distance* (D) *away. For an islet that is 900 feet across, the pencil moved 300 feet, so your distance off is about 3,000 feet or 0.5 mile. A is the distance between the eyes; B is an arm's length.*

Vertical Angle

For navigation within a few miles of target landmarks it is often more convenient to use the height of an object for distance off rather than its width. A peak location is better localized than horizontal features when viewed from nearby, and the same height can be used from various perspectives without having to remeasure the proper width as the perspective changes. Most peak heights and the elevations of lights are charted. *Coast Pilots* include the heights of some rocks and peaks not specified on charts, and they point out which peaks are conspicuous and thus candidates for this application.

Heights are used the same way widths are to find distance off. The vertical angles that span the features can be measured with fingers—they are generally even better for this than for horizontal angles. Nevertheless, measurements taken with a kamal are still more accurate and preferable. The angle to measure is from the top of the peak to the shoreline directly below the peak, as shown in figure 6-21. It does not matter that the shoreline is closer to you; the answer obtained is the distance to the charted peak location. The distance formula is the same as for widths:

$$\text{Distance off (in miles)} = \frac{\text{Target height (in feet)}}{100 \times \text{target angle (in degrees)}}.$$

Again, the distance off is just the charted elevation of the peak expressed in hundreds of feet divided by the kamal angle in centimeters. A 240-foot-high peak that spans 2 centimeters on the kamal must be 2.4 divided by 2, or 1.2 miles off. Usually this calculation can be done adequately without resorting to notes on the chart.

The formula is not so nice when the elevations are given in meters, since the factor of 100 in the formula must be changed to 30. A peak 200 meters high that spans 4 centimeters on the kamal must be 200 divided by 30 times 4, which equals 50 divided by 30, or 1.7 miles. In feet or meters, however, even if the division must be approximated, the answer will be more accurate than an unaided guess.

If it is known ahead of time that a particular peak will be useful for keeping track of position, the chart can be prepared with circles of equal distance from the peak that correspond to specific heights on a kamal. This way no calculations at all are required to use the peak for a reference. With a few bearing lines also drawn on the chart, as shown in figure 6-22, accurate position can be maintained with a few quick observations and a glance at the chart. This can be an easy and accurate way to navigate along an exposed coastline toward one large rock, offshore island, or peak on a headland.

Unlike the horizontal-angle methods, this method is restricted to distances fewer than 2 miles or so. If the answer is 2 or more miles, then it must be considered approximate until you get closer to the target. The restriction occurs because the mathematical approximations

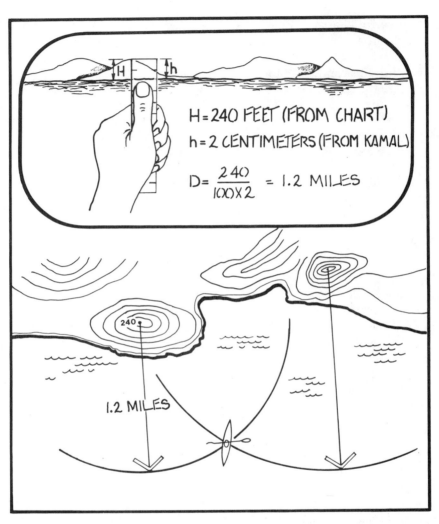

6-21. *Finding distance off by vertical angle using a kamal. A position can be found from the distances off of two landmarks. H is the height of the land, h is an angle or distance on the kamal.*

used in this application of the formula required that the true shore-line below the object be in view. From the seat of a kayak, the earth's curvature blocks the shoreline view at about 1.5 miles off, and at 2 miles off this begins to interfere with the results.

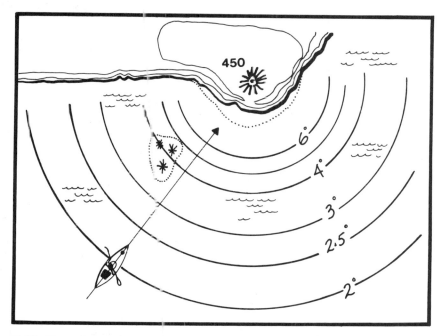

6-22. *Preparing a chart with circles of equal distance off to keep track of position. You will be approaching the rocky shoaling when the peak appears 3° high on a kamal.*

Doubling the Bow Angle

The methods covered so far require information from a chart. Distance off an uncharted feature also can be figured from its change in bearing as you paddle by it. The accuracy of the result depends on the accuracy of your estimated boat speed, which means the method is less reliable in strong wind or uncertain current. A related condition is that the reference landmark must be within a mile or two, so that its bearing changes significantly in a reasonable time. In these somewhat special circumstances, the method works when called for. A common application is to find distance off a shoreline when there is no urgency for the answer and no identifiable charted landmarks along the shore—to find, for example, where you are relative to an underwater shelf or shipping lane.

Any landmark, charted or uncharted, that lies within 20° to 50° (one to two outstretched hand widths) off the bow can be used (see fig. 6-23). Start by reading the compass heading of your course and then temporarily alter course toward any mark in the proper range (like a conspicuous tree) to get its bearing. Turn back to the original heading and figure the bow angle of the tree by subtracting the two compass readings. If the course is 100 and the bearing was 140, the bow angle was 40°. Start a stopwatch and paddle the original course at an average pace of known speed until the bow angle to the tree has doubled. When the bow angle has doubled, the distance off the mark is equal to the distance you had to travel to double it. In this example, the bow angle would have doubled when the bearing to the tree reached 180. If this took ten-minute paddling at 3 knots (twenty minutes per mile), the tree is 0.5 mile off at the time of the second bearing. If the mark was a charted rock instead of a tree, you could get a fix from the distance off and bearing. Figure 6-23 includes another

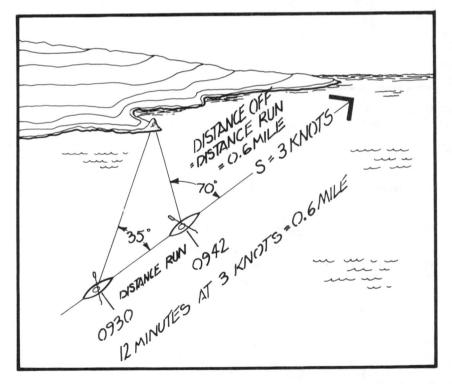

6-23. *Finding distance off by doubling the bow angle. A distance off a charted landmark and a bearing to it is a fix. This method can be applied to uncharted landmarks as well.*

numerical example of this technique.

Paddling along a straight shoreline, this can be done without altering course to measure bearings by doubling 45° to 90°, using nothing more than a diagonal line across the chart mark. Just take for a mark whatever happens to line up with the 45° line, and then time how long it takes for this mark to reach the beam. Distance off the shoreline is then the distance you had to travel to move the mark from 45° on the bow to 90° on the bow, which is on the beam.

As another example, suppose you are paddling along a floating bridge and notice a sign on the bridge that says, "All boats stay 200 yards off the bridge." Start a stopwatch, note which mark on the bridge is 45° off the bow, and keep paddling at what you figure is 3.5 knots. The mark passes the beam in fifty seconds. How far off the bridge are you? A speed of 3.5 knots is 350 feet per minute (since 1 knot is 100 feet per minute), so without further figuring, you know you are too close. The actual answer would be 50 divided by 60 times 350, which is just under 100 yards.

CHAPTER 7

Electronic Navigation

This chapter covers practical use of relatively new technology in electronic navigation that can readily be applied to kayaks. As mentioned in the Preface to the second edition, however, these new developments and associated procedures will not be of interest to all kayak navigators.

This technology is presented here because those who elect to use technological aids will better understand how these aids can be used in conjunction with the basic aids and skills discussed later on if they know ahead of time what they can do. (The remaining chapters of this book, it should be pointed out, are still written as if high-tech tools did not exist—which remains, in fact, the prudent approach to navigation.)

The Global Positioning System, known universally as "GPS," is an extensive satellite-based navigation system developed through Department of Defense contracts during the past twenty-five years. It was conceived as a military system and remains under military control. The loss of the Korean airliner that was destroyed when it wandered into Soviet air space in 1983 was influential in making the system accessible to civilian use to prevent similar disasters. As of about 1989 it was available for public use on a limited basis; today it is the primary electronic navigation system for all large vessels and many smaller ones, commercial and recreational. Within a few years it will undoubtedly be the dominant system used on all vessels and vehicles of any size that carry electronic equipment.

This system can tell you where you are (in terms of latitude and longitude) anywhere on earth and in any weather with astonishing precision—along with the direction you are moving and the speed of your motion, accurate to a tenth of a knot. It also tells the course and distance to any other location, your elevation, and just about any other navigational data you might care to know.

Anyone can use this system for any application. GPS receivers are readily available at marine electronics stores or general chandleries. In early 1999, hand-held units sell for some $100 to $300 (depending on brand and features) from several manufacturers. The price may appear high relative to other kayaking expenses, but once its functions, utility, and engineering are understood, the price can be appreciated as remarkably low.

Before getting to the practical use of this tool, I will share the personal conviction that GPS is one of the most dramatic technological developments in history. It is the first example of space-science technology that will ultimately have significant influence on several aspects of modern life. Its application to guiding boats around the waters of the world is just the beginning of its public use. It has, for example, already revolutionized the fields of surveying, mapping, and exploration. GPS instrumentation mounted near geological faults and volcanoes is being used to measure otherwise imperceptible motions of the earth's surface to forecast earthquakes and eruptions.

In the near future it will likely be standard equipment on motor cars and could be linked to miniature on-board computers. Such equipment can produce electronic maps with encyclopedic indexes to services and addresses. With a few keystrokes, for example, you could call up a map of the shortest route through one-way streets to the nearest Italian restaurant in a town you have never visited. Ambulances or other emergency vehicles could travel directly to any address in the most efficient manner. Combined with automated position broadcasts from moving GPS-equipped vehicles, tracking systems could be developed to warn of collision courses between cars, planes, or boats. Right now there are GPS units available that have stored in their memories the precise location of most navigational lights and buoys in the United States and Canada. New applications are being developed or dreamed of hourly. There are national monthly magazines devoted exclusively to news and features about GPS. See Further Reading and Appendix B on Internet links.

On the down side, the more efficient any tracking capability becomes, the more the question of privacy arises, not to mention hostile or terrorist use of automated precision navigation. Or, who is liable when a freighter from one country collides with a tanker from another country when both were navigated by American satellites that temporarily failed? (Anyone can buy the equipment, and no licenses or permits are required to use it.) Political, social, and legal issues develop in parallel with this, as with all high-impact technologies.

Use of GPS Underway

Physically, GPS receivers look a bit like cellular phone with its keypad and display screen. They easily fit in a shirt pocket. A small integral antenna communicates with satellites, so the unit must be placed on deck when in use, with as much view of the sky as possible. Obviously, kayak use calls for completely waterproof operation. Several brands meet this requirement; others will need a custom protective case. Figure 7-1 shows one secured on deck. The task is to arrange it so that the antenna is vertical, with the unit close enough that the output screen can be read and the keys pressed, but not in the way of the paddle during regular or special strokes.

When first turned on, the unit should be programmed with an approximate position, the time and date, and height above the water along with choices such as preferred units for distances and true or magnetic headings. You also must specify two-dimensional (latitude and longitude) or three-dimensional (includes altitude) position fixes. The obvious choice is two dimensions; this mode requires communications with just three satellites. To measure altitude requires "seeing" four satellites, which is sometimes difficult near steep shores that limit the view of the horizon.

Once programmed, the unit must accumulate basic almanac data from the satellites. This takes a few minutes extra on the first run of a new unit. After that, simply turn it on and in a minute or so it is functioning; from then on, all navigational data are available in seconds. If you transport the unit a long distance or do not use it for a long time, it might be necessary to reprogram it. For daily use it can be turned on and off with no delay in operation.

The units typically run on six AA batteries, which will last up to ten hours depending on brand. Since the units need to be run continuously only in special circumstances, this working lifetime could cover many days of typical touring. All have a battery saver mode that shuts the unit off in a minute or so if no key is pressed. Care must be taken, of course, if this mode is disengaged for longer operation such as for crossing currents. For expedition paddling away from civiliza-

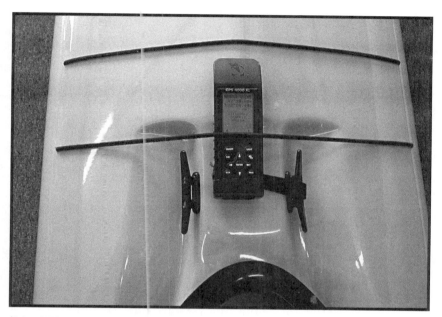

7-1. *GPS receiver secured to the deck of a kayak.*

tion, rechargeable batteries and a solar-powered battery charger are invaluable. Such a system has been used successfully on solo kayak expeditions in the Arctic by Gail Ferris. (She also found that the course over ground determined by GPS was helpful for steering in the fog in high latitudes, where the magnetic compass was not reliable.)

Position Navigation

Your position is indicated on the display screen in latitude and longitude, specified to the nearest one-hundredth of a minute, such as 47° 38.53' N, 122° 24.79' W. Recall from chapter 2 that 1' of latitude is about 6,000 feet, so a precision of 0.01' corresponds to about 60 feet. The remarkable thing here is that the numbers you see on the screen are usually correct. This small hand-held gadget can tell you where you are on the 200 million square miles of the earth's surface to within some four or five kayak lengths!

If the unit suspects that the data may not be good, it will provide various warning signals or icons on the screen, with codes that tell of the problem, such as missing satellites, weak signals, and the like. Although most interactions with the satellites are done automatically, you do have the option in some cases to adjust satellite choices or erase calculations and start the position determination all over. These user interactions, however, are very rarely called for. This is truly a "black box." You turn it on, and it tells you where you are.

Using GPS, position navigation reduces to plotting your known latitude and longitude on the chart—to find out where you really are! This is not a trivial task in a kayak underway, especially if you wish to retain anywhere near the actual accuracy you know. In fact in most cases, you cannot plot the accuracy you know, no matter how or where you do it, because of the limitations of the chart scales. On a 1:25,000 chart (the largest scale typically available), a pencil dot one sixteenth of an inch across spans 130 feet on the chart. If you can get that dot on that chart in the right place, you know you are in the middle of it. Plot the position wrong by one dot width, and you have thrown away accuracy. On a 1:40,000 chart, that dot is 208 feet across.

The only reasonable approach underway in a kayak is to have latitude and longitude lines already drawn on the chart at convenient intervals and then to locate your position relative to them, either by simply estimating the place or using a special tool. Some lines are, of course, printed on the chart to begin with, but they are too far apart to be convenient. On a 1:40,000 chart, the parallel lines of latitude are typically printed only every 5', which spaces them about 9 inches apart. If you draw the lines in by hand every 1' of latitude and longitude it is much easier to estimate where your position lies by interpolation. (It is presumed here that the standard use of dividers and the scales along each edge of the chart will not be usable underway.)

The procedure can be improved by constructing a special plotting tool using waterproof cardboard or plastic and waterproof ink. The plotter is illustrated in figure 7-2. It must be customized for each chart in use, and it requires that the chart be prepared with latitude and longitude lines. The tool can be tied to the chart case along with a china marker or other waterproof pen. I have used this plotting technique extensively in sailboat racing whenever quick plotting was essential. It is much faster than conventional methods, regardless of the tools or space available.

A reminder, though, that no matter how you plot it, or even how you obtained the position fix in the first place, recording that position on the chart and labeling it with the corresponding time remains the key to good navigation. The more often you do it, the more you will learn from it, and the better off you will be when you need it. In Chapter 6 we called this "Rule No. 1."

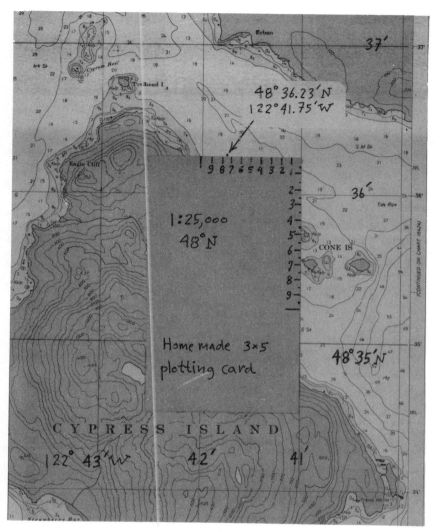

7-2. *Homemade tool for quick plotting of GPS positions. The chart must be pre-pared with Lat-Lon lines at each 1' interval. To use the card: (1) align the right edge of the card with the minutes part of your longitude on the chart; (2) adjust the vertical position of the card to align the tenths part of your latitude minutes (read on the card) with the whole-minutes line of your latitude on the chart; and (3) mark the chart at the minutes part of your longitude read from the card. At this scale, the hundredths of minutes parts of latitude and longi-tude must be interpolated by eye. Separate plotting cards (or separate sides or corners of the same card) are needed for each chart scale and latitude region.*

And one last important point: The operational accuracy of GPS is not constant. GPS remains a military system, and the Defense Department controls the ultimate accuracy available for civilian use with a control called Selective Availability (SA). With the "SA knob" turned full up, a *Standard Accuracy* of just 100 meters is available for civilian use; with the "knob" turned down, the accuracy is much better. Marine users who have made such tests find accuracies closer to 20 meters or so in cases I know about, although the system is capable of even greater accuracy. Generally, civilian users do not know how SA will affect their accuracy at any given time or place. Worse still, civilian access—meaning anyone but the U.S. military—could be deteriorated much more than Standard Accuracy if deemed important in a military conflict.

There is considerable debate going on about the role of SA in this important technology, funded by U.S. taxpayers and used at no charge worldwide. One inevitable solution to the problem is called Differential GPS, whereby satellite signals are coordinated with land-based signals from precisely known locations. These systems (already in use many places) provide accuracies independent of SA better than 1 meter (!) and offer various ways to ultimately charge for the service, directly or indirectly. Full information about GPS services is available at the GPS page of the Coast Guard's Navicenter Web site. See Appendix B.

Speed over Ground and Course over Ground

A GPS receiver includes a computer and a clock. The clock is updated continually from the satellites and displays the precise GMT.

With computer memory and a clock, the unit not only knows where you are, it knows where you were. From this it can figure your true course and speed at any time. It is important to understand that the speed and course it tells you are your true speed and true course, called speed over the ground (SOG) and course over the ground (COG). This is not the same speed that a knotmeter would read and not the course that your compass would read. SOG and COG are measures of your true motion that take into account your paddling speed, the speed of the current, and any leeway you might have if the wind is blowing. In most cases, to navigate these are the primary values you care about.

If you were paddling at 3 knots through a tidal stream moving at 2 knots, the GPS would show a SOG of 5 knots, assuming the current was flowing in the same direction you were paddling. In this case, your COG would be the same as your compass course. If, on the other hand, you were paddling at 3 knots due north magnetic (000 on the compass), across a current flowing toward the northeast at 2 knots, the GPS would show a SOG of 4.6 and a COG of 018. It has told you very plainly you are not going the direction you are pointed (which is what the compass reads).

On a long passage or in dangerous waters, it is the COG and, to a lesser extent, the SOG, that you really care about, not so much your actual position at any one time. This is the information that warns you immediately that you may be getting into trouble, or that you are at least not doing what you think you are. It is, nevertheless, the high accuracy of the position data that allows the instrument to figure the course and speed accurately and quickly.

Since the COG and SOG are so crucial to navigation, it is important that they be displayed in the most useful manner. The high accuracy of the instrument can work against you in some cases. When paddling in gusty winds or bigger seas, your actual course and speed change every few minutes or even every five or ten seconds as you adjust or respond to the seas or gusts. But since the instrument is so accurate it measures each of these intermittent changes. Each time you look at the screen you see a new course, which means you are back to not knowing which way you are going. To correct this, reprogram the GPS to display the *average* value of the COG and SOG over the past thirty seconds or few minutes.

Waypoints and Routes

Navigation with GPS, or by any means for that matter, is facilitated by setting up specific locations called waypoints and sequences of these called routes. A planned trip would begin at home or on the beach, by selecting from the chart various points (usually turning points) along the intended route, and then entering the latitude and longitude of these points into the GPS unit. Most models will accept several hundred such points, which can be numbered or even given alphabetic names. The sequence itself then can be named and stored as a specific route. Waypoints also can be copied from a previously stored route and built into a new one. Or you could define, say, waypoint 22 as 2.4 miles NE of waypoint 57. The format is versatile. It is also possible at any time when you are underway to store your present position as a numbered waypoint. With this option, you could travel a route you have not programmed and store key points along the way to use for a programmed return trip.

Once a route is entered, you can review it (still sitting at home), asking for the course and distance between each waypoint to sum up the trip or for other planning. And this is exactly what you would do underway as you proceed from point to point. From your starting position, you call up the route of interest and the first waypoint on it. Then from your present position, the unit tells you the course and distance to that waypoint. As you proceed in that direction, it will figure your speed and tell how long it will take to get there at that average speed. If you wander off the direct line route to the waypoint, it will tell you so, but regardless of where you are it continually tells you the course and distance to the assigned waypoint. When you arrive at the waypoint, select the next one, and carry on; or use the automatic mode, which will switch to the next waypoint when you pass within a certain distance to the first one.

In Chapter 10 section on paddling in traffic, there is discussion of a useful GPS trick for locating your position relative to shipping lanes. That method makes use of routes and cross-track error, discussed below.

Currents, Cross-Track Error, and Plotters

There are two basic ways to navigate with GPS using waypoints. The first is to call up the desired destination, read the course to it, and head in that direction. As you proceed, set up the display screen to show your course over ground (COG) and then watch how this compares to the desired course to the waypoint. (Most units can show these two courses on the same screen.) If you are in current, your compass is wrong, or you are simply not paddling the course you intended to, the COG will show that you are not making the desired course, and you must alter course until these two agree.

For example, suppose the computed course to the waypoint is 050 and paddling that course for a few minutes you notice the COG is 070, although the compass still reads 050 and you have held this fairly well. You are getting set to the south, most likely by a southerly current. In this case, you will have to point north of the desired course, into the current, in order to track straight to the waypoint. (More general discussion of crossing currents like this is covered in chapter 9.)

As a first guess, since you are getting set 20° south, you could just steer 20° north of 050, toward 030, and then watch how that develops.

If you are then tracking to the mark, you are done—assuming you remain paddling at the same rate. If you speed up or slow down, the numbers will change, but in any event the unit will tell you immediately what course to steer to achieve your desired course. Or stop paddling all together and let the COG and SOG be a measure of the current speed and direction—providing there is no significant wind pushing you across the water.

When crossing currents in this manner, using just one waypoint and the COG, it is important that you monitor both courses (desired course and COG) simultaneously during the process. This is important for fairly close destinations, since the desired course will change as you get set off the original track line.

The way around this problem, which is most important in crossing strong currents or when setting off on a long passage with hazards to either side, is to use the second approach mentioned above. Choose not only a destination waypoint, but also a departure point, from which the computer will establish the straight line track between them. With this method, you can guide the boat along that track through all sorts of hazards, in strong current, or in thick fog. It is the mariner's version of flying by the instruments.

Using this option, you can steer by what is called *cross track error* (XTE). This display shows how far you are off to the right or left of the intended track. In some circumstances this is a convenient way to navigate. Typical displays that you could select under way might read:

TO SMITH ROCK	ROUTE 10 LEG 3
050° M 2.48 NM or	47° 38.41'N 124° 35.03'W
XTE 0.03 NM RIGHT	COG 057 M SOG 3.9

The first shows that you have called your immediate destination "Smith Rock" and that it is located 2.48 miles away in magnetic (compass) direction 050, and at the moment you are 0.03 nautical miles to the right of the track you planned to travel. As often is the case, it pays to recall that 1 mile is about 6,000 feet, so this means you are 180 feet (0.03 x 6,000) off course to the right. It remains impressive: you can draw a precise line mathematically between two points that are, say, 10 miles apart, and at any position along that route know immediately whenever you wander more than 60 feet off that line.

The alternative display shows that Smith Rock is the destination of the third leg of what you have numbered the tenth route of your travels. Your present position is shown, along with the fact that at the moment you are making good a course of 057 at a speed of 3.9 knots. If you want to get back on track, you will have to point more to the left.

Note that in this case if you happened to be steering 050, and then used the previous reasoning, you would alter course to steer some 7° high to correct for the set. What would likely happen, though, is when you steadied out paddling toward 043, you would indeed start making good the course you wanted of 050, but you would not be back on the track you wanted. You just straightened out your course over ground to be parallel to your desired track. You will have to overcorrect for a while to get back on to the actual track, and then fall back to 043.

Remember that these are all *average* courses. You cannot, usually, steer a course of, say, 043 precisely; in all circumstances your compass course swings around as you proceed. But you can get fairly close, especially when you have such a powerful tool as GPS to help. Just do whatever you are doing, and watch the average course on the GPS; if it is not quite right, do a little more or little less of it.

As an alternative to using digital values of cross track error, most models these days offer a graphic plot display. The same screen used for numerical display becomes a blank chart or plotting sheet of the region around your present position. The extent of the plot can span hundreds of miles or just a few tenths of a mile. You can show an entire route, traced between many waypoints, or zoom in on the display to show just 200 yards or so either side of your position. Usually the present position is marked with a dot with an emanating arrow that clearly points in the direction of your present COG. As you proceed along the route, the computer leaves a trail of dots to show the route you followed. At any time, you can tell at a glance where you are relative to the track line and which way you are making good at the moment.

This can be a very convenient option. Depending on the format of this feature, which varies among the brands, actual tracks of a trip can be saved, rather than just a series of waypoints along it. A saved track can then be reversed to use as a guide (actual path) for a return trip, or later scanned at home and transferred to a chart for a precise record of your outing or expedition. Despite the potential conveniences of this feature, however, it remains prudent and still of utmost importance to record your position on a real chart with the corresponding time as frequently as possible ("Rule No. 1"). If you put all your eggs in one little plastic box, you might get caught up the creek with your batteries down.

How It Works

GPS finds position from the intersection of circles of position that indicate ranges to satellites whose locations are known precisely. The procedure is analogous to that shown in figure 6-18, which uses an ancient kamal to measure the ranges. High technology enters in the way the satellite ranges are determined: measuring the time it takes the radio signals to travel from the satellites to the receiver. Time measurements accurate to nanoseconds (billionths of a second) are used, with timing errors removed using a third satellite for the fix. This is the reason three satellites are required for a two-dimensional fix that could otherwise be done with just two, as shown in figure 6-18.

The worldwide system consists of a constellation of twenty-one active satellites with three operational spares. The Coast Guard coordinates civilian use of GPS. Latest information is available from the USCG Navigation Center Web site (see Appendix B). Policies and goals are officially presented in the Federal Radionavigation Plan, which is updated every two years. This publication is available from the Web site.

Excellent introductions to the complex subject of GPS are: *Everyone's Guide to Satellite Navigation* by Steven Thompson (1991, ARINC Research Corporation, Annapolis, Md.) and *GPS—A Guide to the Next Utility* by Jeff Hurn (1990, Trimble Navigation, Sunnyvale, Calif.). See also valuable links in Appendix B.

Other Electronic Aids

In this section we review other electronic aids that are either new or remain as options for use in a kayak underway. The technologies are not so far reaching as GPS, but nevertheless impressive in the convenience and precision they offer. Before covering new developments, we will briefly review Loran, an electronic navigation system that will eventually be completely replaced by GPS. But for the next few years Loran may be useful in some kayak applications. Please note, though, this is very likely the last edition of this book that will cover Loran. It is almost a thing of the past, but not quite yet. The oldest of all electronic aids is radio direction finding, which is covered in chapter 10 in the High Seas Navigation section. Although this is in an entirely different class of electronic navigation, it will long remain a valuable method to know about since it can be applied with an inexpensive pocket radio using commercial AM radio broadcasts. New high-tech developments in communications are covered in the Marine Radios section of chapter 10.

Loran

Loran is a land-based navigation system operated by the Coast Guard. It has been in operation, with several upgrades, since World War II. It was intended solely for coastal waters, but it has been used extensively and successfully on inland waters for the past decade and was crucial to the fishing industry until GPS came along. The name derives from "long-range navigation," which, in some senses, is outdated these days.

The system works by determining lines of position from the observed arrival times of radio signals broadcast simultaneously from two stations several hundred miles apart. The lines of position are hyperbolic curves that trace out across the chart the path of all points with the same arrival-time difference between the two signals. The intersection of two such curves (from one "master" station coordinated with two "slave" stations) produces the fix. Programming within the individual Loran units then coverts this information to latitude and longitude. The precision of this last step varies among the models and manufacturers and from region to region for the same unit.

Regions are covered by separate groups of four or five stations each. The West Coast from Alaska to California, for example, is covered by three such groups. Positions can be determined up to 1,000 miles from the stations, but the stations themselves are often hundreds of miles inland.

We include notes on this older system because hand-held waterproof Loran units exist that look and operate almost exactly like the GPS units discussed above. And they will likely be around and usable for several years to come—if you can find one. The low cost of GPS units has essentially driven them out of the marketplace. Loran signals are available in all coastal waters of the United States and Canada and their connecting inland waters, as well as in Japan, Europe, and Scandinavia; but they are not available in Mexico, the Bahamas, or the Caribbean, nor anywhere in the Southern Hemisphere.

Although Loran measures the same things as GPS (position, COG, SOG, XTE) and uses waypoints in the same manner, there are still very important differences, and these differences are only slowly being appreciated by new users of electronic navigation. If you know how to use GPS, as outlined above, you automatically know how to use the functions of Loran—although historically the statement should be reversed; all the convenient user interface design applied to GPS was developed with Loran.

But though the outputs are the same, the accuracy of the data and dependability of its operation are different. Loran has, indeed, a high *reproducible accuracy* (60 to 100 feet) but it has significantly less *intrinsic accuracy*. That is, if you store a present position as a waypoint and then travel away from it, the unit will guide you back to that precise point very accurately. But if you compared the latitude and longitude of that location read from the Loran with that read from a large-scale chart, you would find the instrument might be off as much as a couple tenths of a mile. This places limits on its use in confined waters and also on the accuracy and immediacy of its derived data, such as COG and SOG.

There are ways around the intrinsic accuracy problem for position navigation, either by relying on repeated routes that have been directly stored when at the site of each waypoint, or by entering "fudge factors" to offset the errors for specific locations. But there is no way around its influence on COG and SOG, which, again, is the primary information required for careful navigation.

It takes a Loran unit a minute or two and sometimes longer to figure your COG and SOG, because it must average over a longer period to compensate for its lower position accuracy. If you were paddling at a constant rate, in constant current and constant wind for five minutes, then the COG and SOG it shows will be as accurate as that of GPS. But the moment you turn or the current changes, you will get inaccurate readings on the Loran until things have stabilized for a few minutes. In contrast, GPS takes just a few seconds to detect new motion, although even GPS results (without differential corrections) should also be averaged over at least thirty seconds for reliable speed and course information.

Another drawback with Loran is its much higher vulnerability to local electromagnetic noise or static. This is not nearly the problem for kayak use as it is for larger vessels with engines, fluorescent lights, televisions, and so forth, but it still influences operation in some areas because ambient noise levels in the environment outside of the boat depend on location and time of day. Likewise, electric storms interfere with Loran but have little influence on GPS. There also are other factors that inhibit the use of Loran that can all be traced to the fixed geometry of the land-based transmitting stations. Many of the problems that arise from these factors can in fact be corrected for by user adjustments, but the vast majority of Loran users, on any size vessel, do not get involved in this level of its operation. GPS, on the other hand, provides what most users want—a true black box, with no required tuning or adjustments.

There is no doubt at all that Loran remains an extremely valuable aid to navigation. In thick fog and strong currents it will get you where you want to go. The key to using it safely and efficiently is understanding its limitations and learning to work with them, which to a large extent is accomplished by plotting your position on the chart and labeling it with the corresponding time as frequently as practical ("Rule No. 1").

Hand-held Tide and Current Computers

At the time of the first edition, several computer software programs related to tide and current prediction were available from several sources, but their cost was either high or their features low. They were not used by many mariners. Today there are scores of programs advertised in nautical publications, with all-inclusive features. They can predict tide and current at any NOAA reference station and all subordinate stations, at any time (not just the turning points listed in the NOAA tables); plot graphs of tide or current versus time; or tell just about anything you want to know about these things. And the same programs can do it for the entire hemisphere, on any date to the year 2030 or beyond. The software is typically inexpensive, at least relative to the cost of the books required to duplicate the data and the time saved not having to use them. Nevertheless, this software still is not used by many mariners, primarily because not all mariners (kayakers or ship captains) use computers as a personal resource away from their employment. The percentage that do, however, is increasing rapidly with time.

In the meantime, though, the gap has been bridged with a small black box called the "Tide Finder," from Conex Electro-Systems in Bellingham, Washington. It takes no special training or equipment to operate (the computer and software are hidden inside).

This is definitely a luxury item for many (prices are about $350), but for those whose paddling must be fit into a tight schedule, this device can save much time. When a trip must be planned around a complex tidal current pattern, this is the most convenient way to compare data for alternative days and times. It also has virtue for long trips with no definite itinerary. Wherever you end up and when, you can call up the local data at a keystroke and not have to carry extra books or paperwork along.

It would be a fair guess that eventually this technology will be built into every GPS unit as just one more bell or whistle, but for now, more and more of these small dedicated computers are showing up at the nav stations of commercial and recreational vessels.

The latest developments in this area are found in the same place as all others: on the Internet. See Appendix B for links that will provide tides and currents in tables and graphs for all U.S. waters and many places elsewhere.

Electronic Compasses

And now let's enter further into the luxury arena—as much for completeness as for anticipated popularity in kayaking—to report on hand-held electronic instruments for high precision bearings and range finding.

The basic electronic-compass technology is not new. It has been used for twenty years in science laboratories to measure magnetic fields; but only recent developments in miniaturized electronics and other engineering have made compass technology feasible for small hand-held instruments, and thus for marine application. A popular model is called the "DataScope" by KVH Industries in Middletown, Rhode Island. The commercial instrument (which sells for about $300 in 1999) evolved from custom designs made for the 1987 America's Cup yacht racing team.

Unlike conventional compasses, which find magnetic north from gimbaled needles pushed that way by magnetic forces (as wind vanes line up with the wind), electronic compasses find the field direction using gimbaled circuitry that figures that direction without actually pointing anything toward it. The underlying principles are the same ones that make electric motors work, though highly refined here with extensive microprocessing of the signals. The circuit design that senses the field is called a "flux gate," which is why these units are often called flux gate compasses.

This technology has widespread applications on larger vessels where it is used for inputting digitized compass courses into other electronics for computing currents or for dead reckoning. (If a computer knows the compass heading and the knotmeter speed, and also knows the actual course and speed over ground from GPS, then it can calculate the current, which is what causes these two sets of data to be different.)

Bearings with the DataScope compass are taken by viewing the target through a 5x30 monocular, with the bearing, specified to a tenth of a degree (i.e., 247.5°), showing continuously below a hairline sight. Press a button to lock the display, store the bearing and accurate time (internal quartz clock), and assign a number to the sight. Later, scan the list to transfer the bearing to a chart or logbook. This procedure can be used to take a series of sights to obtain the best average, or to measure how a particular bearing changes with time, which is used in several standard piloting methods.

Precision in readout, however, does not guarantee a corresponding accuracy in the actual measurement, especially with such sensitive measurements as magnetic bearings. The instrument has built in a convenient way of calibration and compensation, which you perform much like swinging ship to check and compensate a conventional compass. Nevertheless, regardless of its electronic nature and accurate calibration it still measures the magnetic field around you and therefore is just as susceptible to stray magnetic influences as any conventional magnetic compass is. Using one of these, for example, in my left hand with my watch on, I can consistently get measurements to a distant peak that are 1.2° higher than with my watch off. It would be nearly impossible to learn such things with any conventional hand-held compass. Chapter 4 covers pertinent care in compass use.

An equally valuable function of this same instrument is the accurate range finder it includes. This is especially true for kayakers, because it offers a one-handed way to find distance off a landmark of known height. The principle of this range finder is the same as that of the simple kamal discussed in chapter 6, as is its role in navigation. This one is just easier to use, more accurate, and it does the numerical distance calculation automatically.

Again, though, I would *never* head off on any voyage that might require any level of navigation without a conventional magnetic compass, regardless of the kind or size of the vessel, and especially regardless of what other electronic wonders I might have along. Fundamental prudent seamanship requires that all electronics in a marine environment be regarded as luxuries (regardless of their costs), to be used when convenient but not to be depended upon.

Trends in Electronic Publications

Historically marine resources have all been books or other printed publications: charts, *Coast Pilot, Light List, Notice to Mariners*. This is changing in the marine field, just as it is in all walks of life. Telephones, fax machines, and computers allow communications on a much more rapid scale. Information is more timely, more compact, and better indexed. Even very specialized publications are accessible from remote locations

Though we have only covered it briefly here, in Chapter 2, nautical charts are themselves now available as computer files on disk or CD-ROM. Used with good graphic display and zoom options they are truly a space-age way to navigate, especially with GPS interfaced to the charting software so the computer screen shows your position on the chart, along with the track of your past motion, and an arrow showing your COG. A simple slide and tap on a touch pad gives range and bearing to any point as well as other functions. Perhaps someday waterproof palm top computers might make this feasible technology for kayakers.

But there are numerous resources kayakers can tap into with nothing more than a phone or fax machine as well as those accessible by Internet links between computers. Just a few are mentioned below, presented with the fair warning that it is difficult to stay up to date on the resources.

In earlier editions of this book we stressed the use of voice telephone and fax lines for obtaining up-to-date navigation information to supplement printed data that might be outdated. Those processes, however, have definitely been replaced now by Internet resources that you tap into with a computer and modem. Chart catalogs; *List of Latest Editions*; wonderful, thorough weather information; data on navigation aids; *Rules of the Road*; USCG Notices to Mariners; tides and currents; *Sailing Directions*; massive nautical glossaries; kayaking magazine articles; discussion groups on kayaking topics; even extensive courses on navigation itself, and many other related matters are all available with a simple Internet connection. If you do not have this facility at home, it is available at nearly all public libraries and schools these days. Appendix B has an extensive section on the features and use of the Internet.

CHAPTER 8

Tides and Currents

All waters that lead to the ocean are subject to the rise and fall of the tides. In many waters, tides and tidal currents have dramatic impact on many aspects of kayak navigation. Tide height must be known when planning to put in or land because the tide height determines how much beach will be exposed. Changes in tide height can turn an easy landing into an impossible one. Striking examples occur in areas with rocks or islets connected to dry land by spits (called tombolos) that cover and uncover with the tides: A sheltered landing site on the connecting spit might only exist at low tide. (The reference water depth, chart datum, used to define tide heights and soundings is discussed in chapter 2.) Knowledge of tide height is also critical for planning crossings over tideflats. In some circumstances many miles can be saved by crossing a tideflat at high water rather than going around it when it is dry—although it is still important to cross in water as deep as possible because very shallow water is harder to paddle through (see chapter 5). When approaching a rocky shoreline, it is also important to know the tides in order to avoid rocks that cover and uncover with the tides (see chapter 2).

In contrast to tide height, which must be known only in special circumstances and is usually easy to predict, some knowledge of tidal current is needed at all times, and it is usually not so easy to predict. If you plan to go through a pass or across a channel that has strong currents, you need to know when the current will be weakest at the crossing site and also the state of the current along the route to the crossing site from your present position, because that determines how long it will take to get there and whether you will make it there by slack-water time. Furthermore, current flowing against the wind in any waterway causes a dramatic increase in the steepness of the waves, often causing breaking seas that make paddling downwind comparable to paddling in surf—except that the wave crests are closer together. When paddling upwind in strong favorable current, the short steep seas caused by the opposing wind, along with the adverse force of the wind itself, often hinder progress more than the favorable current aids it. Changes in tidal current in just a few hours can turn an easy paddle at 4 or 5 knots made good into drudgery at 1 or 2 knots.

Only when paddling in landlocked lakes or reservoirs (where there are no tides) or in specific areas where it has been confirmed that tides have minimal influence can a paddler get by without an ongoing awareness of the state of the tidal cycle. Although tidal current has more significant influence on navigation than tide height does, the tides drive the currents so they are the starting point to understanding navigational implications of both.

The gravitational force of the moon pulls the oceans up into a bulge on the moon side of the earth as shown schematically in figure 8-1. This leaves the ocean surface slightly depressed on the sides of the earth and (relative to the sides) another bulge is created on the backside of the earth opposite the moon due to centrifugal force. As the earth rotates daily beneath the moon, the two bulges and the two hollows between them tend to hold their position relative to the moon. This causes the tidal wave envelope made up of the bulges and hollows to circle the earth as long waves causing the tides to rise and fall twice a day. Under the influence of these moving tidal bulges, water depths at specific locations oscillate between deeper than average and shallower than average approximately every six hours. The range of water depths on inland waters can be quite dramatic in special locations—40 feet or more in extreme cases—even though the actual height of the tidal bulge in midocean is only about 18 inches: The extremely long wavelength of the tidal bulge causes the height of the wave to build as it enters the shallower water of the continental shelf. It then builds even more in funnel-shaped tidal channels inland, just as small ocean swells build in height before breaking as they run up a beach. In special cases, the size of coastal embayments "match" their tidal periods, which also causes large tides by resonance, just as there is an optimum speed to slide back and forth in a bathtub to create large waves.

Peak water elevations in the tidal oscillation are called *high waters;* minimum water elevations are called *low waters.* The terms, however,

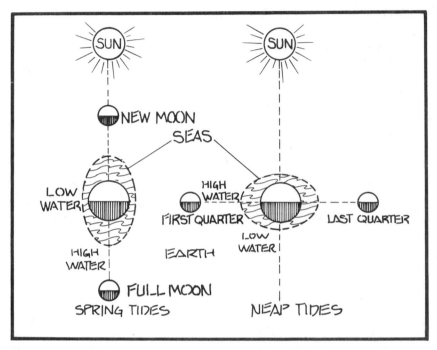

8-1. *Tidal bulges on the oceans are caused by the gravitational attraction of the moon and sun.*

are relative to successive water levels in the tide cycle; it is possible for the actual water depth to be greater at low water on one day than it was at high water on another day. The heights and times of high and low waters vary slowly on successive cycles at specific locations, and they can vary considerably from place to place around the world. The height difference between high and low waters is called the *range* of the tide.

As the earth rotates daily, the moon rises in the east and sets in the west. At its peak height in the sky it bears either due south or due north, depending on your latitude. This moment is called the meridian passage of the moon, because the moon crosses your longitude at this time. The time period between successive meridian passages is called the lunar or tidal day; it is about twenty-four hours and fifty minutes long. A high water typically occurs one or two hours after the moon's meridian passage. The precise time lag depends on location, but it remains fairly constant from day to day at specific places. The time lag occurs because friction slows down the tidal bulge, so it does not follow directly under the moon, but some distance behind it. The sun also influences the tides (its gravitational pull on the water is about one-half as strong as that of the moon), so the relative orbital positions of the sun and moon (the moon's phase) also affect the tide height. In broad terms, the location of the more important moon determines the time of the tides, and the phase of the moon determines the range of the tides.

If the water goes up and down at the coast, it must at some time go in and out of coastal embayments. The up-and-down motion causes the *tide height* to change; the in-and-out motion causes the *tidal current* to change. It is important, however, to distinguish in language and thinking between tides (vertical motion) and the resulting tidal currents (horizontal motion). These two motions are not as simply related as might be guessed, because the size and shape of a tidal basin affect the flow or water within it. The common practice of referring to tidal currents as "the tides" is misleading and should be avoided.

Tidal current flowing into an estuary is called a *flood* current; when it flows out it is called an *ebb* current. The direction into or out of an estuary is not always clear from charts, so the direction as well as speeds are always specified in tidal current tables for each referenced location. The brief time between flood and ebb currents when no current flows (or current speed is minimum) is called *slack water*. Most tidal currents of inland waters are *reversing currents*, meaning the flood current at a particular location flows in one specific direction, and the ebb current flows in the opposite or near opposite direction. Starting from slack water, the current speed increases to a maximum value, called *maximum ebb* or *maximum flood*, and then diminishes as the next slack approaches. Maximum flow in each cycle occurs approximately halfway between successive slack water times. The phrase "a 2-knot flood" usually refers to the entire flood cycle that peaks at 2 knots.

When considering the relationship between tide height and the associated tidal current, it is tempting to guess that slack water occurs at high water and at a low water—based on the reasoning that when the water stops going up, it stops coming in; and when it stops going down, it stops going out. This oversimplified common guess of the general behavior of tidal current is usually wrong, and it has gotten numerous kayakers into serious trouble. This type of current behavior is actually characteristic of the fairly specialized circumstance of a *standing wave* in the local tidal basin. In a standing wave pattern, the water responds to tidal forces by sloshing up and down in the local tidal basin as it might in a large bathtub. When one end of the basin

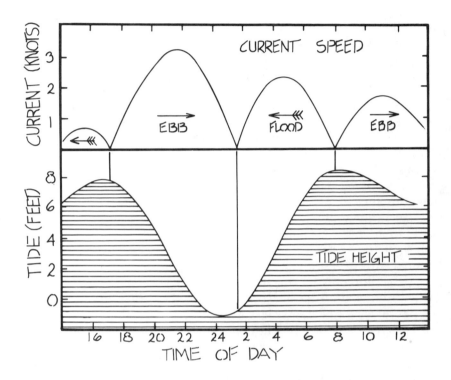

8-2. *Tides and currents off Bush Point, in Admiralty Inlet, between Puget Sound and the Strait of Juan de Fuca, Washington, on October 20 and 21, 1986. This is predominantly a standing wave tide with slack waters near high and low waters and peak flow about halfway between slack waters. Compare this behavior with figure 8-3 for the same period in the Strait of Juan de Fuca.*

is high and slack, the other is low and slack. Some location near the center of the basin behaves as a pivot point (called the nodal point) in that it has a near-zero tide range even though current flows through it. In a standing wave tide, peak flow at any location along the "tub" occurs halfway between high water and low water. Standing wave patterns are established whenever two identical waves are running in opposite directions, which occurs in long dead-end tidal basins that reflect the incoming tidal bulge from the inland end of the basin. Consequently, in some large, partly enclosed waterways this common guess of tidal behavior is, indeed, a fairly close description of the relationship between tides and currents (an example is shown in figure 8-2). In many other places, however, this guess could be seri-

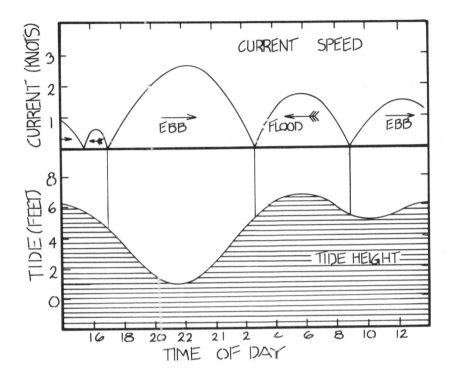

8-3. *Tides and currents off Angeles Point in the Strait of Juan de Fuca, Washington, on October 20 and 21, 1986. This is predominantly a progressive wave tide with peak flows near high and low waters, and slack waters closer to the time of midtide. Compare with figure 8-2.*

ously wrong and lead to danger, particularly where currents are strong.

Instead of a standing wave, an inland tide can behave more like the *progressive wave* of the oceanic tidal bulge that brings the tides to the estuary. In a progressive wave there are no nodal points; the wave shape moves forward just as wind waves and swells do, and the associated current flow reflects the normal horizontal flow associated with the circulation of water particles in waves. In an undisturbed progressive tide wave, the peak forward flow (flood) occurs at the crest of the wave (high water), and the peak backward flow (ebb) occurs at the trough of the wave (low water). Large open waterways exposed to the ocean often show tidal behavior strongly influenced by this pattern, as shown in figure 8-3.

Tides in most areas, however, are to some extent a mixture of both standing waves and progressive waves and consequently behave in an intermediate manner, with no simple relationship between tides and currents. In some inland waterways with strong currents, the water continues to run out in the ebb direction long past the time of low water. Toward the end of the ebb cycle in these cases, the water level is actually rising while still running out. The same occurs on the flood cycle—the water runs in long past being "full" at high water, and continues to run in for some time after the water depth begins to fall. Although several factors contribute to this behavior, the basic causes are momentum of the flowing water and differences in tide ranges and times at the two ends of the waterway—differences that are often amplified over long obstructed waterways.

Looking at this behavior in more detail, as the progressive wave of the tidal bulge enters the waterway it raises the water level at the entrance sooner than it does the more inland end. This puts a slope on the surface of the waterway that causes the current to flood inward as gravity pulls the water level to equilibrium. (The opposite slope is created in basins where the water all rises at about the same time, but the inland end rises much higher.) The momentum of the flowing water then keeps it flooding inward, even after the slope on the surface of the waterway reverses—which it does as soon as the trough following the tidal wave crest enters, lowering the level of the entrance end. Slack water occurs only when the driving force of the new slope can overcome the momentum of the flowing water. Because the shape of a waterway affects the progress of the tide wave and water flow through it, it also affects the specific relationship between tide times and current times. In some channels, the flood can continue for three hours past high water (mostly progressive wave); in others, it persists for only a few minutes (mostly standing wave). The same is true with the ebb at low water. It is impossible to simply look at a chart of a complex waterway and guess this behavior.

A third type of tidal behavior—distinct from standing waves and progressive waves—occurs at narrow passes leading into large confined bodies of water. In these cases, guessing that slack water at the pass occurs at high or low water at the pass could be as wrong as possible because these could be the times of maximum flow, not minimum flow. The constricted channel keeps the inside water level more or less constant as the seaward side rises and falls with the tides. Low water on the seaward side then corresponds to the maximum water slope across the length of the pass and consequently the peak current

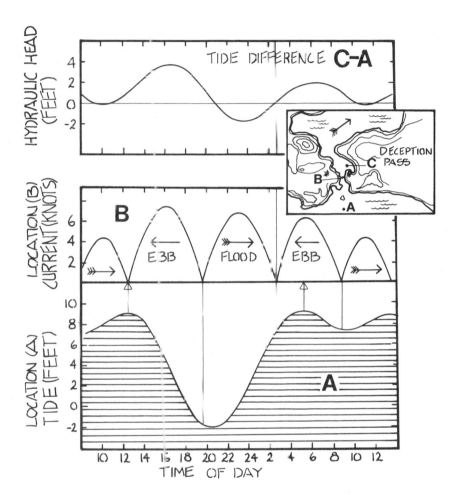

8-4. *Tides and currents at Deception Pass, Washington, on May 21, 1986.
This current is driven predominantly by the difference in tide height (hydraulic
head) across the pass (location A to location C), which also is shown in the figure. Notice that at the first high water (location A) the pass is near slack, but
at the second high water of the same height, the pass is near peak flow at 6
knots (location B). It is not possible to judge the timing of current flow from the
timing of the tides in many places. In most cases, the shape of the current rise
at this pass is probably closer to that of the dashed lines in figure 8-5 than it is
to the one pictured above.*

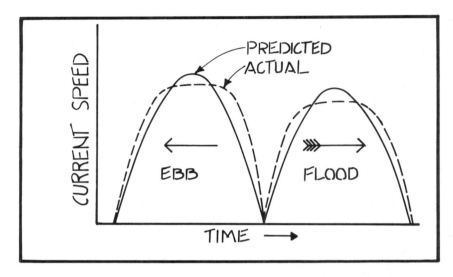

8-5. *Current versus time in a constricted pass. The solid curve is the shape predicted in current tables, but the dashed curve is likely to be closer to the actual currents. The difference is due to the different driving force of a hydraulic head, further influenced by friction and momentum.*

strength out of the pass. The same happens at high water with peak flow inward through the pass. On the other hand, in open water just a few miles from this type of pass, the timing of the tides and currents could be completely different. An example of tidal behavior at a pass showing these effects is illustrated in figure 8-4.

The difference in tide height that drives a current through a channel in this manner is called a *hydraulic head*. Hydraulic currents do not vary with time in a smooth sine function shape as wave-driven currents do, but instead they increase more rapidly after slack water (proportional to the square root of the developing hydraulic head) and remain at maximum flow for longer periods. For this reason, current tables or charts often have separate listings to describe the time dependence of currents in passes dominated by the changing hydraulic head. A comparison of the tide dependence of hydraulic current and wave-driven current is shown in figure 8-5.

Besides the separate mechanisms that drive tidal currents, other geographic details of the tidal basin can cause prominent anomalies in current behavior. One example is the persistent absence of one half of the current cycle in some places. In some specific locations

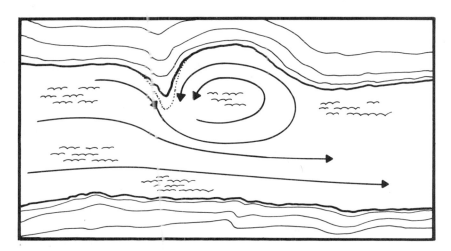

8-6. *Current flow near a point or spit. Sand shoals off the point are often a result of this flow pattern.*

within complex waterways, the tidal current can ebb continuously or flood continuously regardless of the state of the tide or of other tidal flow in adjacent waters. In such cases, flow only weakens during the time it should have reversed. These conditions can usually be traced to a unique flow of strong current into the region—a small-scale analogy would be the unidirectional current adjacent to a narrow point; because of back eddies that develop during both floods and ebbs, the net flow at the point is straight off the point most of the time, regardless of whether the midchannel current is flooding or ebbing (see fig. 8-6). Another anomaly in flow pattern can occur on a temporary basis (for different reasons) in areas where flood and ebb strengths are significantly different. In these locations, the weaker cycle can periodically diminish to zero, leaving the current either ebbing all day (as occasionally happens in Puget Sound, Washington) or flooding all day (as occasionally happens in the Aleutian Islands, Alaska).

With these various examples in mind, it should be clear that guessing the time of slack water or peak flow, or even the direction of the flow, from the time of the tides is risky business without precise local knowledge. The relationship between tides and currents can change from day to day as the range of the tide changes, and it can change from place to place along the same waterway. The common terms "ebb tide" and "flood tide" are ambiguous when considering the relationship between tides and currents. Even the relationship between tide range and current speed must be considered carefully. The only safe rule is that the maximum speed of a current *at a particular place* is proportional to the range of the tide at that place: If the range of the tide today is 10 feet and last week the corresponding range was 5 feet, expect the associated current to be roughly twice as large today as it was last week. It is not possible, however, to estimate the relative current strengths between two *separate places* by comparing their tidal ranges. A location with small tide range could have much larger currents than another place with large tide range.

There are separate tables for predicting tide heights and tidal current flow. When tides are needed, check the tide tables; when currents are needed, check the current tables. Remember, also, that predicted tides and currents may not yield the actual values encountered. Winds, river flow, and atmospheric pressure also may affect the tides and currents, and unforeseen variability in these factors cannot be included in the tabulated predictions.

Predicting Tide Heights

The shape of the curve of tide heights throughout the day depends on location, time of month, and time of year. On the Atlantic coast of North America the tides are predominantly *semidiurnal,* which means there are two high waters and two low waters of approximately the same heights each day. This is the most common type of tide throughout the world. Along the northern shore of the Gulf of Mexico, and in several individual locations such as Victoria, British Columbia, the tides are predominantly *diurnal,* with just one high and one low water each day. This is a much less common tide pattern. Tides along the Pacific coast of North America are called *mixed* because they include both semidiurnal and diurnal wave forms; the typical one having two high waters (called the *lower high* and *higher high*) and two low waters (called *lower low* and *higher low*) each day, with significant inequalities in the two high-water heights and two low-water heights. The shape of the pattern at various places around the world is determined by the shape of the entire ocean basin exposed to the tidal waters, as well as that of the local water basin. In the Pacific Northwest, the pattern changes significantly in the 70 miles between Victoria, British Columbia (often diurnal), and Seattle, Washington (mostly mixed), as shown in figure 8-7 along with the data from an intermediate station at Port Townsend, Washington.

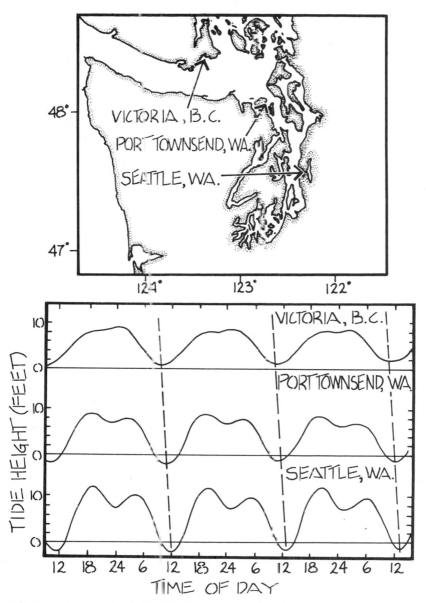

8-7. *Tide patterns in the Pacific Northwest on July 12, 13, and 14, 1984. Victoria, British Columbia, tides are often diurnal, similar to those in Louisiana and Texas; Seattle, Washington, tides are mixed with large inequalities, which is more characteristic of West Coast tides.*

The *mean* range of the tide at any location is the difference between the average high-water height and the average low-water height at that location. Mean ranges vary with latitude, being generally larger for inland waters at higher latitudes. Places in the Magellan Strait in southern Chile and Alaskan waters near Anchorage have mean ranges of over 30 feet; whereas coastal waters around Hawaii and Florida have mean ranges of only 1 foot. Another tidal range called the *diurnal* range is useful in describing mixed tides. It is the average difference between the higher high and the lower low each day. Diurnal range is always larger than mean range. Some references list alternative tidal ranges called *spring* range and *neap* range. Spring ranges are average values of the large tides that occur near new moon and full moon, when the tidal wave forms of the sun and moon are aligned crest with crest. Neap ranges are the average values of the weak tides that occur when the sun and moon produce tide wave forms that are at right angles to each other, near the times of quarter moons (which appear in the sky as half-moons). Tidal currents are smallest during neap tides and largest during spring tides. *Spring* in this usage has nothing to do with the season; it is from the Saxon word *springan*, meaning to swell. *Neap* is from the Saxon word *neafte*, meaning scarcity.

The times and heights of high and low water are listed in the official NOAA *Tide Tables* and in various commercial tables made from these. The times and heights of high and low water are given daily for primary reference stations, while tides at other places must be found by applying corrections to the data from the nearest primary station. Time and height corrections for a large number of subordinate stations are listed in the back of the book (see fig. 8-8). An example of the use of these tables is given in figure 8-9. When daylight saving time is in use (summer half of the year), you must add one hour to the standard times used in the tables. There is only one sentence in the instructions that warns of this correction, so it pays to write a reminder of it on the cover of the book. Commercial tide tables often make this correction in the data themselves, so it is always important to verify which time system is used.

How to Use Tide Tables

Step 1. Locate the position of interest on the chart. Find the nearest subordinate station in the back of the *Tide Tables*. Do not worry if you cannot find your exact location; tides are fairly constant over large

ANCHORAGE, ALASKA, 1986

Times and Heights of High and Low Waters

JULY

Day	Time h m	Height ft	m
1	0228	26.1	8.0
	0935	2.7	0.0
	1601	23.3	7.1
	2127	8.0	2.4
16 Tu	0119	27.6	8.4
	0834	1.4	0.5
	1421	23.9	7.3
	2034	6.7	2.0

AUGUST

Day	Time h m	Height ft	m
1 F	0329	24.0	7.4
	1054	1.8	0.5
	1726	25.4	7.7
	2310	9.0	2.7
16 Sa	0417	27.0	8.2
	1044	0.2	0.1
	1707	26.9	8.2
	2251	7.5	2.3

SEPTEMBER

Day	Time h m	Height ft	m
1 M	0502	25.6	7.8
	1207	-0.2	-0.1
	1811	27.6	8.4
16 Tu	0001	3.5	1.1
	0526	29.4	9.0
	1236	-2.1	-0.6
	1827	30.1	9.2

NO.	PLACE	POSITION Lat.	Long.	DIFFERENCES Time High water h. m.	Low water h. m.	Height High water ft	Low water ft	RANGES Mean ft	Diurnal ft	Mean Tide Level ft
	Kenai Peninsula, outer coast-Cont. Time meridian, 135°W			on ANCHORAGE, p.132						
1923	Fire Island................	61 10 N	150 12 W	-0 25	-0 28	*0.94	*0.94	24.4	27.0	14.2
1925	Sunrise, Turnagain Arm <11>............	60 54	149 26	+0 32	+1 12	+4.2	-0.2	30.3	33.3	17.1
1927	ANCHORAGE, Knik Arm.;....	61 14	149 53	Daily predictions				25.9	28.8	15.2
1929	Eklutna, Knik Arm <12>........	61 28	149 22	+1 11	- -	- -	- -	- -	- -	- -

8-8. A section of the NOAA Tide Tables showing daily predictions for a primary station and the corrections to be applied for a subordinate station.

MORNING TIDES ON SEPTEMBER 16, 1986 AT
SUNRISE, TURNAGAIN ARM, AK. (STATION 1925)

<u>HIGHWATER</u>

	0526	ANCHORAGE	29.4 FEET
+	0032	CORRECTION	+ 4.2 FEET
+	0100	DAYLIGHT SAVING	
	0658	YUKON DAYLIGHT TIME	23.6 FEET

<u>LOW WATER</u>

	1236	ANCHORAGE	−2.1 FEET
+	0112	CORRECTION	−0.2 FEET
+	0100	DAYLIGHT SAVING	
	1448	YUKON DAYLIGHT TIME	−2.3 FEET

8-9. *Numerical examples of figuring tides at a subordinate station using the data from figure 8-8.*

unobstructed areas. Any place within 10 miles or so of open water from your location should be adequate; in coastal waters the nearest station could be 100 miles away. Note the time and height corrections and the name and page for the primary station listed above it. The height correction can be a multiplicative ratio (tabulated as *0.86), an additive factor (+2.9), or both (*0.75 + 2.3). In the latter case, the height at the subordinate station would be 0.75 times that at the primary station plus 2.3 feet. A positive time correction tabulated as "+ 1 36" means the tide at the subordinate station occurs one hour and thirty-six minutes later than it does at the primary station; negative time corrections mean an earlier tide.

Step 2. Turn to the daily pages for the primary station to find the times and heights of high and low waters. If daylight saving time is in use, add one hour to each of the times; then apply the corrections to find the tides at the subordinate station. Bear in mind, however, that the practical accuracy of these predictions is not as high as their tabulated precision implies. Actual tide heights might deviate from these predictions by 1 foot or so, and the times could be off by one hour or so, although more often they will be within thirty minutes of the predicted times. It is not prudent to plan routes that require predicted tide heights to be more accurate than 2 feet, although the largest deviation (during storm surges) add water depth rather than subtract it. Extreme surges add over 2 feet to the predicted tides.

Step 3. Figure the tide level at intermediate times as explained below.

Tide tables give data only at the predicted extremes of high and low water; it is your job to interpolate the tide height at intermediate times. It is best to do this before departing, so that at any time you can glance at your own table or graph of tide height versus time to learn the state of the tide—it also saves weight if you can get by with notes and leave the books behind. Tide variation between high and low water is not a straight line decreasing in proportion to time, but instead it takes the form of a bell-shaped curve (a cosine function) with the tide height lingering at the high and low depths. Tides at intermediate times can be found from special tables in the back of the *Tide Tables*. These interpolation tables are quite easy to use, although many navigators prefer to make their own corrections using the *rule of twelfths*, which is illustrated in figure 8-10.

To use this rule divide the range of the tide by 12 to get the size of the range step and divide the duration of the rise or fall by 6 to get the size of the time step. The rule gives the tide height at 5 time steps across the duration. During the first time step, the tide changes 1 range step; during the second tide step, the tide changes 2 range steps; and during the third time step, the tide changes 3 range steps. After 3 time steps out of 6, you are halfway through the duration, and the tide has changed by half the range (6 steps out of 12). The second half is symmetric to the first half. Most tide changes are similar to this pattern. (This rule is usually presented with the assumption that the duration is exactly six hours, which makes the time steps exactly one hour. Very often this is an adequate approximation, but for large tides with durations longer than seven hours or so, it is necessary to use the proper time step in order to get the tides right to within 1 foot.)

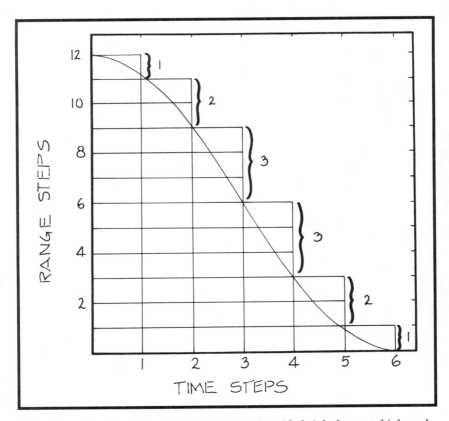

8-10. *The rule of twelfths method of determining tide height between high and low waters. The time steps are each one sixth of the time between high and low waters (which can often be approximated as one whole hour). The range steps are each one twelfth of the difference between the high-water height and the low-water height. This is an arithmetic method, as opposed to the graphic method of figure 8-11.*

An alternative method is to plot a graph of the tide heights on graph paper using the *one-quarter, one-tenth rule,* which is illustrated in figure 8-11. Using any convenient scale, plot the heights of high and low water at the appropriate times for the location of interest. Draw straight lines between them; then at the quarter duration points, adjust the curves by one tenth of the range to get the approximate bell shape of the curve. This is a fast way to prepare tide predictions for long periods and, though literally "sketchy," it is adequate for all applications.

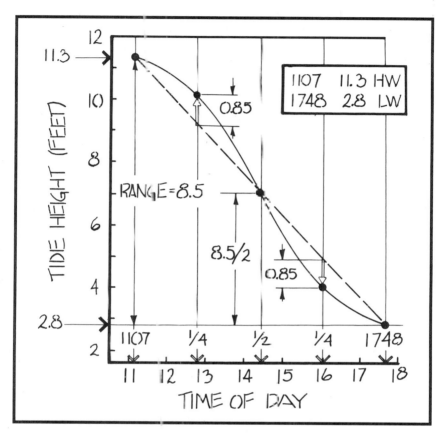

8-11. *The one-quarter, one-tenth method of determining tide height between high and low water. After choosing a convenient time scale, such as one-eighth inch per ten minutes, and a convenient height scale, such as one-half inch per foot, plot the high and low water points on the graph and draw a line between them. Use a ruler or fold the paper to divide the fall time of the tide into four parts. At the first quarter, mark a point one tenth of the full range above the line and mark a similar point below the line at the third quarter. Mark a point at the midtide position and then draw a line through these points to get a graph of the tides at all times. Tides for several days can be sketched this way for quick reference under way.*

Guidelines for Guessing the Tides

There is no substitution for doing your homework on tide prediction; but if you should end up navigating by the seat of your pants and get caught without your resource, the guidelines below might help with a guess.

- Know the local pattern (semidiurnal, diurnal, or mixed). With a mixed tide, a large range will be followed by a smaller range; in the others, successive ranges are similar.

- Look around (at shoreline, pilings, breakwaters) for signs (barnacles, seaweed, beach rubble) that mark the high-water line.

- The typical duration between high and low water is six hours and fifteen minutes (mixed, semidiurnal) or twelve hours and thirty minutes (diurnal).

- High and low waters on successive days are fifty minutes later each day, and the next day's ranges will not be much different than the previous day's—ranges change only slowly from day to day. If high water is 10 feet at 0800 today, expect a high of about 10 feet tomorrow at about 0850.

- Spring ranges (new and full moon) are about 20 percent larger than average; neap ranges (half-moons) are about 20 percent smaller than average.

- The largest spring ranges (higher highs and lower lows) occur near the solstices (21 June and 21 December); the weakest neap tides (smallest diurnal inequalities) occur near the equinoxes (21 March and 23 September).

- In many places along a coast or not far from it, high tides occur within two hours of the moon's meridian passage. For spring tides this will be near midnight and midday; for neap tides it will be near 6 A.M. and 6 P.M. local time.

- In many places, the compass bearing to the moon (when visible) will be nearly the same for that location on alternate high waters, regardless of the moon's phase. The intermediate high waters will be about twelve hours and thirty minutes later, but the moon will not be visible.

- Over a long enclosed waterway, tide range on the inland end is usually larger, and the tide times later than at the seaward end.

On the Washington State coast, for example, the mean tide range is 6 feet and high water closely follows the meridian passage of the moon; whereas in Olympia, Washington, at the base of Puget Sound (168 miles inland) the mean range is 11 feet and high tide trails the moon by an average of about five hours.

- Final rule: any of the above could be wrong. A good navigator is not the one who can guess the tides, but one who has looked them up ahead of time and has proper information at hand at all times.

Predicting Tidal Currents

The NOAA *Tidal Current Tables* are arranged similar to its *Tide Tables.* Times and speeds of maximum flow and the times of slack water are given daily for certain primary reference stations, with time and speed corrections for a large number of subordinate stations listed in the back of the book. In contrast to tide predictions, however, it is very important to note the precise location of the subordinate current station, which is specified in the tables with latitude and longitude and often further described as, for example, "Golden Gate Bridge, 0.8 mile east of.' This description of the location is usually more helpful than the coordinates, which are only specified to the nearest whole minute of latitude and longitude (almost 1 mile accuracy). Sometimes the coordinates will actually locate the reference point on land!

The published current predictions apply to these precise locations; current speed, direction, and timing could be significantly different just a few hundred yards away. Furthermore, most of the reference stations are located in midchannel so they do not necessarily represent current flow along the edge of a waterway where kayakers do much of their paddling. Consequently, these on-station predictions are often just the starting point to current predictions in the waters you plan to traverse. Although it is difficult to speculate on how well you might estimate the current locations away from these stations, it is fair to assume that the tabulated predictions at or very near the locations of the reference stations will be accurate to within 30 percent on the strengths and 30 minutes on the times. Daylight saving time is not used in the tables, so when applicable you must add one hour to the tabulated current times. Sample tables and an example of the use of these tables are given in figures 8-12 and 8-13.

ADMIRALTY INLET (off Bush Pt.), WASHINGTON, 1986

F-Flood, Dir. 180° True   E-Ebb, Dir. 005° True

JULY

Day	Slack Water Time h.m.	Maximum Current Time h.m.	Vel. knots	Slack Water Time h.m.	Maximum Current Time h.m.	Vel. knots
1 Tu	0817	0405	3.1E			
	1412	1102	1.5F			
	2000	1700	1.1E			
		2208	0.7F			
16 W	0713	0303	3.3E			
	1320	1003	1.7F			
	1858	1602	1.2E			
	2318	2116	0.8F			

AUGUST

Day	Slack Water Time h.m.	Maximum Current Time h.m.	Vel. knots	Slack Water Time h.m.	Maximum Current Time h.m.	Vel. knots
1 F	0902	0455	2.9E			
	1545	1212	1.9F			
		1836	1.2E			
		2328	*			
16 Sa	0836	0437	3.5E			
	1531	1152	2.6F			
	2149	1821	1.6E			
		2322	0.5F			

TABLE 2. - CURRENT DIFFERENCES AND OTHER CONSTANTS

NO.	PLACE	POSITION Lat. °' N	POSITION Long. °' W	METER DEPTH ft	TIME DIFFERENCES Min. before Flood h.m.	Flood h.m.	Min. before Ebb h.m.	Ebb h.m.	SPEED RATIOS Flood	SPEED RATIOS Ebb	AVERAGE SPEEDS AND DIRECTIONS Minimum before Flood knots deg.	Maximum Flood knots deg.	Minimum before Ebb knots deg.	Maximum Ebb knots deg.
	ADMIRALTY INLET				on ADMIRALTY INLET, p.16 <1>									
	Marrowstone Point													
985	1.1 miles northwest of..........	48 07	122 42		-3 31	-2 20	-1 02	-1 42	0.8	0.5	0.0 --	1.3 100	0.0 --	1.3 275
990	0.4 mile northeast of <8>......	48 06	122 41		-1 20	-1 03	-0 04	-1 03	1.1	1.1	0.0 --	2.4 122	0.0 --	3.1 338
995	0.3 mile northeast of..........	48 06	122 41		-0 53	-1 36	-1 13	-0 13	1.2	1.1	0.0 --	2.0 170	0.0 --	2.8 015
1000	1.6 miles northeast of <8>.....	48 07	122 40		-0 16	+0 07	-0 03	-0 17	1.2	1.2	0.0 --	2.3 152	0.0 --	2.6 344
1005	2.5 miles northeast of <9>.....	48 08	122 38		-- --	-- --	-- --	-- --	--	--	-- --	-- --	-- --	-- --
1010	Nodule Point, 0.5 mile southeast of...	48 02	122 40		-1 27	-0 47	-0 59	-0 24	1.2	1.0	0.0 --	2.0 160	0.0 --	2.5 339
1015	ADMIRALTY INLET (off Bush Point).......	48 02	122 38		Daily Predictions						0.0 --	1.6 179	0.0 --	2.6 003

8-12. *A section of the NOAA Current Tables showing daily predictions for a primary station and the corrections to be applied for a subordinate station.*

MORNING CURRENTS ON AUGUST 16, 1986 AT
1.1 MILES NW OF MARROWSTONE POINT, WA. (STATION 985)

EBB

0437	ADMIRALTY INLET	3.5 KNOTS EBB
_0142	CORRECTION	X 0.5
+0100	DAYLIGHT SAVING	
0355	PACFIC DAYLIGHT TIME	1.8 KNOTS EBB

SLACK

0836	ADMIRALTY INLET	
-0331	CORRECTION	MINIMUM BEFORE FLOOD
+0100	DAYLIGHT SAVING	
0605	PACIFIC DAYLIGHT TIME	SLACK

FLOOD

1152	ADMIRALTY INLET	2.6 KNOTS FLOOD
-0220	CORRECTION	X 0.8
+0100	DAYLIGHT SAVING	
1032	PACIFIC DAYLIGHT TIME	2.1 KNOTS FLOOD

8-13. *Numerical example of figuring tidal currents at a subordinate station using the data from figure 8-12.*

In a similar fashion with the *Tide Tables,* the *Current Tables* list only slack water and peak current values; current speed between slack water and peak flow must be interpolated. There is a special table in the back of the *Current Tables* for doing this, but it is adequate to use an abbreviated rule (see fig. 8-14): Separate the duration between slack water and peak flow into three steps. During the first time step after slack, the current speed increases to 50 percent of its peak value; during the next time step the current increases to 90 percent of its peak value; and during the last time step the current increases to its peak value. Following peak flow, the current decreases in a similar pattern: During the first time step it drops to 90 percent of what it was, and during the next time step it drops to 50 percent of what it was. The only thing that might change is the size of the time step. Although most currents rise in about three hours and decrease in about three hours, there are exceptions. If the time between slack and peak flow is three hours and the time between peak flow and the next slack is four hours, the time step going up is one hour and the time step going down is one hour and twenty minutes (4 times 60 divided by 3). For example:

Tabulated data		Interpolated data
Slack water	1230	
1230 + 0100 =		1330 2.0 knots (0.5 x 4.0)
1230 +0200 =		1430 3.6 knots (0.9 x 4.0)
4.0 knots ebb	1530	
1530 + 0120 =		1650 3.6 knots
1530 + 0240 =		1810 2.0 knots
Slack water	1930	

Unusual current behavior at any of the stations is pointed out in the endnotes of the tables. It is important to check these notes for all stations near the area of interest, and at some point, it pays to read all the notes—even for areas you do not plan to visit—to get a feeling for the types of variations that can occur. It is also important to check the *Coast Pilot* or *Sailing Directions* for further notes on local current behavior. These publications often add information that is not included in the *Current Tables*. When you find such notes, write them on the chart at the proper places as reminders.

Small-craft charts show current flow with arrows pointing in the flow direction and labeled with the average values of the maximum currents. The points on the chart where the arrows are located mark locations of reference stations listed in the *Current Tables,* and in this sense these charts are convenient guides to telling where the currents

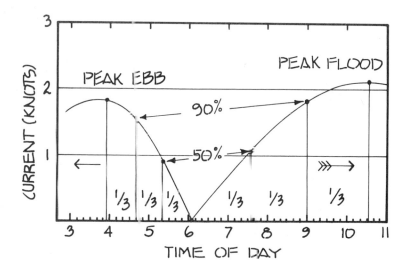

8-14. *The 50-90 current rule for figuring current speeds between slack and peak flow. Divide the time between slack water and peak flow into three steps. In many cases, each step will be approximately one hour long. During the first step the current increases to 50 percent of its maximum value, and during the next step it increases to 90 percent of its maximum value. The same procedure will reproduce the fall in current speed after maximum flow.*

are predicted. Unfortunately, not all subordinate stations are included on the small-craft charts, so it is still necessary to check the list in the *Current Tables* to see whether uncharted stations might be more appropriate and then mark their locations on the chart to save doing this again.

For a few areas around the country, there are commercial current guides or atlases that show strength and direction of current flow plotted on charts of the regions. One example is the *Cap'n Jack's Current Atlas* by Randel Washburne, published by Marine Trade Publications in Port Ludlow, Washington. These include additional notes on current flow from the *Coast Pilot* and *Sailing Directions* along with very convenient tables that show what chart applies to any hour and day of the year. When such aids are available, they greatly reduce the problem of figuring currents and planning around them. The first practical step toward current prediction in areas without these guides available is to plot these data in a similar fashion on your own

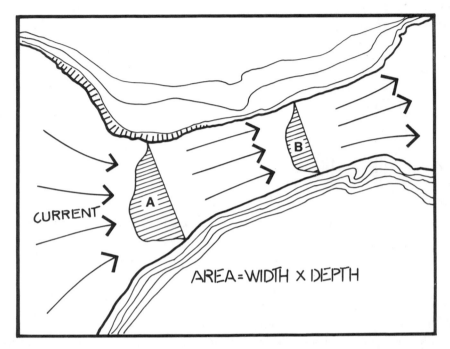

8-15. *Current speed is often inversely proportional to the cross-sectional area of the waterway, which depends on its depth profile as well as its width. In this example, area A is twice as large as area B, so the current at B would be expected to be twice as fast as it is at A. Whenever the location of the reference station used in the* Current Tables *is not at the most constricted point of a channel, peak currents in the channel can be significantly larger than predicted.*

chart. With this overview of the distribution of stations, use the following guidelines to help you interpret and extrapolate these predictions into the actual areas you plan to paddle through.

Guidelines for Judging Current Flow

- If a confined waterway narrows, horizontally or vertically, its current speed increases. This happens because the current tends to pile up at the constriction, and the developing hydraulic head adds a new driving force that pushes the water through faster. The speed increase in many areas is proportional to the reduction in cross-sectional area of the water, which often can be estimated fairly accurately from the average cross-channel depth and the width of the channel read from a chart. An example is shown in figure 8-15. Because the current accelerates in narrow channels, the easiest route across current in a narrowing channel is usually not the shortest route.

- Current in shallow water along a shoreline is slower than current in deep water farther offshore, because a larger proportion of it is slowed down by the frictional resistance of the bottom. (To appreciate the illusive effect of surface drag on a fluid, consider how fast a cup of water might run down a sheet of glass compared to a sheet of sandpaper.) Because of this effect, paddling *against* the current is best done in shallow water along the beach. The best ride *with* the current is in deep water away from the beach.

- Current along the outside edge (concave shore) of a smooth turn in a waterway is faster than it is along the inside edge (convex shore), provided the water depth is uniform across the width of the channel at the turn and the shorelines are similar on both sides. The effect is caused by centrifugal force that throws the water to the outside edge of the curve. In principle, when paddling with the current in no wind through such an idealized turn, it does not matter which side of the turn you take, because the increase in current speed along the outer edge is proportional to the extra length of the route, so the transit times are the same. When paddling against the wind, however, the inside of this ideal turn is favored because the seas will be less enhanced due to the weaker contrary current. Paddling against the current, on the other hand, the outside edge is doubly bad: The route is longer and the current stronger. Bear in mind, however, that this is an idealized waterway. Usually the depth and shorelines are not the same on either side, and these differences can dominate the current flow around the corner and the best choice of routes. The inside or middle could be deeper, which would make it faster water, or, as is more likely, the inside could be shallower, which would cause steeper waves even though the current was weaker. In short, there are not many turns in open tidal waterways that fit this idealized description. Turns in meandering rivers or narrow channels provide more pertinent examples.

- Back eddies (circulating toward the shore) develop in bays downstream of points protruding into the waterway. At maximum flow in the main channel, a reverse current can be expected inside the point-to-point line across the bay. A sandspit at a point is usually a good sign that back eddies are common and well developed on either side of it, because sand deposits from the eddy circulation are what build the spits. If the eddy current is significant, however, there likely will be tide rips at the points, so getting into favorable back eddies when trying to progress against the mainstream flow must be done with caution. On the other hand, when riding with mainstream flow, it is best to stay offshore enough to avoid the bays and inlets that might have contrary current. The sizes of shoreline back eddies are proportional to the perturbations in shoreline contour that created them. They can be several boat lengths across or several miles across. Small ones are more often found along steep shorelines. Current eddies of all sizes also are found well offshore, formed when opposing currents collide or when slack water allows the nearshore eddies to wander out of their bays into the mainstream. It is usually difficult, however, to predict the locations of offshore eddies, and consequently, their effect on navigation cannot be anticipated.

- When a waterway changes from flood to ebb or vice versa, it does not often do so uniformly across its width. Current usually changes directions first in the shallow waters along its edge, because the water in the deeper midchannel region has more momentum to be overcome by the new tidal forces. This process often leaves a current shear line on the surface (parallel to the shore) that separates currents flowing in opposite directions. As the main flow proceeds to reverse, this current line moves out toward midchannel. In this manner, currents often change directions from the edges in, as much as they do from one end to the other. Spotting this line when present and getting onto the proper side of it can make a difference of 2 or 3 knots in your speed made good.

  In shallow water, the directional trend of anchored seaweed shows the current direction as does the wake behind buoys or rocks in deep water. In light winds, the set of an anchored boat or crab pot marker shows the current flow. Paddling hard but not moving relative to the shoreline is an obvious sign of an opposing current direction, as is a fast passing shoreline when paddling easy—although it is usually simpler to tell that you are not moving than to tell you are moving too fast. (Ways to quantify these observations are given in chapter 9.) When paddling farther offshore,

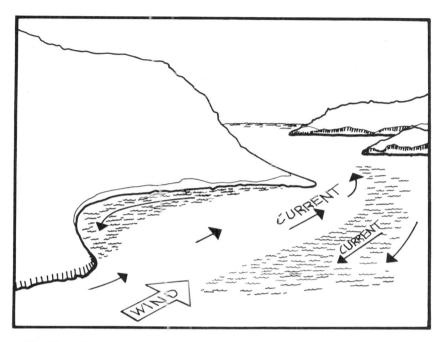

8-16. *The effect on surface texture of opposing wind and current. The direction of current flow can sometimes be determined this way even in light winds. In strong winds and fast currents, this "texture" turns into terrible water, with steep breaking waves.*

current lines can be detected from a change in the texture of the water surface (see fig. 8-16). Water on the rough side of the line is flowing into the wind; the smooth side flows with the wind. In winds of about 10 knots, you might see occasional whitecaps in water flowing into the wind and none in water flowing with the wind. In winds of more than 15 knots and currents of more than 2 knots, there is a dramatic distinction in sea state between current flowing with or against the wind. Some surface effect, however, is noticeable in nearly all conditions because current flowing against waves always steepens them and current flowing with the waves always smooths them out, regardless of whether the waves are 6-foot ocean waves, 3-foot swells from a passing freighter, or 1-inch ripples from a 3-knot wind.

• Current lines are also present along the edges of back eddies (called eddy line in this case) as they migrate toward midchannel during slack water when the main flow reverses. Even before the current starts to change directions, these eddies have current along their shoreward side flowing opposite to that in midstream; so when the current starts to change directions, which it does first along the shore, the increasing speed of the new current does not counteract the eddy circulation; it just pushes the eddy offshore. Large eddies that have drifted offshore often trap floating debris in their centers, which is a good sign of their presence. On the other hand, debris is also often seen lined up *along* a current line. If the opposing currents are strong enough, small particles or patches of foam along this line spin in circles, showing the flow directions clearly. As you paddle across a prominent line, the torque of the opposing currents will tend to turn the boat toward the flow direction you are entering. Judging flow direction this way, however, is like noting that a storm is coming when the wind picks up and it starts raining. Nevertheless, if the new current is not favorable, you can turn and get back out of it.

- Current flow often follows the paths of deep underwater trenches, which are only discernible from depth contours on a chart. If a prominent shelf, for example, extends well off the end of a point, expect the main current flow to follow the contour of the shelf around the corner as opposed to the contour of the shoreline. Current in such areas is usually strongest just at the edge of the shelf. Paddling with the current, stay just off the shelf; paddling against it, stay well onto the shelf. Similarly, current that flows around and over shallow underwater banks is often significantly accelerated over the mainstream flow. If published current predictions show irregular behavior in open water, check the shape of the bottom for a possible clue to understanding it.

- Current flowing out of a pass acts much like water from a hose. If unobstructed, it fans out and weakens; but if it is directed toward a shoreline, it will pile up against it, creating larger than average downstream currents along that shore or in the deeper water just off that shore.

- To guess current behavior at points intermediate to those where published predictions are given, sketch flow lines parallel to the predicted directions at the nearest stations, then interpolate the current strengths between the published points. In open areas where nearby predictions differ significantly (speeds differ by 1 knot or more; times by 30 minutes or more; or directions by 45° or more) the current flow is clearly complex and probably sensitive to the range of the tide. Check the tide range at the time of your current prediction and compare it with the mean tide range for the place. If these ranges differ by some 30 percent or more, it is likely that the current predictions will be off in some details. Read the *Coast Pilot* and study the timing and directions of the predictions to look for any indication of eddies in the area that could be potentially dangerous. Charted notes of tide rips are further warnings of questionable predictions for the area. Areas with charted tide rips will likely not go slack at all, but remain erratic ("weak and variable") throughout the slack period.

- If published current predictions for a particular place or time seem unusual, plot the tide height versus time for the period in question to see if some clue is to be had.

- If the water is brown or gray instead of its usual blue or green, it has probably changed colors because of the silt from excessive river runoff. Normal runoff is included in the published current predictions; excessive runoff (after long rains or unusual snowmelts) is not. When present, this extra fresh water adds to the ebb strength and reduces the flood strength of tidal currents. It also extends the duration of the ebb cycle (it starts earlier and ends later, leaving maximum flow at about the predicted time) and reduces the duration of the flood cycle. In extreme cases, or at particular points near the source of the river water, weak flood cycles might be completely masked by runoff, leaving the water ebbing all day. During periods of drought, ebb currents will be weaker than predicted.

- If a steady wind blows over any body of water for half a day or longer, it starts a surface current flowing at a speed of approximately 3 percent of the wind speed. Twenty knots of wind for half a day creates a wind-driven current of about 0.6 knots. In confined waters this current flows with the run of the waterway; in open waters of the Northern Hemisphere the wind-driven current is deflected about 45° to the right of the wind direction by the Coriolis force. Along a coast or on inland waters, the deflected current may meet a shore and elevate the water level. Once this occurs, the wind-driven flow follows the wind direction more closely. Local winds can create wind-driven current in lakes that have no tidal flow, and in tidal waters the wind-driven current must be added to the normal tidal flow: When the wind flows in the flood direction, for example, it lengthens and strengthens the flood cycle and shortens and weakens the ebb cycle. A crude estimate of the increase or decrease in tidal current speed could be 3 percent of the wind speed. The change in slack-water times depends on the current strengths. As a rough rule of thumb, a steady 15 knots of wind will shift the slack-water times by sixty minutes divided by the peak current strength in knots: A 2-knot current cycle flowing with the wind would start roughly thirty minutes earlier than predicted and end thirty minutes later than predicted.

For nine large waterways around the country (including Long Island Sound, New York; Tampa Bay, Florida; and Puget Sound, Washington), NOAA publishes special current charts that show pictorially the speed and direction of current flow throughout the waterway for each hour of the flood and ebb cycles. The charts can be used on any day of any year; the time and speed scales that apply to each page for a specific day are determined from *Current Table* data at a particular reference station in the area. The charts available are listed in the appendix to any *U.S. Coast Pilot*. The Canadian government also publishes current charts for specific regions. Current charts and diagrams for specific areas also are included in many *Coast Pilots* and *Sailing Directions*. Whenever they are available, current charts are a convenient way to get an overview of the flow pattern for large areas and long periods of time, which is useful for planning long trips through variable currents.

Coastal Currents

Current flow within a mile or so of a coastline is typically the result of a complex set of forces. Contributing factors include tidal current, wind-driven current, prevailing offshore ocean circulation, and local currents running parallel and perpendicular to the shoreline, which are caused by the surf. Unusual hydraulic currents also might flow along a coastline following long storms. These hydraulic currents can occur with no wind, no waves, nor any tidal changes as the sea-surface slope readjusts to calm conditions. Near headlands, bays, or entrances to inland waters, the coastal flow also is strongly affected by the shape of the coastline.

Because so many forces influence the flow, it is difficult to predict coastal currents of interest to kayakers without local knowledge. Nevertheless, these currents are important to kayak navigation because they can severely hinder progress along routes that are exposed to sudden weather changes. The height and direction of swells also can change in a few hours with no change in local weather, as wave remnants of distant storms first reach the coast. Coastal currents can vary significantly in speed and direction at any one location and vary rapidly and irregularly from point to point along a coast. Although in many areas the currents farther offshore are fairly well understood by local mariners and documented in *Sailing Directions*, it is questionable whether much of the knowledge gained from extensive traffic of larger vessels farther offshore can be extrapolated shoreward into the "kayaker's domain" nearer shore.

Because there is so little data for the region that lies just outside of the surf zone, it is important to measure the current yourself (as explained in chapter 9) as often as possible when paddling along coastal routes. It might then be possible to correlate this information with the state of the tide, wind speed and direction, lay of the land, and state of the surf, and gain some insight into the local current behavior that might help plan the rest of the trip. Nearshore current is a difficult subject in oceanography. When dealing with currents in these waters, your surprise threshold must be fairly high.

The tidal part of coastal current is typically *rotary* as opposed to the reversing currents found inland (see fig. 8-17). A pure rotary current changes directions without changing speed, so there are no slack waters. *Current Tables, Sailing Directions,* and some nautical charts provide diagrams that can be used to predict the speed and direction of rotating tidal currents based on the times of high and low tides at coastal reference stations. Examples are shown in figure 8-18. Tidal currents in coastal waters rarely exceed 1 or 2 knots, and well away from the entrances to inland waters, the average values are much smaller—although as with all currents, coastal currents accelerate near headlands and diminish at the mouths of bays. The rotations are also not purely circular near long open coastlines. The current direction does rotate (clockwise in the Northern Hemisphere) through 360° every 12½ hours or so, but the rate of rotation is not uniform and the speeds are not exactly the same in all directions. Most tidal streams well removed from inlets into inland waters flow faster and

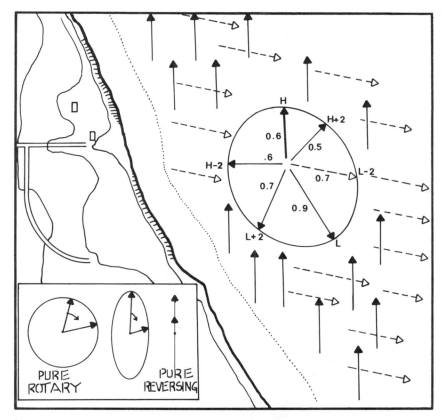

8-17. *A rotating current diagram that describes coastal currents. As opposed to pure reversing currents found inland, which alternate their direction, coastal currents tend to rotate their direction with little or no change in speed. At the time of high water, this coastal region has a north current of 0.6 knot; at two hours before low water, the current flows east-southeast at 0.7 knot. Note that the coastline shown could be 50 miles long or more. The arrows on these diagrams are usually scaled to the current speeds, but the location and overall size of the diagram has no significance. The current is not in any way emanating from the location of the diagram on the chart, nor is the behavior it describes limited to that area. The diagram describes currents throughout that region of the coast. Also, the timing of the currents is not necessarily associated with the local tides. The tide stations used to reference the currents could be far from the current site. If a particular tide cycle near the current site is much different from its mean value, the rotation diagram could be wrong in both current speed and rotation rate.*

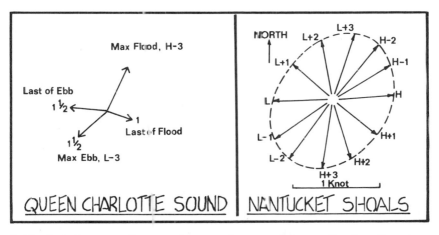

8-18. *Actual current diagrams for coastal waters of Queen Charlotte Sound, British Columbia (51°N, 129°W, from the* Canadian Sailing Directions *and for Nantucket Shoals, Massachusetts (41°N. 70°W), from the* NOAA Current Tables. *The styles of the two diagrams are different, but they convey similar information. The currents in Queen Charlotte Sound are much larger. In areas with mixed tides, the corresponding diagrams have two loops, reflecting the inequality of the highs and lows.*

longer parallel to the coastline than perpendicular to it. Their rotation diagrams are not circles, but ellipses with the long axes lying parallel to the coastline. Near entrances to inland waters, on the other hand, the ellipses are more aligned with the inlet due to the flow in and out of the waterway.

In many areas, however, the rotary tidal flow is completely masked by wind-driven current whenever the wind blows steadily for half a day or longer. Expect this contribution to be approximately 3 percent of the wind strength, directed some 45° to the right of the wind direction in the Northern Hemisphere. Wind-driven currents tend to be stronger in heavy rains because brackish water slips more easily over the denser salt water below it. If *Sailing Directions* predict north-flowing currents of 1 or 2 knots, for example, expect the stronger end of the prediction when the wind blows toward the north and the weaker end of the prediction when the wind blows toward the south.

When waves strike the shore diagonally, they set up a current along the shore, inside the surf zone, flowing in the general direction of the wave motion. These currents inside the surf zone are not strong—0.5 knot might be typical for large waves—so these currents would rarely have direct influence on navigation. Nevertheless, water accumulated shoreward of the surf zone has to periodically escape seaward forming large rip current cells that can contribute to the prevailing flow outside of the surf. See Current Hazards below for further discussion of this topic.

Although nearshore coastal currents are difficult to predict with much dependability, every effort should still be made to establish the range of potential currents when planning coastal routes. *Tidal Current Tables* help in some locations, but *Coast Pilots* and *Sailing Directions* are the primary references in many areas. Whenever possible, also check with local fishermen who work both on and below the surface. In some areas, for example, commercial divers (who gather sea urchins, abalone, geoduck, kelp, herring roe, or sea cucumbers) are an excellent resource because they work daily in precisely the waters you might paddle, and they are aware of the current under many circumstances. Sport divers contacted through local diving shops also might be a source of local knowledge. Kayaking schools that do regular tours in an area you might visit are naturally the best source when available.

Current Hazards

The most common and illusive current hazard to kayakers is fast water flowing into strong wind. This is an ever-present concern to paddlers in tidal waters. The rapid increase in wave steepness that accompanies these conditions can, quite literally, stop you cold. You might be surfing downwind, for example, with a 15-knot southerly at your back in 2 knots of favorable current and get lured offshore with waves that tended outward; the apparent wind would be a comfortable 10 knots or less, depending on how fast you were going. In some areas, however, atmospheric convergence zones can reverse the wind direction in a matter of minutes. If this happened in this example, a brief lull would be followed by a sudden, cold northerly of 15 knots full on your face, which would feel even colder due to the enhanced spray and wind-chill factor. In ten minutes or so the water would change from gentle rollers with occasional "surfers" going your way, to short, steep waves coming straight at you and breaking over the bow every few minutes. Your fun ride would suddenly change to an unpleasant and potentially dangerous struggle just to get to shore.

Always keep in mind the relative wind and current directions that lie ahead. These conditions can change suddenly where a waterway turns, and they always change when the tidal current reverses. Do not let yourself get caught very far offshore when the current reverses. Current flowing with the wind actually smoothes out the seas, so the potential sea state is deceptive before the current turns. The effect of current on wave steepness is shown in figure 8-19; average values of deep-water waves are given in table 8-1.

The second most common hazard is simply fast water that occurs in narrow passes. For "navigable" passes used by larger vessels, *Current Tables, Coast Pilots,* and *Sailing Directions* provide ample warnings and speed predictions. Kayaks, however, can go through narrow openings between rocks that will not be covered in these publications. So it is important to remember that whenever current is flowing and the waterway narrows significantly, the current speed will increase proportionally (see fig. 8-15). Furthermore, in most cases of accelerated current, there are associated fast back eddies and whirlpools that can be sudden hazards to safe navigation. These usually occur downstream of the constriction, so they might be detected only after you have committed yourself to going through. Even worse, you might find hydraulic jumps or standing overfalls at the constriction. If you are not prepared for this type of water, it is best to avoid fast currents in narrow openings or passes, even when the current is flowing in the direction you want to go.

Tide rips are another source of potential danger. They are always associated with fast water but they are not restricted to narrow passages. A tide rip is a localized region (typically an acre of so in extent) of fast, turbulent water with steep waves that occurs whenever the smooth flow of strong current is abruptly altered. Rips occur over isolated shoals well offshore and at points of land along the shore; consequently both of these areas are always potential danger points to kayakers during strong currents—in fact, prominent points and spits are potentially dangerous to kayakers even in slack water if any waves are present, because wave and swell energy is concentrated at the points by reflection and refraction. Rips also can occur in deep offshore water wherever opposing currents meet, either head on or in passing as along a current line. Channels with very irregular bottom topography also will have tide rips in strong current. Tide rips are always most prominent when the current flows against the wind, because the rips effectively trap the approaching waves, and as they slow

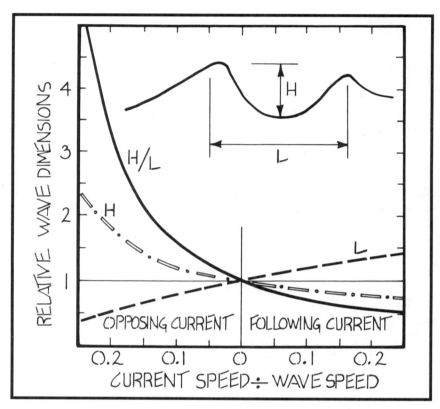

8-19. *Wave steepness as a function of current speed. Developed wind waves move in the direction of the wind at about 0.7 times the wind speed (average properties of the waves are given in table 8-1). When they meet opposing current, they steepen according to the graph, where* H *is the height of the wave and* L *is the length of the wave. A wave in 10 knots of wind would be moving at about 7 knots with a length of about twenty-five times its height. If this wave traveled against 1.5 knots of current (0.2 times the wave speed), it would steepen by a factor of 3.5, according to the graph, making a wave whose length is only seven times its height. Waves break at this steepness, so the gentle waves of a 10-knot wind in still water would be breaking in 1.5 knots of current. The graph also applies to swells from ships. These are already steep when produced and moving at the relatively slow speeds of the vessel. Those that are not breaking already will certainly break in opposing current.*

Table 8-1. Average Values of Fully Developed Deep-Water Waves.

Wind speed (knots)	10	15	20	25	30
Period (seconds)	3	4	6	7	9
Length (feet)	28	62	111	173	249
Speed (knots)	7	11	14	18	21
Height (feet)	1	2	5	9	14
Required duration	2	6	10	16	23
Required fetch (miles)	10	34	75	150	280

down they increase in height, just as swells steepen and break on beaches when the shallowing depth of the shore slows them down. A relatively mild rip can become more exciting when a freighter passes by, and the swell from its wake is trapped and amplified in the rip zone. (All waves steepen when they slow down—by dragging on the bottom in shallow water or when they meet opposing current—because the kinetic energy they lose with their speed must be converted to the potential energy of height.)

Areas of prominent tide rips are shown on charts with symbols or words (see fig. 8-20). These warnings should definitely be heeded as they imply potential hazard for vessels much larger than kayaks. In some cases, tide rips are not shown on all charts of the same area; these are charting errors that should be corrected on your chart. Kayakers, on the other hand, will frequently find areas of rips significant to them that are not shown on charts. These also should be marked on your chart, along with a note of the current speed and direction at the time. Even severe rip zones near points or rocks are often left uncharted because they are too close inshore to be of concern to larger boats. When approaching any point or shoaling, look ahead for signs of whitecaps. Rips at gently sloping points or spits often can be circumvented in shallow water right next to the beach (or on the beach!); but if the point is steep or rocky, the safest route is likely to be outside of the rip zone, not inside of it.

Overfalls are related current hazards that occur along the interface of two colliding current streams. Sometimes a standing wave is formed when one current "falls over" the other, which can be quite impressive (in sight and sound) and a real boat spiller. The range of severity of charted overfalls is as large as that of tide rips, so it is especially important to check *Coast Pilots* or seek out local knowledge

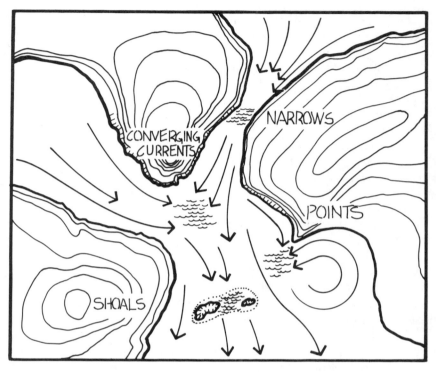

8-20. *Typical locations of tide rips. The rips are more severe when current and wind are in opposing directions and when swells from a passing vessel enter the rip zone. Remember that the current flows through the rips, so you will eventually come out the other side if you happen into one.*

when they are marked on a chart. The same chart notation ("overfalls") is used for the mild and the mighty. Overfalls also are formed on occasion when strong currents first meet strong head winds at the mouth of an outlet or when a waterway turns.

Coastal routes present current hazards that are frequently more severe than those found inland because the waves are bigger—at major headlands the currents might be bigger as well. For coastal routes, especially, charts typically do not warn of even very severe conditions close to points and near rock groups because they do not expect vessels to be there.

Coastal routes also have certain unique current "concerns," which may or may not present an actual hazard if anticipated. *Rip currents* are one example to keep in mind when paddling just offshore along beaches with surf. The water that piles up along shore inside the surf zone with each breaking wave must run back out. Part of it usually does so in fast narrow streams at specific places where the surf is weakest, such as points of land, localized rock formations, or where a trough cuts through the offshore bar (see fig. 8-21). Rip currents, however, also are present at regular intervals along straight, uninterrupted beaches. Along such beaches, the surf usually alternates between regions of high surf and regions of low surf. Expect an outward flowing current in narrow regions offshore of where the surf remains consistently weaker. Rip currents can reach speeds of 2 or 3 knots and typically increase with a falling tide to peak values just before low water. Outside of the surf zone this current weakens and turns parallel to the beach as it flows back to the regions of larger surf on either side.

A special type of rip current occurs frequently in waters around tropical islands enclosed by reefs. The waves continually break over the windward side of the reef so the water trapped inside must flow out of the passes. In these cases, the flow is nearly always directed out of the pass regardless of the state of the tide cycle. Similar effects are occasionally found in higher latitudes where a reef or other natural breakwater has waves breaking over it into a confined area. Water that gets into it must come back out.

The interaction of current and waves is a much more important concern where a river enters the sea. Notorious breakers can occur at the bar (just off the mouth of the river) whenever the tidal current is ebbing at the river entrance. Conditions are even worse with any swell running offshore. The swell steepens as it enters the current and breaks at the bar. River bars that look timid during the flood can have huge breaking waves during the ebb. These conditions are deceptive when viewed from seaward, because beaches to either side of the river might be calm, and viewed from the back, breakers at the bar might be difficult to detect. (A popular maritime poster on the West Coast shows an 82-foot yacht standing on its stern totally engulfed in a breaking wave about to capsize it. The vessel attempted to head out across the bar at Moro Bay, California, in defiance of Coast Guard warnings not to. Similar incidents occur yearly at several dangerous bars along the West Coast.)

Naturally, a kayaker would not plan to enter or exit a river over the bar and against the ebb. It simply would not be possible in most cases; even close shoreline routes into a river must be planned carefully. A more realistic problem is the route *across* the mouth of a river that might take you near the bar in transit. Such a crossing always

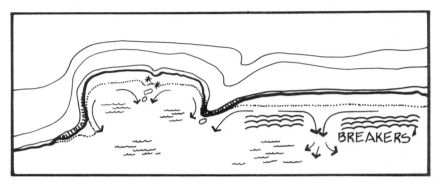

8-21. *Typical locations of rip currents. This current is from water trapped against the shoreline from onshore waves and swells. With no waves or swells there will be no rip currents. When approaching a calm beach, look for sandbars offshore. This is where the breakers will develop the next day if swells roll in; rip currents run out in the deep water between the sandbars.*

should be considered potentially dangerous due to the drastic change in sea state that can accompany the change from flood to ebb. When crossing river entrances, be certain you can make it across during the slack before the flood and not get caught near the bar during the ebb, especially when there is any swell running. Similar cautions must be taken at the mouths of inlets through the barrier islands that separate the ocean from the inside waters along the East Coast.

In any fast current flow, the upstream side of any obstruction in the waterway also presents a potential hazard to kayakers if it is approached too closely. The water is fast and turbulent where it abruptly changes directions to go around the obstruction. Examples include rocks in midstream, buoys, or bridge pillars.

Tidal rapids are another phenomena that might be considered current hazards in some areas. These are steep, narrow embayments that fill at high water. They are easy to enter at high water, but when they ebb the water flows back out to sea as fast rivers. There can even be rapids and waterfalls along them that are unpassable at certain times. Side trips along such waterways should be done with local knowledge or at least the awareness that you might get stuck or have to carry the boat around the dangers on the way back out.

And then there are places like Devils Hole and Dent Rapids in British Columbia, where violent tidal whirlpools develop as large as 100 feet across and 12 feet deep. Navigation, however, is not an issue in waters like these; seamanship, boat handling skills, and common-sense, along with Edgar Allan Poe's *Descent into the Maelstrom,* would be more to the point.

Randel Washburne, in his book *The Coastal Kayaker's Manual—A Complete Guide to Skills, Gear, and Sea Sense,* discusses practical approaches to current hazards based on much experience in and around them.

CHAPTER 9

Crossing Currents

Navigating in currents using GPS electronic equipment was covered in chapter 7. Here we return to the fundamentals of traditional navigation using compasses, natural ranges, and so forth.

Currents usually flow parallel to shorelines. Consequently, when paddling along shore, you are moving directly with or against the flow of the current, so progress along the shore is figured simply from paddling speed plus or minus current speed. Your direction of motion is not changed by current flowing parallel to the boat. Navigation while *crossing* strong current, on the other hand, is not as easy. Diagonal current affects both your direction and speed, and the resulting speed cannot be figured from simple addition or subtraction. The solution begins with determining the strength of the current that must be crossed.

Resources listed in chapter 8 provide current predictions for many places, but when at a specific place at a specific time it is seldom possible to tell at a glance whether these predictions were right, or even close enough to be valuable. Your motion when riding along with the current flow of deep, offshore water is rarely detectable. Only in fast current close to a steep shore or close to something attached to the bottom (like rocks, seaweed, or buoys) can you actually see the water move, or watch the shoreline fly by without paddling at all. Even these observations are qualitative. It might be obvious that the current is strong, but you cannot tell just by looking whether it is 2 knots or 4 knots, unless you are actually paddling against it nearshore.

Floating objects (other boats, birds, parts of trees, loose seaweed) tell nothing about the current when you are all floating in it together.

Objects might drift toward or away from you, but this is due to differences in leeway (windage) between you and them, not current. Everything floating in the water moves with the water at the same speed—assuming the current is the same everywhere you are looking. When the current is not the same everywhere in sight, its presence might be detectable, even in open water without fixed references. Floating objects would then move at different speeds, depending on the currents they were in, or they might even spin when trapped near the boundary of two adjacent currents flowing in opposite directions. In extreme cases, colliding currents form overfalls that you can hear, as well as see. But it is especially difficult to judge strengths of colliding currents from the churning water around them.

In most circumstances, precise current speeds are not needed. Just knowing whether the current is strong (over 1.5 knots), moderate (0.5 to 1.5 knots), or weak (less than 0.5 knot) is usually enough to navigate safely and efficiently. When you are in continuous sight of landmarks, even strong currents can be crossed on a desired track without knowing current speed. But navigation of large open waters where there are few useful landmarks, or navigation through currents at night or in the fog, relies on tabulated predictions, educated guesses, or actual measurements of current strengths. All tricks for crossing currents without knowing current strength require visible reference points on shore. Without these reference points, the accuracy of the crossing depends on knowledge of the currents.

If you anticipate losing landmarks during a crossing, it is best to learn as much about the current as possible before leaving. Because currents flow parallel to the shoreline, this can be done riding the current along the shoreline you plan to leave, using for references whatever charted landmarks are visible at the time. The same measurements would be needed to plan progress along the shoreline, if that were the route.

Measuring Current Strength

To measure current speed, you need to know where you are now and where you were some time ago. In piloting terms, you need two position fixes and two times. One approach is to measure the time it takes to drift (without paddling) a determined distance. You might, for example, drift along the edge of a channel—being certain that you are in the faster deep water you care about—past an islet that is 0.2 mile long. If it takes five minutes to go from one end of the islet to the other, the current speed is 0.2 mile per five minutes. To convert this speed to knots, multiply the drift rate in miles per minute by 60:

$$\text{Current (knots)} = 60 \times \frac{\text{Drift (miles)}}{\text{Time (minutes)}}$$

$$= 60 \times \frac{0.20}{5} = 2.4 \text{ knots.}$$

This formula is a convenient way to find current speed when headed downstream. It is not as handy otherwise, but learning the current strength could well be worth a short drift in the wrong direction. The method, however, requires fairly calm wind. If a tail wind pushed you along this run at 0.4 knot even without the current or paddling, your net speed during the run would be 2.8 knots (0.4 knot from the wind plus 2.4 knots from the current). The measured time would be proportionally shorter, and you would wrongly conclude that the current was 2.8 knots. With wind in the problem you are in effect sailing, not drifting, which is equivalent to slowly paddling the route. Because it is difficult to estimate a sailing speed in a kayak, this method is not an accurate way to measure current in wind strong enough to move the boat (winds over 10 knots or so). Nevertheless, the combined effect of wind and current might still help planning in some circumstances.

Current strength can be measured when paddling, but the accuracy of the answer depends on the accuracy of the estimated boat speed during the measurement. As discussed in chapter 5, boat speed is not just paddling speed, but paddling speed plus the effect of wind and waves. The procedure is to measure your actual progress along the shoreline (called *speed over ground*) and compare it with your estimated boat speed through the water. The difference is the current speed. If you are progressing faster than you are paddling, the current is with you, flowing in the same direction you are paddling. Otherwise it is against you. When paddling at a speed of 3.5 knots, but progressing at a speed of only 2 knots, the current is flowing against you at a speed of 1.5 knots.

For example, while paddling at 3.5 knots in calm wind, you time a run past a cove that is 0.5 mile wide. You do this far enough offshore that the current is not influenced by eddies around the headlands. It takes fifteen minutes to pass the cove. Figure the current as:

Boat speed = 3.5 knots.

$$\text{Speed made good} = 60 \times \frac{0.5 \text{ mile}}{15 \text{ minutes}} = 2.0 \text{ knots}$$

so

Current = Boat speed − Speed over ground
= 3.5 − 2.0
= 1.5 knots (against you).

Whenever the measured speed over ground equals your estimated boat speed through the water, there is no current—or at least the current is small compared to the uncertainty in boat speed.

This measurement has taught two things: the speed over ground along this route in the prevailing current is only 2 knots when paddling at 3.5 knots, and the current speed at this specific time and place is 1.5 knots.

The first result shows that a planned 4-mile run along this shore will take 2 hours in this current when paddling at a steady pace of 3.5 knots. Tidal current flow on inland waters, however, usually changes direction every six hours or so, with speed increasing during the initial three hours and decreasing during the final three hours. Even if the current does not change directions, its speed is likely to vary along a 4-mile run over a two-hour period.

The second result, measured current speed at a specific time and place, may be equally valuable. Comparing this measurement to the predictions for the area can help you plan the next leg of the trip. If the measured current is close to the prediction, you might have more confidence in believing predictions for later times in neighboring waters. On the other hand, if it is significantly different than predicted, you must be more careful and carry out similar measurements as you proceed.

Often a quick check of the current just to get its direction and approximate speed is valuable near slack-water time when you are not sure if the current has turned or not. When near a stationary mark within the main current flow (such as a buoy, the edge of a rock, or the end of a piece of attached kelp), you can make a quick check of the current by timing your drift past the mark. Without paddling, start timing when the bow goes by and stop timing when the stern goes by. With a boat length of 17 feet and a drift time of ten seconds, the current speed is 17 feet per ten seconds. This speed can be converted to knots using the approximation that speed in knots equals 0.6 times the speed in feet per second:

$$\text{Current (knots)} = 0.6 \times \text{Drift (feet/second)}$$

$$= 0.6 \times \frac{17}{10} = 1.0 \text{ knot.}$$

In 2 knots of current it would take a 17-foot boat five seconds to pass a mark; in 0.5 knot of current it would take twenty seconds.

When holding onto an anchored object, you can, even more easily, reverse the process and time the passage of anything that happens to float by the boat, even a patch of foam. From shore you can get some idea of the current this way by throwing a stick into the water and estimating how far it drifts in ten or twenty seconds—if you can throw it out far enough to be in the main current. A stick that drifts 30 feet in ten seconds must be in a current of 1.8 knots (0.6 times 30 divided by 10). To get a more accurate result from any of these quick methods, however, they should be repeated several times, and the results averaged.

Current speed also can be judged by how much it pushes you downstream as you start to paddle across it. Imagine a line drawn across the current from your starting point to your destination. With no current, you would paddle straight along that line, with the bow continuously pointed to your destination, and the stern continuously pointed to your departure point. This will not be the case, however, with current flowing against the side of the boat; it will push you downstream of that line as you paddle across. The angle between the way you go and the way you are pointed is informally called your *set,* or the *set of the boat.* (This use of the word "set" must be distinguished from its formal definition as the direction toward which a current flows.)

When paddling straight across a current, a set of 6° means the current speed is 0.1 times your paddling speed (small-triangle rule). A set of 12° implies a current of 0.2 times your paddling speed, and so on, up to a set of about 30° corresponding to a current of 30 divided by 6, or 0.5 times your paddling speed (see fig. 9.1). This convenient mathematical approximation takes part of the guesswork out of paddling in currents. The trick does not work for larger sets, but for those you need an anchor, not a trick.

Whenever current speed, boat heading, and boat speed remain constant, the set angle also remains constant. With a known paddling

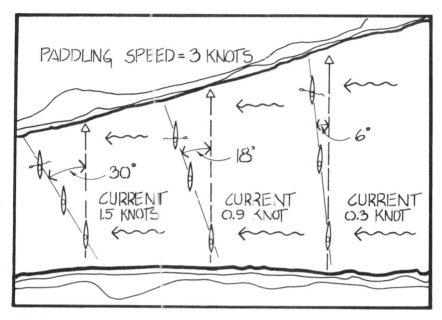

9-1. *When crossing current, the set angle can be approximated from the small-triangle rule presented in figure 4-4. Each 6° of set corresponds to a current of one tenth of your paddling speed.*

speed and an estimate of the set angle, you can get a good estimate of the current speed. The set angle at the start of a long crossing, however, must be judged by looking back over the stern, toward the closest landmarks. As soon as you enter the current and begin to get set downstream, your departure point (viewed over the stern) will shift upstream by the set angle, and remain stationary at that bearing. Looking over the stern, the set angle should be obvious after just a few minutes of paddling in the current (see fig. 9-2).

Distant landmarks viewed over the bow are not nearly as useful for warning of current set. Because they are farther away, they will not shift suddenly and remain at constant bearings, but they will only slowly move upstream of the bow as you proceed across on a constant heading. You will not detect your full set looking forward until you are halfway across, which is perhaps the worst time to discover you might be in trouble.

For example, after five minutes into a crossing, you notice your departure point is no longer on the stern, but 24° (a hand width)

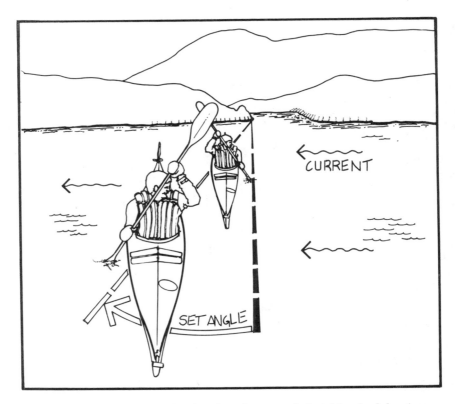

9-2. *Detecting a current and estimating the set angle by taking back bearings over the stern. With no current, the departure point stays on the stern; with current it moves upstream. Paddling at the same speed, it will stay at the same relative angle off your stern, but if you paddle slower or the current increases, it will move farther upstream of the stern.*

upstream of the stern, where it appears to remain stationary. From this you can conclude that you must be crossing a current that has a speed of 0.4 times your paddling speed. If the current remains constant, after ten or twenty minutes the same observation would lead to the same conclusion—but looking back you did not have to wait that long. What you would see looking forward, on the other hand, depends on how far across you were. At the start of a crossing, bow bearings shift with current set in direct proportion to your progress across. Paddling at 3 knots on a 2-mile crossing, you will be one eighth of the way across in five minutes, so bow bearings to the shoreline ahead would have shifted only one eighth of the set, or 3° in this example. Such a small shift in compass bearings is imperceptible; you would not even know you were in a current. To check for current set, look back.

One convenient way to judge your set looking back is to use the angular span of your hand. A typical outstretched hand at arm's length is approximately 24°, though it is useful to check your own with compass bearings. After entering the current, and on steady course across it, check the landmarks directly astern. Paddle for a few minutes on a constant heading by keeping an eye on the compass or distant landmarks on the bow. Then, keeping the boat on the same heading, twist around in the upstream direction and point your arm back toward the stern. Extend your hand with the little finger aligned over the stern and see where your thumb falls on the shoreline relative to your departure point. If the departure point is one hand width upstream of the stern, you are being set 24°, which means you are paddling across a current of approximately 0.4 times your paddling speed. If the current is not expected to weaken or change directions during the crossing, something must be done about this set now, or you will end up well downstream of your destination when you reach the other side.

Ferrying

When you know you are being set 24° downstream, the way to correct it is to alter the compass course 24° upstream. If the set is known in handspans, without a compass available, then alter the course upstream of the original target by the same number of units. This should take you straight across the rest of the way, assuming still that current and wind do not change much as you cross. This is not mathematically exact—the proper correction is not exactly equal to the set itself (see fig. 9-3)—but it is close enough for practical purposes. What you are doing is called *ferrying*—paddling a course upstream of your destination that will result in a straight tack across the current. As you paddle upstream, the current continually sets you downstream, so you end up going straight across.

But keeping track of where you are as you cross this way can be tricky without natural ranges available, because when ferrying you are not moving in the direction you are pointed, and you are not progressing at the speed you are paddling. Furthermore, ferrying may not be the best way to cross the current in the first place. Deciding how to cross a current requires a closer look at how current moves the boat.

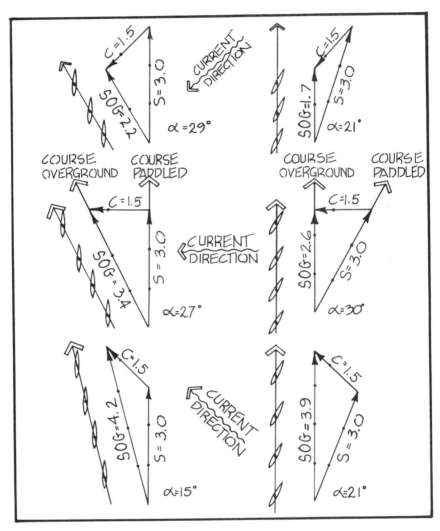

9-3. *Proper vector solutions to current problems for bow, beam, and quarter currents. Boats to the left are paddling straight across, allowing themselves to be set; boats to the right are ferrying straight across by picking the proper angle in the current.*

First consider what happens if you ignore the current, point the boat to the other side, and start paddling (see fig. 9-4). You know you will be set downstream, but where will you end up? The answer is easy to figure. If you paddle at constant speed straight across a current of

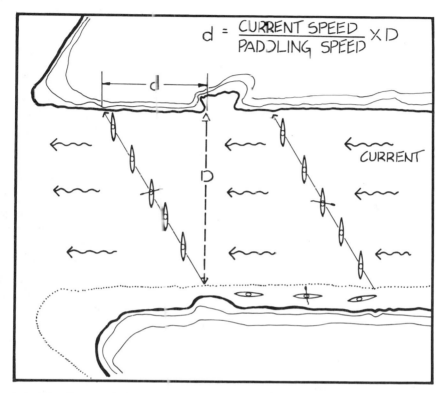

9-4. *The distance* d *that a boat is set downstream when crossing a current for a distance of* D *can be figured accurately from the equation shown above, provided the paddling and current speeds are constant. The "up-and-over" method of current crossing also is shown, wherein a paddler makes his way upstream in the slower shallow water along shore.*

constant speed to a landing site located straight across the channel from where you started, you will be set downstream during the crossing by a distance that can be found from:

$$\text{Distance set} = \frac{\text{Current speed}}{\text{Paddling speed}} \times \text{Crossing distance.}$$

By paddling at 3.0 knots across 1.2 miles of current flowing at 1.5 knots—keeping the bow pointed toward the opposite shore, not the landing site, which will appear to move upstream as you proceed across—you will land downstream of your target by 1.5 divided by 3 times 1.2, or 0.6 mile.

This is a big, and in many cases, intolerable error. It could, for example, put you into still stronger currents leading out into open water. But you learn a lot from this simple calculation. If you could paddle at 5 knots, for example, you would still be set downstream by just less than 0.4 mile—which is not much of an improvement for the extra work it would take. If 0.4 mile downstream still puts you too close to danger on the other side, another approach should be considered. It might be possible to paddle upstream for a half-mile on this side of the channel and then head straight across. The current in shallow water near shore would likely be much weaker or even flowing in the opposite direction from the deep water in the channel. Starting from upstream, the downstream set during the crossing would put you on target. Also, if there is strong wind flowing with the current in midchannel, the route upstream along shore might offer resting places in shelter from the wind, whereas in strong winds you cannot rest very long when ferrying across strong current. If you stop, you get set and pushed downstream.

This "up-and-over" method may not be the best choice or even a possible choice, but it is an alternative to ferrying that should be considered. The time it takes to get across open water this way, for example, also is easy to figure. Do it just as if no current were present: 3 knots is twenty minutes per mile, so 1.2 miles would take twenty-four minutes. When the boat is kept perpendicular to the current (current on the beam), as when paddling straight across a channel, the time it takes to cross is figured using the distance straight across. It does not matter that the boat, in fact, travels farther during this time, ending up downstream. Current on the beam pushes the boat downstream, but does not alter its forward speed.

If you choose to ferry, or circumstances force you to, the task reduces to measuring the ferry angle as explained earlier. When this is not possible, but you do have a reasonable estimate of current speed, the ferry angle can be estimated from this approximation:

$$\text{Ferry angle} = \frac{\text{Current speed}}{\text{Paddling speed}} \times 60°.$$

The formula applies to paddling straight across, with current on the beam. Paddling at 3 knots across 1.5 knots of current, the set would be 1.5 divided by 3.0, times 60°, which equals 30°. When starting across, point the boat toward your destination (assumed here to be straight across the current), read the compass, and then head 30°

upstream from that course. If you cannot see your target, read the compass course that leads across from a chart and apply the correction to it. By paddling the corrected compass heading all the way across, you should track straight toward the target, even though you are not pointing at it (see fig. 9-5).

When the current you cross is not on the beam, but closer to "on the bow" or "on the quarter" (45° forward or aft of the beam), then the same ferry-angle formula will work with the factor of 60° replaced with 40°. The proper ferry angle is the same for bow and quarter

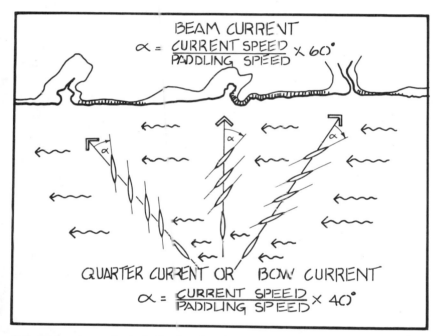

9-5. *Approximate formula for figuring ferry angles. The rule works adequately well for ferry angles up to 42° or so, which is equivalent to limiting its use to currents that are less than some three quarters of your paddling speed. In most cases, knowledge of current speed and direction is not accurate enough to justify precise vector solutions. This formula is useful and easy to remember. Bow and quarter currents take less of a correction, but they are the same in each case. The only difference is the resulting speed over ground. Bow currents slow you down, quarter currents speed you up. Bow, beam, and quarter current directions are defined for this application with the boat pointed toward the destination, as in the starting position shown on each route*

currents, although bow currents slow you down while quarter currents speed you up.

The ferry-angle formula is an approximation to an exact vector solution (see fig. 9-3), but for currents less than some three quarters of your paddling speed it is good enough for all practical purposes. Current strength (or direction) cannot be known precisely, so there is no need for precise solutions. The formula, however, does not warn of the natural limits to the method. You cannot ferry straight across a current that is faster than your maximum paddling speed—even though the formula claims that a ferry angle of 60° would do it. This formula simply cannot be used for current speeds approaching three quarters of your maximum paddling speed. In practice this is not a serious restriction on the value of the formula.

Ferrying lets you cross in the direction you choose, but you sacrifice open water crossing time. Ferrying speed across the channel will be slower than your paddling speed, so the actual exposure to the channel is longer than when going straight across while getting set. Generally, the best way to cross depends on what is going on around you. If the goal is just to get across the channel as quickly as possible, and it does not matter if you get set downstream, then let the current carry you downstream as you cross. This would be the case when going that way to begin with, and when there were no downstream hazards on the other side—but you still wanted to get across fast open water (of windy shipping lanes, for example) as quickly as possible.

On the other hand, to go straight across to a specific place on the other side, ferrying is usually the fastest way to get there, even though crossing speed is reduced. Not much speed is lost when ferrying unless the current is strong enough to require a large ferry angle. The largest ferry angle that might be used is approximately 60°, corresponding—in real terms, not the approximations of the formula—to a current of just under 0.9 times your paddling speed. In this case, speed over ground would be about one half of the paddling speed. Crossing speeds in terms of paddling speed (S) when ferrying across beam currents are:

Current Speed	Ferry angle	Crossing speed
0.97 x S	75°	0.3 x S
0.87 x S	60°	0.5 x S
0.71 x S	45°	0.7 x S
0.50 x S	30°	0.9 x S
0.26 x S	15°	1.0 x S

To ferry across a 2-knot current when paddling at 4 knots calls for a ferry angle of 30°. At this ferry angle the crossing speed would be 0.9 times 4 knots, or 3.6 knots. Notice that crossing speed does not deteriorate much for angles less than 30°, but then it drops rapidly.

The alternative method of letting yourself be set downstream and then paddling back up the other side to your destination, or paddling up this side and then riding down as you paddle across, is usually slower in total time under way than a direct ferry across—especially if the current is not slack along the shoreline and you have to paddle against a weak current as you make up for the midstream set. Nevertheless, the time difference between these two methods is rarely the critical factor in choosing how to cross. The midchannel wind also can have a strong influence on the crossing, but it is difficult to predict its effect on the time it takes to cross. Wind with the current smooths the seas you meet while crossing, but its added leeway is equivalent to increasing the current speed that must be compensated for. Wind against the current pushes you in the right direction, which effectively reduces the current, but it steepens the seas you must cross, which slows you down.

It is interesting to note that for crossing very fast or very slow currents, ferrying is not any quicker in *total* crossing time than going up and over the current. To go up and over a weak current requires only a short run upstream to compensate for the set; so net crossing time is just slightly longer than a straight slack-water crossing. Likewise, to ferry across a weak current requires only a small ferry angle, which only slightly reduces speed over ground, so this crossing time also would be just slightly longer than a slack-water crossing.

In the other extreme, currents approaching paddling speed require ferry angles of approximately 60°, which reduces crossing speed to one-half of paddling speed, so it would take twice as long to ferry across as it would to paddle straight across in slack water. Going up and over this current, on the other hand, requires paddling upstream a distance equal to the width of the crossing, because this is how large the set would be when current equals paddling speed. The total trip would be twice the crossing width, so the net time to cross also would be twice the slack-water crossing time—the same as when ferrying—providing the beach was indeed near slack.

Only when crossing currents of intermediate strength (1 to 2 knots) is there any significant time difference between the two methods. Even in these cases, ferrying is only faster by approximately 30 percent, on the average. When planning to cross a current of 1 or 2

knots, first figure how long it would take in slack water, and then figure that it will take approximately twenty minutes longer per hour of
slack-water crossing time to go up and over than it would to ferry
across. Then judge whether the time factor has any bearing on your
choice. Related factors that influence the choice include prevailing
wind, crossing distance, shape of the waterway, and state of the tidal
cycle.

When planning to cross strong currents, it should not matter, as
far as crossing time is concerned, which method is used. But for
strong currents that lead past a headland into open water, it is clearly
prudent to use the belt-and-suspenders approach: paddle upstream
for some way, and then still ferry as you cross, making every possible
use of natural ranges to monitor progress along the way.

Using Natural Ranges

When paddling within continuous view of landmarks, it is often possible to cross currents in a controlled manner without knowing precise
current strengths or paddling speeds—although it always helps to
have estimates of both—and without having to rely on calculated
ferry angles. The best way to do this is to use natural ranges to mark
the route and to monitor progress as you cross. The two range marks
can be on either side or on opposite sides of the waterway.

Figure 9-6 shows a "front range" made from a nob near shore and
a distant mountain valley. This type of range would not be found
from the chart, but by simply looking toward where you want to go
and seeing what lines up. To progress straight along the range, you
must point the boat upstream of your destination by an amount (the
ferry angle) that depends on paddling speed and current speed.
Accurate knowledge of these is not needed with a range for a guide,
but it still pays to use what is known to decide if it is closer to 5° or to
50°. For quick guesses, just multiply the current speed in knots (C) by
a constant angle that depends on your maximum paddling speed (a
simplified form of the ferry-angle formula discussed earlier):

Paddling speed	Ferry angle
3 knots	C x 20°
4 knots	C x 15°
5 knots	C x 12°

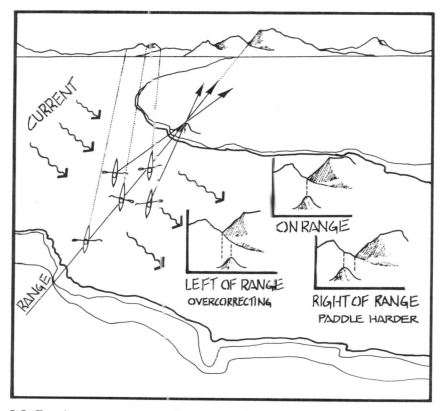

9-6. *Ferrying across current using a natural range in front of the boat. Once the proper ferry angle has been found, distant landmarks can be used for a steering guide, as shown. With waves or swells running, your course also can be maintained by the relative angle at which you meet the waves. This can help in the fog when no landmarks are in sight.*

The paddling speed to consider depends on crossing distance. You might, for example, feel that 4 knots is fine for a 1-mile crossing, but that 3 knots would be a better choice for a 5-mile crossing. For this example, assume you can make 4 knots for the entire distance. In this case you would reason that the angle you need is roughly C times 15°, the chart (or tables) shows that spring floods here are 2 knots, and so the most it should take is 30°. With a compass, you would point the boat at the target, head upstream 30°, and start across. Without a compass, point about one and one-quarter hand widths upstream of the target.

It will not matter if these guesses are wrong. The range will tell. As you start across keep an eye on the alignment of the nob and valley. If your ferry angle and speed are not adequate to hold the range against the current, you will notice it immediately as you slip downstream of the range. The nob will shift left of the valley. This calls for harder paddling or pointing more into the current. If neither one of these corrections gets you back onto the range, then turn around and head back or choose another acceptable destination downstream and range on that one. You are not making it as planned.

On the other hand, if you start creeping significantly upstream of the range as you proceed, then you are overcorrecting and could, in principle, reduce the ferry angle and head more toward your destination. It is always prudent, however, to "put a little in the bank" by making way upstream of the range on the overcorrected course—especially if you are not yet to midchannel where the current is likely to be strongest. What is an overcorrection at the start might barely hold the range at midstream. More generally, if you can barely hold the range at the start, assume you will not be able to hold it at midstream and turn back. Also keep the wind in mind. Wind on your back can aggravate the problem. It gets you out there faster, but makes going back against it harder.

Once it is clear that the crossing is under control and you have settled in on a good course that holds the range, check your compass or look for distant landmarks on the bow for steering guides, such as saddleback peaks shown in the figure. These then mark the heading that will keep you on range. Such marks must be at least ten or twenty times farther away than the length of the crossing; otherwise their bearings will change as you proceed across. A deck-mounted compass is clearly an asset when no distant landmarks are in sight. Without landmarks or a steering compass it takes continual course adjustment using close landmarks to hold the range. Hand-bearing compasses are not of much value in this important application.

Front ranges are the easiest to follow, but they may not last all the way across because your perspective on the shoreline changes as you get closer. Figure 9-7 shows how a front range might be lost as you get closer. Keep this potential problem in mind when picking front ranges, and also remember that the range marks need not be prominent things like peaks and nobs; they could be a bush and a gray spot on a bluff behind it, or an inshore rock and a log on the beach. A *back range* on the shore you leave also would do the job if it could be seen all the way across, but it is less convenient for small ferry angles.

9-7. *Losing a front range. Keep this common problem in mind when relying on front ranges alone. When you lose a front range, choose another guide range or look for other ranges to the side to check your progress across.*

On longer crossings toward a shore that is barely discernible, you might find only one mark on the far side. In this case pick the second mark on the shore you leave and use the range that lies between them, as illustrated in figure 9-8. Again, estimate the ferry angle, set off, and check the range as you proceed. The best way to check this range is with the aid of the paddle shaft. Point the paddle at one of the marks—whichever is the most convenient—and see where the other mark is relative to the other end of the paddle, as shown in the figure.

With either kind of range, however, it pays to have some backup means of checking progress. Always ask yourself what you would do if the range you plan to follow somehow disappears. You cannot use a rock on one side, for example, that you could not see from the other side. Or consider what would happen if you lost your glasses halfway across. A general rule of navigation is never to rely on any single aid to navigation. In other words, do not put all your boat in one basket. This means choosing more than one potential range for any crossing, using what you can see by looking around, and noting what the chart shows that might be seen when partway across. Checking the chart before crossing is important in any event, because it helps a lot with interpreting what you do see by just looking around.

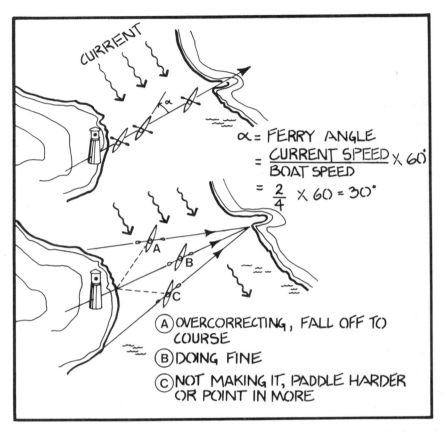

CURRENT

α = FERRY ANGLE

$= \dfrac{\text{CURRENT SPEED}}{\text{BOAT SPEED}} \times 60°$

$= \dfrac{2}{4} \times 60 = 30°$

A) OVERCORRECTING, FALL OFF TO COURSE

B) DOING FINE

C) NOT MAKING IT, PADDLE HARDER OR POINT IN MORE

9-8. *Use of a crossing range with marks on each side of the waterway. Sighting along the paddle shaft is an accurate way to check back bearings to judge your progress.*

For this type of planning, you can consider various kinds of ranges: guide ranges to mark the route, checkpoint or cross ranges to monitor progress across, and safety or danger ranges that warn of hazards. Examples are shown in figure 9-9. Here the guide range is from the 1,000-foot nob to the 600-foot ridge. As you start across, you can see the bay at point A behind the bluff in front of it. If you hold the range, you expect the bay to gradually fall behind the bluff and disappear. If you continue to see the bay as you cross, you know you are not making it, even if you lose your guide range. The cross range from spit B to the Twin Islands marks the halfway point on the crossing. With a good crossing on range, when you see daylight between spit B

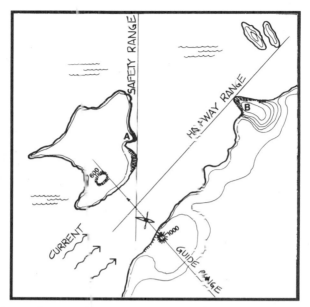

9-9. *Use of several ranges for crossing current. When the Twin Islands align with point B, you are halfway across. At this point, the bay at point A should be obscured by the cliff.*

and Twin Islands, point A should be gone. This type of planning makes the crossing safe. It is good training in chart reading and an enjoyable part of the sport of navigation. Each crossing presents new challenges to your ingenuity in choosing these ranges from the chart.

Time and Place to Cross

Time and energy can be saved by crossing currents at the right time and place. In some circumstances the right choices are obvious; in others they must be found from quick calculations. Fast currents generally go slack for only a short period every six hours, so without careful planning and some luck, it is not likely that a channel will be slack when you want to cross it. Furthermore, on a downstream route you might not want to be crossing in slack water; with no current hazards in the area, you might want to spend as much time as possible in the faster water. To optimize both getting across and getting downstream, you could cross headed slightly downstream (the opposite of ferrying), with the start timed to put you in midchannel at maximum flow—a maneuver that might require paddling along shore at first, to wait for the current to develop fully in the favorable direction.

Currents that threaten progress, however, take more consideration than those that aid it. Slack water is usually the best time to cross dangerous or adverse current, but even this choice depends on the nature of tidal cycle. In areas where flood and ebb strengths are much different, the slack before a strong adverse current might not be the safest time to cross. Strong currents accelerate after slack water more rapidly than weaker currents do, which makes getting caught in fast water more likely if the slack-water timing is off. Starting the crossing well into the preceding cycle of slower current might be more prudent.

The best time to start this type of crossing depends on the maximum current strengths on either side of the slack and the length of the crossing. Current tables list the times of slack water and the times and strengths of maximum flow, but this alone does not tell whether the water will be "slack enough" for "long enough" to get across without ferrying. The tabulated slack-water time is the *moment* the water is predicted to change directions. Technically it never stops flowing; it just slows down in one direction then speeds up in the other. Even this is an idealized picture, because large eddies can persist throughout the slack-water period. In areas known for strong current, *slack* water is rarely *still* water. To plan crossings in such areas, it is not so much the actual direction of the weak current near slack that matters, but rather how long it remains weaker than some specified speed.

This can be determined from Table 4 (the Duration of Slack) in the NOAA *Tidal Current Tables,* and when traversing or crossing dangerous channels this table should be consulted for specific predictions. For more general planning, a rule of thumb should suffice. This "slow-water rule" tells how long the current speed will remain less than 0.5 knot as it approaches slack or as it builds in the new direction following slack. The answer is sixty minutes divided by the peak current speed in knots, which quite accidentally is the number of minutes it takes the water to move 1 mile at its peak speed. An easy way to remember the rule is to think of the slow-water time in terms of the peak current speed in minutes per mile. The current of an ebb cycle that peaks at 3 knots will spend twenty minutes (60 divided by 3) less than 0.5 knot at the start and end of the cycle. A current cycle that peaks at 10 knots will take six minutes (60 minutes divided by 10) to build to 0.5 knot just following slack, and will decrease to 0.5 knot at six minutes before the next slack.

As an example of the use of the slow-water rule, consider the question of how long the current will remain less than 0.5 knot during the transition from a 2-knot flood to a 5-knot ebb, although it

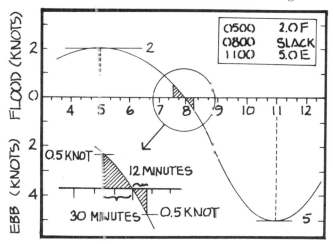

9-10. *The slow-water rule for estimating the duration of slack water. Current will typically stay below 0.5 knot on either side of slack water for the length of time it takes the water to move 1 mile at peak flow (sixty minutes divided by the peak current speed in knots). Five knots is equivalent to twelve minutes per mile, and 2 knots is equivalent to thirty minutes per mile, so in this example you have thirty minutes before slack and twelve minutes after slack (from 0730 to 0812) to cross the channel in less than 0.5 knot of current.*

does not matter which is flood or ebb in this question (see fig. 9-10). There will be 60 divided by 2, or thirty minutes of slow water before slack as the flood diminishes; and 60 divided by 5, or twelve minutes of slow water following slack as the ebb builds. In this case, you have a forty-two-minute window of slow water to cross in, but most of it is at the end of the flood cycle. If the crossing is less than 2 or 3 miles long, it could be done in less than 0.5 knot of current by starting thirty minutes before slack water. Remember, though, that the tabulated slack-water time could be off by as much as thirty minutes, so you would want to start sampling the water about an hour before slack to be sure that you do not miss it.

For longer crossings or to plan progress in current on long passages, it helps to know the average effect of a full current cycle or some part of the current cycle. If you stay in a current from slack to slack, the net effect of the first increasing, then decreasing current is the same as that of a constant current of 63 percent of the peak current strength. This result is independent of the length of the cycle or its peak strength. (The precise solution is twice the maximum current divided by pi, but 63 percent is close enough and easier to use in

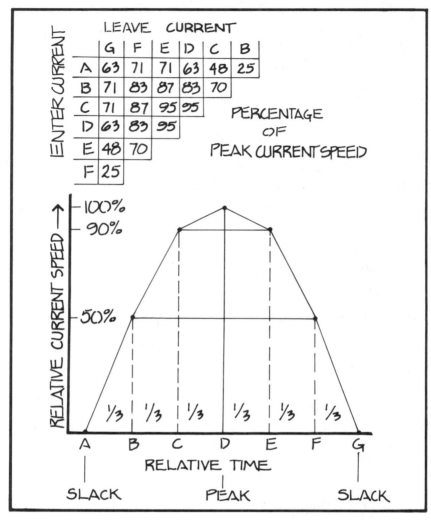

9-11. *Use of the 50-90 current rule to estimate the effect of a changing tidal current on net progress. Divide the duration of the cycle into six parts, then use data from the inset to find the constant current speed that is equivalent to the changing current of the cycle. Paddling in a current with a peak speed of 3 knots from relative point B to point E, the current would be increasing from 1.5 knots to 3 knots and then decreasing to 2.7 knots during this time. From the inset, you can assume that this will move the boat as if in a constant current of 0.87 times 3, or 2.6 knots. Note that staying in a current from slack to peak (A to D) or slack to slack (A to G) is equivalent to paddling in a constant current of 0.63 times the peak current speed.*

quick calculations.) The same result applies to staying in the current for exactly one half of a cycle, from slack to peak or peak to slack, but these time periods are more difficult to judge accurately. If the peak flow is 2 knots throughout the region you plan to traverse, and you stay within this region from slack to slack, you will be moved by the water as if the current speed were constant at 0.63 times 2, or 1.3 knots. If you plan to paddle at 3 knots during this time, you should figure your net progress over the six-hour period (or whatever) of the current as 4.3 knots. This is a convenient way to plan progress in favorable current: choosing resting times, for example, to coincide with the times you want to wait for the current to change or develop in the right direction. It does not help with long-term planning in *adverse* current, because it is natural to avoid the main flow of adverse current whenever possible, which prevents determining a proper average. Figure 9-11 shows how to estimate the net effect of a changing current for arbitrary time periods spent in the current.

It is important to remember that traversing a long pass with strong current is similar to crossing a channel when it comes to timing the currents. In some long passes there is no shelter in shallow water from current along the edges—or worse, the edges might be rocky with dangerous eddies. Such passes might even be dangerous in midstream at full speed, even when the current is flowing in the right direction. If you wait until after maximum flow to traverse the pass, consider the slow-current rule as a guide to how fast the adverse current might build against you, and be certain you can get through in the time allotted. If the current builds to 0.5 knot in ten minutes, it will build to 1.5 knots in approximately thirty minutes. In some passes, however, the current might build even faster than this rule suggests, so it is best to check Table 4 in the NOAA *Current Tables* to be safe. Passes with anomalous current behavior are often footnoted in the tables or given separate data in Table 4.

When crossing channels, remember that current accelerates as the cross-sectional area of the waterway diminishes (see chapter 8), and that this is not always apparent from looking at the surface shape of the waterway alone—the area reduction might be all underwater. It is best to survey the chart to choose the best place to cross whenever you have an option. A longer crossing in slower water can be more efficient and safer than a short one in fast water. Always look downstream of your route across to see what would happen if the current anywhere on the crossing is much larger than predicted. (Specific examples of navigation in currents are given in chapter 11.)

CHAPTER 10

Special Topics

Choosing a Landing Site

Choosing a place to come ashore in a kayak is a fine opportunity to coordinate trip planning with underway skills in navigation, chart reading, meteorology, oceanography, and seamanship. A coastal landing can be a bigger challenge than one in more sheltered waters, but the concerns and planning are similar for all landings. It is always important to have potential sites in mind before you get there; once underway you might have to make these decisions faster than anticipated and with fewer aids. The most valuable aid to this planning is likely to be local knowledge from someone who has been there or a kayaking guidebook that describes the area. But bear in mind the variability of winds and seas that might change the nature of the place, as explained in chapter 3. Good sites in some conditions may not be good in others. The following materials are required to interpret recommendations or find new sites on your own: a large-scale nautical chart; *Chart No. 1* to explain chart symbols; a topographic map of the region; wind, wave, swell, and fog statistics; tide and current tables; and references on the oceanography of beaches. Books on general kayak seamanship such as those by Washburne, Dowd, Hutchinson, and others listed in the Further Reading section at the end of this book include much valuable information on choosing and negotiating landing sites in various conditions.

Usually kayakers want a landing site on a gentle beach of fine sand and no surf, with an idyllic campsite overlooking the beach and a stream nearby to top up the water bottles. Campsite accommodations are not a navigational concern so they will not be pursued here, although they likely will be important to first choices when planning. (Chapter 3 has a brief discussion of the value of topographic maps in picking campsites. Books on kayak touring listed in the Further Reading section have more details.)

With the chart laid out, the first step is to figure approximately where and when you might want to land. Use the methods described in chapter 5 to estimate boat speed and passage times. Do this first assuming fair weather and ideal conditions, then consider bad weather or other emergencies that might call for heading in to shore early. It is important to study the area you will transit for all possible landing sites, not just a preferred destination.

In fair weather with flat seas, any long beach or any of the numerous pocket beaches along an irregular coastline offer good landing sites, approached from any angle. In some areas, however, long exposed beaches should not be counted on at all, because they are more likely to have high surf. Wave and swell statistics from *Sailing Directions* and *Coast Pilots* should tell of this, but coastal conditions can change with little warning in some areas. Pocket beaches are better because they can sometimes be approached in adverse conditions. Pocket beaches appear on a chart as small but conspicuous crescent bays with symbols, letters, or words for sand or gravel on the foreshore of the crescent (see fig. 10-1). Typically there are distinct points or off-lying rock at each end of the crescent that offer some shelter from seas that approach the shore diagonally. The size of a pocket beach is relative—the name refers more to their shape than to their size—but most in Pacific Northwest waters, for example, are less than 1 mile across. Beaches down to 100 yards can be located on a 1:40,000 chart. Canadian charts are especially good for this because of their tendency to use symbols more than words or letters to describe foreshore composition, and symbols can be applied to smaller beaches. The presence of a stream noted from a topographical map also might be a clue to a beach site, even without the symbols, because small gravel beaches often form where streams enter the sea.

Knowing foreshore chart symbols and abbreviations (explained in chapter 2) is crucial to interpreting a site before you can see it. You can estimate the average slope of the beach from the range of the tide and the width of the foreshore. A long foreshore means a gentle slope with finer sand (in some areas), or even mud on longer ones. Steeper slopes have gravel or stones. Other factors, however, also affect beach composition. In the Pacific Northwest there are many flat

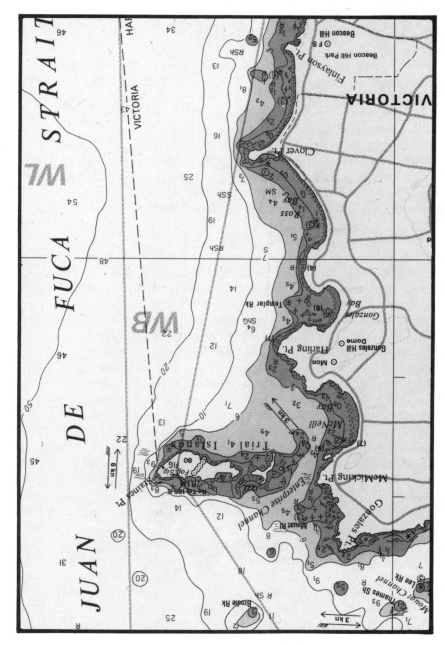

10-1. *Pocket beaches near Victoria, British Columbia. Note the small one above the "I" in Trial Islands; the mouth of Gonzales Bay is 0.2 mile (400 yards) across. Symbols for sandy shore are depicted in figure 2-7.*

beaches of boulder fields. References in the Further Reading section by Thomson, Bascom, and others discuss surf and the nature of beaches. Note in *Chart No. 1* (fig. 2-7 in chapter 2) the subtle differences among the foreshore symbols for stones, sand, and mud. Where little green is shown this must be read carefully. *Stony* can mean big stones, as shown below:

Charted name	Particle diameter (millimeters)
Mud (silt, clay)	smaller than sand
Sand	0.06 to 2
Stones	
Gravel	2 to 4 (buckshot to marbles)
Pebbles	4 to 64 (marbles to golfballs)
Cobbles	64 to 256 (golf balls to soccer balls)
Boulders (rocks)	bigger than cobbles

When beach composition is not given, check the bottom composition just offshore. It could be a sign of what is on the beach. A beach or bottom labeled *stones* means an aggregate of gravel, pebbles, and cobbles. *Shingle* means a mixture of large pebbles and cobbles. *Rocky* or *rocks* means either solid rock or with many boulders. *Rubble* means sharp angular rocks not worn smooth like stones.

Keep the tide height in mind as you choose your spot. Beach composition in some areas changes dramatically with distance from the high-water line. The high-water beach could be sand, while the low-water beach is mud or stones. It is possible to have a wonderful landing right on the beach at high water, but to have to carry the boat over 200 yards of mud or stones to put in at low water. When the slope is steeper near land, which is perhaps more common, you may find sand at low water and stones at high water. When entering on high water, keep an eye on the bottom to see what is down there. When entering at low water, note the apparent tide range on shore along with its composition and slope. Whenever the beach slope changes abruptly, the nature of the surf will change with water depth. A gentle spilling surf at one tide level could be a dangerous dumping surf at others.

Tides are easy to predict long before you leave; they are not sensitive to precise locations as currents are. One approach is to plot the tide height versus time on a graph at home, so the tide height can be found at a glance when needed underway. Some rocks that are quite important to navigation may be covered at high water. Review the rock symbols in chapter 2 and remember that even deep rocks are potentially dangerous because deep swells can break over them (boomers). Locate all charted rocks in the area and look for them or signs of their presence underwater by ripples, breakers, or foam streaks on the surface from big waves passing by. Naturally, if you leave your boat on the foreshore overnight, check the overnight tides, and tie it to dry land in any event.

Finding shelter and getting to it in wind and swell is ultimately a question of seamanship and boat handling. Bear in mind, however, that there are basic navigational considerations that apply even in mild coastal conditions, and remember always that wind and swell are typical coastal conditions, not rare ones. The value of pocket beaches in wind and swell is not their sandy strands, but the rocky end points on either side that protect the beaches. Because they are prominent, they are potential weather shelter on their leeward sides and shelter from the seas as well, which is usually more important. Wind waves and swell diminish in height as they bend around these points, as il-

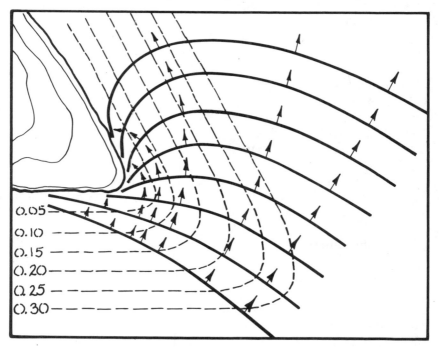

10-2. *The refraction of swells around a point. The dashed depth contours are marked in fractions of the swell's wavelength.*

lustrated in figure 10-2. The trick is to ride the swell in wide on the point and then curve back in behind it as the swell bends around and weakens. Often the slope of the beach also is more gentle just inside the protective point.

Without the protective headland of a pocket beach, you might find some small passage—through outlying rocks—with calmer water inside. Here the tricky part may not be the surf on the beach itself, but the entrance or pass into it. When approaching such an entrance, it is best to stand off for some time to survey the situation: to detect any breakers at the entrance and watch for the cadence of the seas. Often there is a repeating pattern, alternating about every three minutes between isolated larger waves and a series of smaller ones. Then if it looks manageable, try to get in between the big ones. Remember that breaking waves can look deceptively gentle when viewed from their seaward side. Generally such a passage is easier to gauge from inside, so a good procedure might be for a more experienced paddler to go in first to help guide others in with directions from inside. The standard international code signals for giving landing directions are vertical motion of arms, a white flag, or a light as a means of affirming that it is okay to land here; horizontal motion means negative or dangerous to land here.

If the chart shows probable kelp beds just off such a rocky entrance, it might be easier going. The kelp may not absorb all the deep swell, but it should dampen out much of the wind waves. It at least reduces your leeway or gives you something to hold onto as you survey the region. Large outlying rocks or small islands serve the same purpose of breaking up the swell. But the shelter they offer must be judged carefully. It will be most calm just before them, but farther back the seas may get quite confused as the diffraction pattern builds (see fig. 10-3). The shelter provided by rocks also depends on the size to the swell, which can vary tremendously from day to day. Rocks that let you in one day might not let you out the next.

The dynamics of coastal weather patterns tend to make each situation special. Along the Pacific Northwest coast, for example, large swells are typically from the west or northwest (because that is where the storms are that created them), whereas strong winds and waves that generate typically come from the southern quadrant. In such cases, you have to judge which factor causes the biggest hazard at the time and choose the landing site accordingly. It will not always be obvious when planning ahead of time which direction will be the sheltered

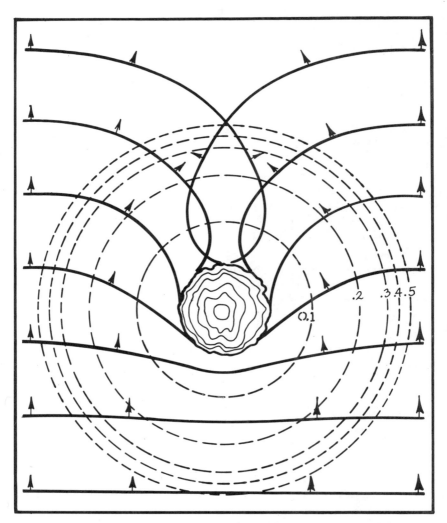

10-3. *The refraction of swells around a circular obstruction. The dashed depth contours are marked in fractions of the swell's wavelength.*

one. Wind and wave statistics, though, should help with the guesses before you get there. Coastal weather is discussed further in chapter 11.

Careful navigation during the approach to a landing site is especially important during actual or anticipated conditions of reduced visibility (darkness, fog, rain, or snow). Large seas also can limit your range of sight on coastal routes. Several examples of the coordination of navigation planning and practice underway are given in chapter 11 for both inland and coastal routes.

Marine Radios

Any long or exposed trip in a kayak is safer with a VHF marine radio on board. Those usable from kayaks are battery-operated hand-held units with similar capabilities as the bigger, more powerful versions used on larger vessels. They can be used for two-way communications with other vessels, Coast Guard stations, or any telephone in the world, for that matter. They are fragile and fairly expensive, and using them to make marine telephone calls to land is expensive. However, it is difficult to place a dollar value on the security or convenience they provide. When a trip is delayed underway, for example, you can call or relay messages to anyone concerned about the delay. Besides, most of the features (programming, scanning, and a large number of channels) of the more expensive models are not required for kayak use. The simplest models will suffice. These radios also receive weather radio broadcasts, although less expensive radios (receivers alone) will do this one job adequately in most cases. A VHF marine radio is a tranceiver, which means it can transmit as well as receive. You can call for help in an emergency, or call to forewarn that an emergency might be developing. One emergency call could make the radio's cost irrelevant.

To take advantage of these radios, however, requires some research and practice. They are essential navigation aids for larger vessels, and as such, there are strict laws on their usage. (The laws vary somewhat in different countries.) References in Further Reading include the details; the discussion here is limited to topics not stressed in the principal reference, F.C.C. Fact Sheet #14 "Ship Radio Stations" available online or by mail (see Further Reading and Appendix B). Articles in *Sea Kayaker* (see Further Reading) cover practical as well as legal guidelines for choosing and using marine radios.

The radio signals used by VHF marine radios are similar to those of commercial FM radio stations, and as such they have a short range of communication that is limited to not much farther than direct line of sight between transmitting and receiving antennas. Because a hand-held unit in a kayak is so low, this range is determined mostly by the antenna heights of those you communicate with. The reception range in miles is geographically limited by the earth's curvature to approximately 1.2 times the square root of the antenna height in feet, although the low output power of hand-held units and an enhanced electrical attenuation of signals so close to the water can cause even greater *electronic* limits. Hand-held radios do not work as well from a kayak seat as they do from the deck of larger vessels.

Usually you can communicate with large ships or sailboats (with antennas on the masthead) that are within 10 miles off—meaning, as a practical guide, when in sight on a clear day—but you might not be able to reach a fishing boat or other small powerboat that is more than 5 or so miles off, even when clearly in sight. The Coast Guard has very good VHF radio coverage throughout American coastal and inland waters; they use repeater antennas, so you need not be near an actual Coast Guard station to communicate with them. Except for a few blind spots between islands or inside of deep coves, the Coast Guard can usually be reached with a hand-held radio within and along most American coastal and connecting waters. You can call them for a radio check when in doubt about a particular area. Any VHF radio communication requires a fairly unobstructed line from your position to the receiving antenna and well-charged batteries. Communications between kayaks is limited to about 3 or 4 miles in calm water (depending on the individual radios) and to even shorter distances in large waves that frequently interrupt the line of sight.

Weather radio broadcasts can be received from anywhere within the geographic limits of the broadcast antennas, but any VHF transmission can be shut off completely by intervening terrain. The locations and heights of NOAA weather radio broadcast antennas are given on NOAA's Marine Weather Services Charts, listed in the appendix. These valuable publications describe all marine weather services in the regions covered.

Because most vessels equipped with VHF radios continuously monitor the emergency channel 16 (an official requirement, although one that is not strictly adhered to by all small craft or kayakers), an emergency call might well be received by other vessels even if the Coast Guard cannot receive the transmission from your location deep inside a sheltered cove along a steep shore. Standard procedures for sending or relaying emergency messages are covered in official and commercial publications on radio use, and it is not legal or practical to use these radios without first studying these references.

In the past the Coast Guard issued $1,000 fines for the use of channel 70 in vessel-to-vessel communications—this was a legal channel before 1985, but now it is not. Be sure you have current rules on radio usage. If you loan or rent kayaks or radios, it could be important to note that the laws presented in *Navigation Rules* clearly state that the owner of the vessel (or the station license) shares the responsibility for any violation of the Rules, regardless of who actually made the violation; the FCC rules on radio usage are also contained in *Navigation Rules*. Sailboat owners who have chartered their boats have been fined and the fines upheld for violations they knew nothing at all about until they received the violation notice.

The range of hand-held radio communications with marine operators for placing telephone calls is difficult to predict without local knowledge; they vary from just a few miles near irregular shorelines to more than 10 miles over some open waters. If you need to place a call when near steep land or listen to weather reports from a campsite, it might be necessary to climb a hill, or paddle past a headland to get better reception. Beaches along steep cliffs are often blocked from inland radio reception. If you cannot reach a marine operator to inform people of a long delay in your trip, then it is best to call the Coast Guard and tell them of your situation. They would prefer that you wait out the storm. It is easier for them to handle this extra radio traffic than to initiate a search and rescue when you do not arrive at your destination as scheduled. See related discussion in this chapter on the use of cellular phones.

The batteries of hand-held VHF radios last about eight hours when listening alone, but they provide only about twenty minutes of actual transmission time before requiring a charge at a standard AC outlet (or a new set of batteries on those units that have optional battery packs of standard alkaline batteries). Calls must be brief and to the point. Backup battery packs and telescoping antennas (which significantly increase radio range) are valuable options, and waterproof carrying bags are essential.

Possible Uses of a VHF Marine Radio

• You can receive weather broadcasts on channels WX1, WX2, and WX3 (the weather channel WX4 is the same as channel 21R; it is used in Canada). The broadcasts are continuous, twenty-four hours a day, with updates of actual reports every three hours, and new forecasts every six hours. American coastal weather broadcasts are given by the Coast Guard at specific times on channel 22A. The times and channels (frequencies) of marine weather broadcasts are listed in the radio-telephone section of the NOAA publication *Selected Worldwide*

Marine Weather Broadcasts. Other countries, including Canada, use channels 67, 26, 25, and 19 for these special broadcasts. See Internet references in Appendix B for updates.

• Use channel 16 to call for emergency help from any vessel or the Coast Guard. Nonemergency calls to the Coast Guard are made first on channel 16, then switched to channel 22A. Coast Guard Broadcast Notices to Mariners (e.g., that a lighthouse is temporarily not working) and special weather broadcasts also are first announced on channel 16, then broadcast on channel 22A.

• To contact other vessels for weather or sea state information, or to check that they see you (in some special circumstances of collision risk), or to talk to other kayakers equipped with radios, make initial contact on channel 16 (or 9, see below). Once contact is made, switch to one of the unused working channels: 68, 69, 71, 72, or 78. Note that channel 70 is not in this list. That channel is strictly reserved for digital transmissions between automated equipment and related distress or safety calls.

• For planned communications within a group, one of the working channels can be chosen ahead to avoid the extra contact through channel 16 (provided that someone else is not using it when you want to call; only one party can use a channel at one time within a given geographic area, and you may not interrupt except in emergencies).

• Channel 9 is an alternative to channel 16 for calling between recreational vessels. At present, its use is encouraged in areas with high traffic, where extensive use of channel 16 by noncommercial vessels has interfered with operations. The use of this channel is not so well known to recreational boaters, so you may have to try 16 as well if you can't reach a passing vessel on channel 9. Channel 16 remains the emergency channel, however, even where 9 is actively used for calling.

• Channels 13 or 14 are available for monitoring ship traffic locations, port operations, and the visibility reports they frequently provide. Although you can make contact with ships or the Coast Guard on these channels, it should be strongly avoided. These are busy channels intended only for navigational matters of large vessels. Channels 11, 12, 74, and others also are used for this purpose in some areas. (Channel 13 or 67 is often the main working frequency of drawbridges and locks, although they could be called on 16 for initial contact.)

• To make telephone calls through the local marine operator on specific channels with n 24 to 28 and 84 to 88, check with the telephone company or local cruising guides to learn which channels are used in specific areas. If you plan to make VHF marine radio phone calls, it is best to call your local marine operator ahead of time and set up a calling card account in the name of your vessel—make up a name for your kayak. This will greatly facilitate the actual placement of phone calls underway.

• In an emergency situation that has left you in an unknown location in thick fog, the Coast Guard can locate you by radio direction finding on your transmitted signal. This service should be reserved for real emergencies.

• Practice with your radio before setting off on a trip that might depend on its use. Contact other kayakers to test its range; talk to passing fishing vessels or recreational craft; or call the marine operator to place a call. Also whenever you are near the water or in VHF range of vessel communications, turn on your radio and eavesdrop on the various channels to learn the protocol. And be sure to study the FCC rules before transmitting. The rules are enforced, the fines are expensive, and Coast Guard vessels can easily track down a transmitting radio.

Other radios to consider for use on kayak trips are weather radio receivers, shortwave receivers, AM receivers, EPIRB (emergency position indicating radio beacon) transmitters, CB transceivers, and two new options described at the end of this section.

Weather radio receivers are small, inexpensive radios that receive only channels WX1, WX2 and on some models WX3. They typically do not include channel 21R (WX4) or channel 22A, which provide valuable weather broadcasts in coastal waters. These omissions can be remedied if needed with a regular VHF marine radio (most models receive these channels), or with inexpensive VHF receivers (the kind used to follow police cars, fire trucks, or news helicopters), by inserting the proper crystals for these weather frequencies (161.650 MHz and 157.100 MHz). Every kayaker on an extended trip should carry a radio of some kind that provides marine weather broadcasts in the areas paddled. The contents and formats of the various types of broadcasts are explained on Marine Weather Services Charts.

Shortwave receivers are useful for weather broadcasts in coastal waters. The reports and forecasts are given several times each day (see *Selected Worldwide Marine Weather Broadcasts*). These broadcasts provide local weather and also approaching ocean weather that might not yet be reported on VHF broadcasts. Shortwave transmission is long-range and reaches many places that have no VHF reception.

A small inexpensive AM radio can be used for emergency radio direction finding as well as a secondary source of marine weather. Open the radio to learn the orientation of the antenna bar; then rotate the radio to the point of weakest reception. In that orientation the antenna is pointed toward or away from the broadcasting antenna. This trick can provide constant bearings to steer by in the fog and without a compass, even when the location of the broadcasting antenna is not known. Some AM stations regularly broadcast abbreviated marine weather reports. These long-range broadcasts often can be received where VHF signals cannot be. Marine Weather Services Charts tell which AM stations provide this service.

Earlier editions of this book referred to class-C EPIRBs, but these will be phased out by the end of 1999 and will no longer be recognized as a safety aid at that time. EPIRB stands for "emergency position indicating radio beacon." Once triggered, it emits a signal that will initiate a search and rescue operation by the USCG.

Outside of VHF coverage, you should consider class B EPIRBs or the larger 406 MHz EPIRB. These are used for ocean crossing and isolated waters with no VHF coverage. EPIRBs have established an impressive record of assists with search and rescue. Their distress signals are monitored by satellites and aircraft. Response times are from six hours to a day for coastal calls. The 406 MHz EPIRBs broadcast your personal identification; they must be registered upon purchase. These offer the highest level of safety. See Appendix B for references.

Portable citizens band(CB) radios are a questionable option for communication within a kayak group or for emergency communications to land. They have longer range and are less expensive than VHF marine radios, but they are not made for use on the water (not even splash proof), and the emergency CB channel 9 (not to be confused with VHF channel 9) is not guaranteed to be monitored by the Coast Guard. Some fishing boats (commercial and sport) carry and use CB radios, but this radio is not a dependable way to contact even these few vessels. There are no marine weather services available on them, but near populated areas you might reach someone that would be willing to call the Coast Guard for you in an emergency. In contrast, it is the law that anyone who hears an emergency call on VHF channel 16 must assist you. For radio communications on the water, it is better to spend the extra money and buy a proper VHF marine radio.

On the more exotic side is the use of new hand-held amateur

(HAM) radios designed for the VHF/UHF-FM frequency range. These are very similar radios both technically and physically and in terms of price to hand-held VHF marine radios. They can receive all the marine frequencies (listen only) including the regular marine weather broadcasts, but transmissions are limited to specific amateur frequencies. They are designed for amateur radio communications, meaning no business or commercial matters can be transmitted. General communications from recreational boaters underway or on shore are allowed, and even welcome due to their novelty—a call from "marine mobile" is eagerly answered by land lubbers, especially "marine kayak mobile."

With these radios you communicate with other HAM operators via repeaters (relay stations) scattered around populated and sometimes not so populated areas. Seattle kayakers have reached Idaho from the middle of the San Juan Islands. The calls are free and you can use them on land—VHF marine calls to land via marine operators are relatively expensive and all use of marine VHF on land is prohibited. They are intended for people attracted to radio as a hobby. You must obtain a license for their use, which requires a written test. The Amateur Radio Relay League provides information about local classes on test preparation and other services throughout the country. For more information see Appendix B.

Beyond exotic we come to cellular phones, which can be used from the seat of a kayak as well as from the bridge of a luxury yacht. And for communications to land (from on the water or on shore), to anywhere in the world, they are indeed the most convenient. There is virtually nowhere that you could reach a marine operator by VHF that you could not place a cellular call. On the contrary, there are many waters where you can place cellular calls where no VHF marine operator service is available. The reception is better, the calls are more private, and the cost is about the same or less. Off the California coast, a man called his wife from a life raft to ask her to call the Coast Guard to report that his yacht had sunk. Because this incident is hardly unique, you can now, if in Washington or British Columbia waters, press *CG to reach the Coast Guard by cellular phone—sort of a maritime 911.

Things change. Technology readily available to the public is expanding faster than most of us have time to learn about. Kayakers are a diverse group of individuals, much more so than in any other area of boating. The goal here is just to mention the technical resources that might be of interest to some paddlers in some circumstances. If you were so inclined, however, and you had a notebook computer with modem and a cellular phone (all of which would easily fit into just a corner of a kayak) you could, from the camp fire of an isolated beach, send or receive faxes to any point in the world; receive the same detailed weather maps used by the National Weather Service; or tap into the card catalog of the Library of Congress and load into your computer the titles of every book ever written in English on the topic of the Northeast Passage over the top of Russia.

Navigation in Traffic

Kayaks are versatile, seaworthy craft. They are found in isolated waterways that have never seen another vessel, and in the middle of the congested shipping lanes of the world's busiest ports. Regardless of your paddling preferences, encounters with other marine traffic cannot always be avoided. A long trip in a kayak will likely bring you into close proximity with other vessels: ships, ferries, fishing boats, tugs and barges, or recreational powerboats and sailboats. In some areas, seaplanes, jet skis, or sailboards might be additional concerns. Encounters with other traffic always must be considered a potential hazard because kayaks are difficult to see in some circumstances, and they are often overlooked when they should be seen. As it is for air traffic and for other marine traffic as well, the biggest danger occurs in clear weather. In fog everyone tends to be more careful; there are fewer collisions and near collisions in reduced visibility than there are in clear weather.

Legal Matters

The laws that govern the interactions of all vessels on all waters are collectively called the "Rules of the Road" or just the "Rules." The main body of the Rules appears in the Coast Guard publication called *Navigation Rules*, although further regulations are listed in the *Code of Federal Regulations* (Titles 33 and 46), parts of which appear in each *Coast Pilot*. Additional local and state laws occasionally apply to inland waters, and these supersede federal laws in most cases. Important interpretations of the rules are only available in the records of various admiralty court cases compiled by the International Maritime Organization, Sub-Committee on Safety on Navigation (a body of the United Nations, with headquarters in London). *Farwell's Rules of the*

Nautical Road, listed in Further Reading, is an advanced text on the legal interpretation of the rules, although kayaks per se are not mentioned. Most of these complex laws are of no interest to kayakers; a few are pertinent, however, and kayakers are obligated by law to know and obey them. As with all laws, ignorance is no excuse. When paddling in traffic, your finances are at stake as well as your safety. Small sailboats have been heavily fined for violating the rules, and there is no reason kayakers could not be also. Negligent operation of any vessel that endangers life or property (including your own) costs $1,000; gross negligence costs $5,000. Attempting to sprint between a tug and its tow would be a clear example of the latter.

Some rules on right-of-way refer to specific kinds of vessels: powerdriven vessels, sailing vessels, and vessels doing specific kinds of work such as fishing or towing. Muscle-powered craft such as kayaks, canoes, and rowboats are not specifically mentioned in the sections on right-of-way. Many of the fundamental rules, however, refer only to *vessels*, and a kayak is definitely a vessel (defined in the Rules as "every description of watercraft used for transportation on water"). Consequently, kayakers have certain rights and certain obligations. For those who might read through the official rules, bear in mind that although it would seem true, a kayak is not a "vessel restricted in her ability to maneuver" or a "fishing vessel" when you happen to be fishing. These are special terms, with special meanings. A kayak is just a "vessel," or, as distinguished in some rules, a "vessel of less than 12 meters in length." If you have a sail up on your kayak, however, you become a *sailing vessel*, even if you are not moving. Those who sail their kayaks in traffic must look into the applicable rules; they are not covered here. Sailing rules are more comprehensive than paddling rules.

Before discussing the important practical aspects of paddling in traffic, it is useful to review the formal rules that apply—bearing in mind, of course, that these are legal aspects of navigation that are not always pertinent to actual encounters on the water. If you were run over by a Mack truck or a drunk driver on the highway, you might not care much whether he or you or both of you were technically or even flagrantly in violation of the law. But somebody will care, and somebody will pay the bills. In this sense, some Rules of the Road might be of more interest to your heirs than to you. In any event, when you play with the big boys, you should know the big boys' rules. In the long run you will be safer.

And before getting directly into a subject that might seem dull, or bothersome, irrelevant to some paddlers, I would like to share a personal attitude about the Rules of the Road. If you choose to paddle in traffic, you are truly entering into maritime affairs. You immediately become the "master of a vessel," small as it is, interacting with other vessels and their masters. You begin to share the broad concepts of good seamanship with other seamen. And a key point to good seamanship is your mutual understanding that each knows and obeys the Rules. I want to imply that it is more than just law; it is part of nautical tradition—a tradition that you are choosing to take part in. And I want to suggest that the Rules of the Road, as a body of knowledge, is a fundamental and fascinating part of that tradition.

Studying the Rules can be a very rewarding pastime, both practical and captivating. They constitute a remarkable document with an immense assigned task—the prevention of collisions between a vast array of vessels in a vast array of circumstances: vessels barely visible at 100 yards (a kayak in choppy water) to vessels the size of horizontal skyscrapers; vessels drifting along without power or traveling at 30 knots or more; vessels following unmarked lanes or crisscrossing open waters offering nothing more than an educated guess as to their intended course in all conditions of weather, clear or fog, calm or storm, and often with no common language among their drivers.

But despite this enormous assignment, they do the job. Collisions can always be traced to at least one violation of the Rules. The key to avoiding further proof of this is a thorough understanding of the Rules and how to apply them, including what to do if an approaching vessel does not obey the rules. In the following we cover the basics of right of way, distilled down to the parts relevant to kayaks. I hope the discussion encourages you to think through the Rules and be able to apply them. Sometimes just "staying out of the way of everybody" might not be in your best interest. In these cases it is valuable to know what your rights and obligations are. Remember, too, these are international rules; they apply everywhere in the world.

We first consider the law when you are in open water, outside of traffic lanes, narrow channels, or fairways. Maritime "traffic lanes" are vessel traffic separation schemes set up by governments in the waters approaching major ports around the world. They are discussed later in the text. "Narrow channels" are just that: any place the width of the waterway limits the course of vessels. They can be man-made in the middle of a city or natural passes between two islands in the middle of nowhere. "Fairway" is a more subtle concept in the Rules and calls for more careful attention by kayakers and other small craft. Fairways are simply direct routes from one waterway to another, usually marked by buoys. They are often dredged channels through an otherwise open uniform waterway, but they could be simply a direct route across open unobstructed water between one point and another. Within fairways, the Rules are the same as if the route were a narrow channel. As masters of vessels upon navigable waters, we are obligated to know this distinction and recognize this feature from a chart, from the layout of the buoys, or from simply looking at some ship or boat and asking ourselves "where is he going and why is he going that way?"

The wording of the Rules presented here has been abbreviated and paraphrased.

Your Rights as a "Vessel" *Outside* of Traffic Lanes, Fairways, and Narrow Channels

Rule 2 (b), Responsibility. All vessels approaching you should take into account the limitation of your vessel, which might require a departure from the Rules on their part if necessary to avoid immediate danger.

Rule 6 (a), Safe Speed. All vessels approaching you should travel at a safe speed, meaning slow enough that they maintain full control and could avoid a collision in the prevailing conditions of weather and traffic. Outside of traffic lanes, fairways, and channels, "I couldn't stop" is not a valid defense in a collision.

Rule 7 (a), Risk of Collision. All vessels approaching you should continually assess whether there is a risk of collision. If doubt exists, they must assume that there is a risk of collision and act accordingly.

Rule 8 (a) to (e), Action to Avoid Collision. A vessel approaching you with a risk of collision should maneuver early enough to stay at a "safe distance" when passing by using whenever possible a prominent course alteration that you can readily detect, as opposed to a series of small course and speed changes.

Notice that none of the above rules gives you "right-of-way" over another vessel; they just prohibit other vessels from running over you, just as they prohibit you from running into the way of some other vessel and then claiming categorical innocence of any damages done. *The above rules apply to you as well as to the vessels that approach you.* In a kayak, as in any other small craft, common sense and courtesy are usually reliable guides to what should be done when the proper rule doesn't come to mind immediately. The only time a kayak assumes actual right-of-way over another vessel is when the vessel is passing (overtaking) the kayak as stated in Rules 13 and 16.

Rule 13 (a) to (c), Overtaking. Any vessel approaching you from behind (on a compass course that lies within 67.5° of your own) must stay well clear of you as it passes. From your perspective, that is any boat approaching from an outstretched hand width aft of your beam: If you hold your arm straight out to the side, with your hand outstretched and your thumb on the beam, overtaking vessels are those that approach from aft of your little finger. Vessels approaching forward of your little finger are called *crossing* vessels, and only the fundamental rules listed above apply.

Rule 16, Action by Give-way Vessel. When a vessel is overtaking you, it should take early and prominent action to keep well clear of you when passing. For what it is worth, it is against the law for them to "just miss you" as they go by. When you are being overtaken, however, you become a vessel with right of way (the *stand-on* vessel) and as such have certain obligations included in the list below.

Your Obligations as a "Vessel"

Rule 2 (a), Responsibility. You (and the boat's owner, if different) are responsible for anything that occurs as a result of a violation of the rules or a neglect of any precaution, which may be required by the "ordinary practice of seamen." The good seamanship clause of this rule has been cited in cases where weather reports were not checked ahead of time (so inevitable bad weather could not be used as a defense), and in cases where equipment failures could not be used as defense in a collision because it was known to the skipper that the equipment was faulty before departing. This rule also has been applied to cases in which the skippers were not familiar with the handling characteristics of their vessels. None of these examples involved kayaks, but the analogies are clear.

Part (b) of this rule requires that you be aware of the limitations of your own vessel as well as those of the other vessel when interpreting and complying with the rules. Obvious ones to remember are that kayaks cannot go very fast, and they are difficult to see. Parts (a) and (b) of Rule 2 are interrelated. Often cited in poor seamanship arguments is the failure to plan ahead. In any vessel, planning ahead must take into account the vessel's limitations. It can be useful to consider an analogy of driving a car on a busy freeway. If you know you have to get off up ahead, you must get in the proper lane now, while you have a chance to.

Rule 7 (d), Risk of Collision. You must continually assess the risk of collision by every possible means, but among these *must* be included the angle on the bow (compass bearing) method discussed below in the section on Practical Matters. Every boater is required by law to know and use this piloting technique.

Rule 5, Look-out. In all conditions of traffic, visibility, wind, and sea state, you are required to keep a careful ("proper") watch for other traffic in all directions. This apparently simple rule is actually quite complex, and it is often critical in legal arguments about collisions. "Proper watch" is not defined in the rules, but it has been established in various court cases. Among the many fine points, the one of interest to kayakers is: The person on watch must have no other duties that distract from his watching for traffic. Courts, however, have ruled that a solo sailor standing at the wheel can constitute a proper watch. This nevertheless raises the question of whether rough seas (in open water or narrow channels), which must be continually watched and carefully negotiated to keep from capsizing, constitute such a distraction. Again, common sense is a reasonable guide. When conditions are so bad that you are continually distracted from watching for traffic, you should not be in traffic. This rule simply makes this obvious choice a legal requirement.

Rule 17, Action by Stand-on Vessel. When you do have right-of-way (meaning for kayaks when you are being passed by another vessel), you should maintain course and speed until the other vessel has passed you. This requirement can create tense moments in some cases, but it is a well-motivated law, and it should be adhered to as long as you feel safe in doing so.

If you tried, for example to get out of a passing vessel's way by altering course or speed, regardless of good intentions, you might in actuality increase the risk of collision rather than reduce it. When an overtaking vessel is first detected at some distance off, it is difficult to judge which side it plans to pass on (the rules do not specify this choice). If you happen to sprint toward its intended course, it would not know what to expect from you next, and from then on things only get worse. Have you ever, for example, bumped into someone face-to-face on the sidewalk as you jogged back and forth trying to guess which way the other was going?

On the other hand, if you believe that the vessel is not keeping clear as it passes, you have the right and obligation according to rule 17 (a) and (b) to take whatever action you can to avoid a collision. A kayaker must be especially careful when being passed by other vessels. You are the privileged vessel, but your burden is high.

Rule 9 (a), (b), (d), Narrow Channels. Whenever it is safe to do so, you should transit narrow channels as close to the right-hand side as possible. In any event, however, you are not allowed to impede vessels that can only navigate safely in certain parts of a channel or approaches to the channel (fairways). "Not impede" could be interpreted as meaning not cause them to alter course or speed in order to keep well clear of you. In 1989, however, a new part was added to Rule 8. Rule 8 (f) (i) states that "not to impede" means to take early action to allow sufficient sea room for a safe passage. This restriction applies when you are crossing channels or fairways as well as when following them.

This rule might require charts to identify fairways, even though the use of charts is not required for finding or keeping track of position in the case at hand. Larger vessels, for example, might be following buoys or range marks along a dredged channel through wide open but shallow water. The presence of such fairways are not always apparent from a casual look over the waterway. Nevertheless, as mentioned earlier, it is your obligation to know about them from the lay of the buoys, range markers, or daymarks (as you see them from the boat or on the chart) and treat these fairways just as you would treat narrow channels with steep walls on either side.

Strictly speaking, however, these rules do not apply when you meet sailboats *under sail* in narrow channels. If you are obeying the channel rules—meaning staying to the right and out of the way of power-driven vessels that must follow the channel—they should stay clear of you; they have no rights over you or anyone else when sailing within narrow channels. Likewise, small craft that can maneuver safely within the confines of the channel also do not have categorical right of way over you. "Small" in this case formally means less than 66 feet long, but it is important to remember that many boats in the 30- to 66-foot range can navigate safely only near midchannel in some cases and therefore should not be impeded. Some sailboats, for example, have deep keels that restrict them to deep water. This gives them right of way over kayaks in a channel with shallow sides (as a matter of good seamanship), even though they are officially small-craft powerboats when using their engines, and as such would not otherwise have categorical right of way over you.

Note that Rule 9 does give you the right to travel down the middle of a narrow channel whenever the sides are unsafe due to large waves (clapotis from wakes), but the remainder of the rule still has priority—you must not impede large vessels restricted to the channel. From a practical as well as legal point of view, with other traffic around, you should simply wait, looking forward and backward, for a clear time to go through or across, and then do so rapidly.

If you do illegally impede a large restricted vessel in a channel, it is nevertheless still bound by the fundamental rules. This point has been further emphasized in the new Rule 8 (f) (iii). It cannot run you over if it has the ability to stop (Which a tug and tow, for example, might not have), but it certainly can report you to the local police or Coast Guard and have you fined for impeding it. And even though you do have full rights of an overtaken vessel when approached by a *maneuverable small craft* in a channel, it is prudent to avoid exercising this right—small-craft operators that pass kayaks illegally fast and close along steep-sided channels are among the most serious hazards to kayaking traffic.

Rule 10 (j), Traffic Lanes. You must not impede any vessel following a designated traffic lane; this means ships and other large vessels, since small craft, both power and sail, also are discouraged by the Coast Guard from traversing the lanes just as much as kayaks are. These lanes are established to facilitate safe traffic in busy shipping areas. Just as kayakers do not want ships running around on random courses, the safe navigation of large commercial traffic cannot accommodate "every description of watercraft," undetectable on radar screens and barely detectable by sight, randomly traversing these designated lanes. It would be difficult to defend in any court any of your rights as a vessel if a collision with a ship should occur inside traffic lanes. Think of it as playing in the street. Organized sailboat or kayak events that take place in or across traffic lanes are always prearranged

with the Coast Guard and published in the *Local Notice to Mariners.*
Specifics of the *Navigation Rules* may seem far removed from the
paddling experiences of many, nevertheless, when paddling in traffic
they remain the law for "every description of watercraft used for transportation on water." In maritime court cases liability and fines are
often distributed among the participants. Even if a larger vessel vio-
lated one or more rules in an encounter with you that ultimately led
to a collision and injury, your behavior, down to the last detail, would
still be analyzed strictly according to the *Navigation Rules.* Any violation that could be remotely interpreted as contributing to the collision could be influential, regardless of how impractical the Rule
might have seemed at the time.

On the other hand, not having proper light at night, impeding
traffic in narrow channels or shipping lanes, approaching too close to
fast vessels to play in their wake, and other such things are clear viola-
tions of the Rules that could earn a sizable share of liability in any
case.

To illustrate the rigidity of the Rules and their application, consider the unusual case of *Rumpelheimer v. Haddock* in the British
Admiralty court of 1935 (described in an appendix to *Collision Cases,*
by F.J. Buzek and H.M.C. Holdert, Lloyd's of London Press, 1990).
Damages were sought in an encounter between a rowboat and a
motor car being driven on a flooded road (legally a power-driven vessel upon navigable waters, since the flood was from a river that led
seagoing vessels to the ocean). The rowboat, with legal right of way
according to the Rules of the day, refused to yield this right, and the
car was damaged expensively when attempting to go around it in
deeper water. The court held that the Navigation Rules did indeed
apply and ruled in favor of the rowboat.

Procedures for Paddling near Traffic Lanes

In most of the waters of the world, traffic lanes do not exist, so they
are not a concern. But many miles of wonderful kayaking waters leading to major ports of the world are crisscrossed with a maze of these
invisible maritime streets. In these areas, the lanes cannot be completely avoided, so it is important to know the rules for paddling in or
across them. Each regional traffic system is controlled by the local
Coast Guard district, which usually publishes a pamphlet that describes its traffic system and its rules. (Addresses and telephone numbers for all Coast Guard district offices are listed in the appendix to

each *Coast Pilot*.) The fundamental rules and procedures are common to all systems and serve as a guide for foreign systems as well.

- It is your obligation to know if lanes exist in a particular area and precisely where they are. When in effect, traffic lanes are shown clearly on all nautical charts. Looking seaward, the outbound lane is on the right side of the waterway; the inbound land is on the left side, separated by a *separation* zone that runs down the middle of the waterway in most areas. The waterways on the shoreward side of each lane are called the *inshore zones*.

- Whenever possible, paddle in the inshore zones and stay well clear of the traffic lanes and separation zone. Although no ship traffic is supposed to be in the separation zone, it is still a part of the lane system that should be avoided; it is a particularly dangerous place to travel.

- When you must cross the lanes, do so at a right angle to the lanes so as to cross them as promptly as possible.

- You do not have any right of way in the lanes; when you see approaching ships, you must stay clear of them.

If you were 0.5 mile in front of a ship traveling at 15 knots, for example, that ship would be where you are in two minutes. Paddling at 4 knots perpendicular to its course, it would pass 800 feet behind you (a distance of about two ship lengths for *smaller* ships). You would be illegally close to the ship, and its bow wave and the turbulence in its wake would create potentially dangerous seas in the area. Ship waves are especially hazardous (often steep and breaking) when running against strong current or across prevailing waves. Fifteen knots is a typical ship speed for traffic lanes, but some travel as fast as 20 knots. If you passed a half mile in front of a vessel making 20 knots through rough seas and winds that limited your escape speed to 2 knots, the ship would pass much less than a ship's length behind you, and its bow wave and wake would present a definite hazard to your safety. In short, a half mile is much too close to be in front of a ship. Even 1 mile is marginal for safe navigation. Court cases, for example, have established that when a vessel is directed by the rules to stay clear of another (as a kayak is in traffic lanes), it should do so in such a manner that not only avoids risk of collision, but also avoids any potential *development* of risk. When considering a crossing distance, ask yourself if you could get out of the ship's path with a sudden cramp in your hand, or with your paddle floating away. Neither of these would be a legal leg to stand on.

Remember also that from the bridge of a ship you cannot be seen from much farther than 2 miles off in clear weather and flat water (imagine how close you would have to be to see a kayak riding on the bow of the ship), and that some ships cannot see anything in the water that is closer than a half mile off due to the obstruction of its own bow and cargo. There are also large blind spots on some ships with aft bridges and congested foredecks. A large fast ship might have the opportunity to see you for a period of only three or four minutes (in swells or waves, the time window could be even shorter). With nearby traffic or other navigational matters on the mind of the skipper and pilot during this critical period, they might not see you at all, even in the clearest weather and best of conditions.

When an approaching ship sees you in a potentially hazardous location, it will likely sound its horn but maintain course and speed—in an emergency it will naturally maneuver as best it can to increase the safety margin, but a ship's maneuverability is *very* limited. The usual sound signal for such a warning is one long blast if a developing risk is detected, or five rapid short blasts for imminent risk of danger. When you suspect that you are in a dangerous place and an approaching ship does not sound its horn, then chances are very good that it does not see you—or you have misjudged the risk of a close passing. In any event, do not count on the ship going around you. Modern cargo ships are lumbering giants; they maneuver about as well as a fifty-story office building would when making 20 knots through the water. They turn very slowly and take a mile or more to stop, even when the stop is planned ahead. An unplanned emergency stop poses a threat to the safety of the ship itself. They can go out of control or lose an extremely expensive engine when attempting an emergency stop.

Needless to say, GPS is a wonderful aid to navigation when you must paddle in the vicinity of shipping lanes—as it is to just about every other application of actual navigation. There are numerous ways to apply it in this case, but one slick trick stands out as particularly handy for kayakers who must use this device with the minimum of interaction. This method lets you know if you are in the lanes or not from a simple glance at the screen.

Select two waypoints (A and B) that are located in the center of the separation zone between the inbound and outbound lanes, as shown in figure 10-4. Sometimes you can use the buoy locations that mark the centerline of the lane system, but these need not be the

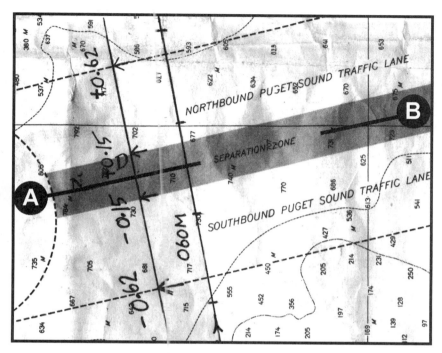

10-4. *Section of a vessel traffic separation (VTS) scheme on a chart that is set up to paddle across using GPS. Waypoints A and B define the "centerline route." Cross track errors relative to this route show at a glance whether or not we are in the lanes. See application of this planning in figure 6-4.*

choices. The main requirement is that there is one waypoint at one end of the region you paddle, and one at the other end, and that they mark the precise centerline between inbound and outbound lanes. Then define a fictitious route between these two waypoints. Next go to the chart and measure width of the shipping lanes relative to this centerline route. For example, you might find that each lane starts at 0.15 miles from the centerline and ends at 0.62 mile from the centerline —shipping lanes are usually symmetric in width and spacing. Here we have two lanes that are 0.47 mile wide (0.62 -0.15) that are separated by a zone that is 0.30 mile wide (2 x 0.15).

Now to use this trick when paddling in the region of these lanes, just take out your GPS, select the fictitious route, and tell it that you are paddling to waypoint A of this route (or waypoint B, it doesn't matter). You won't actually be paddling to waypoint A or B at all, but the GPS will think you are and when you ask it to display the cross track error (XTE) it will tell you how far you are off of that route, which happens to be the centerline of the shipping lanes. Hence, if the XTE is greater than 0.62 you know you are not yet in the lanes. If it is less than 0.62 but greater than 0.15, you are in the lanes, and when less than 0.15 you are in the separation zone. In this application, you will not be using the GPS to tell you your precise position— you could of course get that by asking for Latitude and Longitude—but instead you are getting what you usually care more about, which is where you are relative to the lanes.

Practical Matters

From a practical point of view, the main concern in traffic is judging, as soon as possible, whether you are on a collision course with approaching traffic. The standard way of deciding this is to watch the vessel's angle on your bow (see fig. 10-5). To do this, first check your compass course, a distant landmark, or a natural range in front of you so you can hold a steady course: then check the bearing of the vessel relative to your bow. The vessel's bearing can be noted several ways, depending on the circumstances: by just looking, by using hand widths off the bow, by noting the vessel's location along your paddle shaft, by temporarily altering course toward the vessel to get its compass bearing, or by noting where the vessel lies relative to distant landmarks in its background. Then carefully watch how this angle on your bow changes with time. If the vessel moves forward on your bow from this point, it will pass in front of you; if it moves aft with time, you will pass in front of it. If the vessel does not move on your bow, you are on a collision course. To judge collision risk this way, it is important to be on the same heading (by compass course, natural range, or distant landmark) each time you check the bow angle—although you could paddle on different headings between the checks.

The method of noting angle on the bow while holding a constant heading is just a simplified practical way of taking compass bearings to the traffic. In some sea conditions it is the only possible way from a kayak. it fulfills the requirement of Rule 7(b) that you must take compass bearings to approaching traffic if there is any doubt about collision risk. This measurement is required because a constant compass bearing to a target approaching from a distance means it is headed toward you on a collision course. If its bearing changes as it approaches, it will pass you.

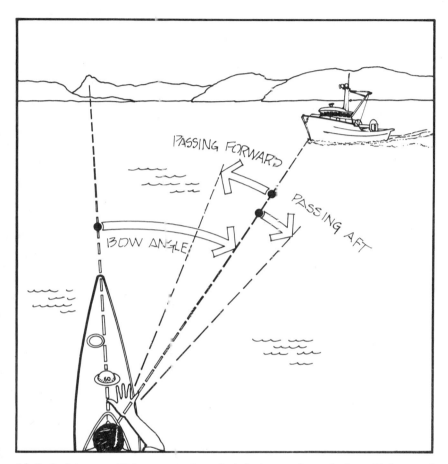

10-5. *Judging a collision course from the relative angle on the bow. If the vessel does not move on your bow, you are on a collision course.*

If you were traveling in a double, and had an accurate bearing compass such as the "hockey puck" or Datascope mentioned in chapter 7, then one person could take accurate bearings to the traffic regardless of your precise heading at the time of the observation. This is a more accurate evaluation of collision risk. In a single, you could do the some in some conditions by turning to point toward the traffic briefly and reading your steering compass. But such measurements are usually not accurate enough to give early warning.

In most cases, this test is not necessary anyway because you can just stop and watch the ship go by. In other cases it would be valuable. You could, for example, be in strong current that is drifting you into collision risk in an area busy with traffic that you are anxious to get out of. Or when evaluating more distant approaches when crossing wide lanes, it is good to know that an approaching ship is going to safely pass astern so you can keep going, as opposed to paddling headlong into a close encounter that you will eventually have to turn and run from.

In any event, the direct compass bearing or bearing relative to your own bow are methods most suitable when the traffic is fairly far off. For very close traffic, on the other hand, it is best to watch the bow of the approaching vessel relative to its own superstructure or cabin top as illustrated in figure 10-6. This is an accurate and easy way

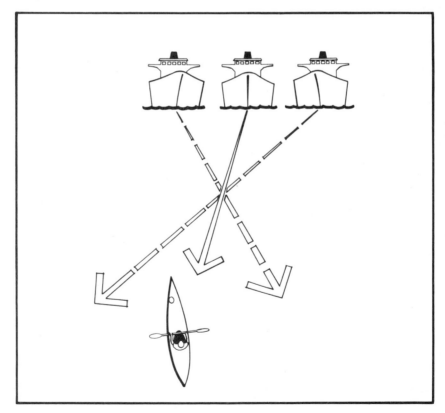

10-6. *Judging relative course lines at close quarters by watching the ship's bow relative to its superstructure.*

to judge relative course lines and course changes at close range, although it is obviously prudent to avoid getting so close that you need to use it.

Either of these checks, however, only tells of the risk of collision; they do not tell how close you will pass of both of you maintain course and speed. The guidelines for judging distance off given in chapter 6 can help with this. A large ship that appears one finger-width high will be somewhere between 0.4 to 0.8 mile off, depending on the sizes of the ship and your finger (practice with docked or anchored vessels to calibrate your fingers this way). You are likely to be dangerously close to any ship that appears two or three finger-widths tall. Another guideline is the appearance of people on board. At about a half mile off they appear as dots or posts; when you can see heads, arms, or clothes the vessel is within a quarter of a mile or so. Any people you see clearly should be going by you, not toward you.

Although vessels following traffic lanes will not alter course to accommodate isolated small craft (they would sound their horns instead), you can be fairly confident that they will follow the lanes. Since the lanes are straight lines between specific turning points, *it is very important to know where the turning points are.* A ship that appears to be safely crossing ahead of you might be approaching a turning point where it will turn to head straight for you. Any time you are in or near the lanes it is valuable to pick out natural ranges or use dead reckoning to keep track of where you are relative to the lane boundaries.

Large car ferries are the same as ships as far as the rules are concerned and as far as kayaking around them is concerned. They do differ, however, in that they have better visibility, and they are much more maneuverable. Their skippers also have more experience in traveling through small-craft traffic. If they see you cannot get out of the way, they will go around you if they can; but if they see you headed into their path, they will sound a warning blast. Ferries cross traffic lanes more often than they follow them, but nevertheless they are participating in the traffic lane system, often following specific fairways, and as such must not be impeded. When paddling in areas of ferry traffic, it is your responsibility to know the ferry routes and anticipate their presence. Be especially cautious when crossing harbors with ferry terminals. Look ahead to see what the cars are doing, and listen for the ferry's horn. It will often sound one long blast or some other prominent signal before departing. As you approach the harbor, watch the horizon for ferries that also are headed that way.

The most common concern in traffic, however, is not with ships or other commercial traffic, but with smaller powerboats traveling at high speed. Some boats in the 14- to 40-foot range can travel at 30 knots or more. When traveling that fast they fly off the tops of even the smallest waves with their raised bows blocking their view more often than not. When all you can see approaching is the bottom of a hull and a bow spray thrown off to each side, the driver most likely will not see you as soon as you see him. My tendency in this situation is to start taking high stokes, with the hopes that they might see the paddle blade flash by once in while, although I am not sure how effective this is.

Most drivers of these speedboats are not familiar with the pertinent details of the "Rules of the Road," so you cannot anticipate that they will pass you at a safe distance. During these encounters, survival is the main concern, not the rules. Nevertheless, it is still much easier and more accurate to judge relative course lines if you hold a steady course yourself as you watch them approach; at the same time be ready for quick paddling at the last moment. Bright-colored vests or a cyclist's flag mounted in a fishing rod holder might help when padding in heavy traffic of this type. Waters used for water-skiing or waters that lie between popular sportfishing grounds and public boat ramps are often riddled with this type of traffic at certain times. In any event, it is good policy to carry flares or smoke signals readily at hand when paddling in any area of potential traffic, day or night.

Sometimes a speedboat that sees you clearly will actually alter course to pass close by for a better look at your unusual craft—or worse, purposely watch you bounce around in its wake. This can be a frightening situation when you are in rough water and requires close attention. Flares provide some recourse in this vulnerable position. I also have seen large sailboats tack around very nervous kayakers in a strong wind purely to harass them. Again, flares serve well to remind such reckless boaters of the hazards they are creating. At least with flares at hand, one does not feel totally unarmed in this situation.

The main hazard of close encounters is not as often the chance of actual collision as it is the chance of being capsized by the sudden waves caused by the boat, and then perhaps being run over by the next one that goes by. When many fast boats cross confined waters (even as large as a mile or more across) the waves from their wakes grow steep and confused, even on waters with no wind or current. The problem is especially serious in narrow waterways or near a steep shore, breakwater, or other obstruction along the edge of a heavily traveled waterway. The passage under a large bridge can present similar conditions. Without proper planning, it is possible to get stuck between a rock and a hard place: You head to the edge to get out of the path of the traffic (likely to be traveling illegally fast according to the rules or local laws), only to find that the reflected waves near the edges are more dangerous than the traffic in the middle. For paddlers with limited experience in chaotic water, some channels or bridges might not be safe to pass through on a sunny Sunday afternoon as masses of recreational boaters head home along that route. When paddling in a group through traffic, keep the group close together; you will be more visible and prevent a boat from hitting one kayak when going around another.

The hazards of traffic always must be considered when planning times and routes of kayak trips. Dangerous encounters with large vessels (ships) are more often the fault of the paddler than the ship, because the routes and behavior of large vessels are usually predictable, and their skippers (in vast majority) know and obey the rules. Dangerous encounters with small craft, on the other hand, are more often the fault of the small-craft operators. The incidents are rarely outright malicious; they are usually incidents of poor seamanship that result from an ignorance of the rules and your safety concerns or drunken horseplay that appears malicious. Paddling amongst small craft must be like defensive driving: Do not watch the street light, watch the cars that are supposed to stop at the street light. In any kind of vessel traffic, remember to look back—a maneuver that takes practice in tippy boats—or occasionally alter course enough to check the view behind you. Also remember that both hearing and vision are impaired when you are looking downwind, and the sun is in your eyes. In the critical end, all rules boil down to the famous tonnage rule: "If it is bigger than you, it has the right of way".

Navigation at Night

Good navigation planning through hazardous waters calls for leaving plenty of time to get to your destination before nightfall. Coastal surf, rocky shorelines in strong current, and tide rips in even relatively sheltered waters are especially hazardous at night when you cannot see what is going on around you. In some circumstances, plans must be changed, and a new campsite found when darkness sets in. In coastal waters it might even be necessary to stay offshore overnight and wait for a landing opportunity during daylight the next morning.

Nevertheless, when planning any trip in a kayak, it is best to be prepared for paddling and navigation at night. Even on local waters, injuries or sightseeing distractions might call for paddling home after sunset. This means carrying the right lights, knowing about vessel lights and navigation lights, and practicing the use of these lights before you are forced to. In protected waters, comfort with night paddling extends the potential range of a trip; it could also get you back on schedule after an unexpected delay. As a side benefit, paddling at night sharpens your sense of feel for a boat because you must rely less on visual aids to balance and steering. Nighttime paddling is also a good way to experience the beauty of marine phosphorescence. The illuminated trails of fish, seaweed, marine mammals or any other form of turbulence are a wonderful part of the marine environment. Besides its eerie beauty, it provides a unique navigation aid in some cases. The flow of phosphorescent kelp, for example, can show the current direction on even the darkest foggy night.

The laws in *Navigation Rules* require that you carry a white light at night that can be shown to warn other vessels of your position "in time to prevent collision." To be effective for this purpose, this should be a light that is much brighter than conventional two-cell flash lights. Options include six-volt lantern lights, three- or four-lights, or special two-cell lights with high-intensity bulbs, good reflectors, and good lenses. Choosing a proper light is an important task with several factors to consider. Several aspects of flashlights and batteries are summarized in the appendix.

Although conventional two-cell flashlights might satisfy the letter of the law for paddling at night, they should not be relied upon for this purpose because that are not bright enough to attract the attention of distant vessels in time for them to alter course or for you to get out of their way. Furthermore, conventional flashlights are not bright enough to illuminate shoreline features, aid a search for another kayaker, or to read the numbers on a buoy. The brighter lights can help with these tasks; they also can be used to check the nature of the bottom as you paddle into shallow water looking for a nighttime landing site. Modern technology in batteries and gas-filled light bulbs has produced remarkably bright lights in very small units. Read and compare the specifications of lights before choosing one. Naturally, all lights used on a kayak should be waterproof.

Practice with the use of a warning light is essential, because without practice it can be awkward to show it quickly and maintain control of the boat, especially in rough water. When struggling to keep clear of traffic, it might be necessary to show the light intermittently between bursts of paddling. A light on a lanyard around the neck is one way to keep it handy or tie the light to the boat so it can lay on the spray skirt. Bright climber's headlamps are another option, but without special care their glare on the deck can destroy night vision crucial to nighttime paddling. Spotlights from larger vessels attempting to identify your light are especially hazardous to night vision. If a spotlight is shined onto you, turn your head immediately or night vision will be lost for some minutes. According to the Rules of the Road, vessels are not supposed to shine spotlights on you in this manner, but they do, so you must be prepared.

Some paddlers prefer the simplicity of carrying one good light for all purposes, and there is virtue in that approach. On the other hand, a light bright enough to safely warn of your position and to use in camping is not well suited for other purposes underway. If you must steer a compass course on a dark featureless night, for example, a dimmer light (penlight) directed toward the compass from under an elastic cord or tape is a better approach. Fortunately, most nights are not featureless, so an occasional compass bearing to a star, cloud, hill, or light on the horizon is adequate, and occasional bearings can be taken with any kind of light. As in daytime compass steering (see chapter 4), take a bearing to the reference mark and then steer relative to it. Most paddlers are surprised to learn how much they can see at night once their eyes adapt to the dark. On clear nights, you can see quite well, except that there is no color perception, and depth perception is very poor. At night it is important to evaluate frequently the distance to shore, ships, or navigation lights. On the other hand, peripheral vision is enhanced at night, which is an asset to paddling in traffic.

Bright lights are also awkward for keeping a group together at night. They blind nearby paddlers and require unnecessary battery consumption. A chemical light—the kind that provides onetime usage after breaking an internal glass vial—fixed to the front or top of a broadbrimmed hat is one solution. The hat blocks the light from your eyes, but leaves it visible to others within a quarter of a mile or so. Chemical lights are available in several options, including six-hour yellow-green, twelve-hour red, and high-intensity thirty-minute yellow and perhaps other forms as well. The red one, however, is not legal for kayak use in traffic as it could be confused with the proper lights of a sailboat (discussed later in this section). The common yellow-green version in this arrangement can illuminate large, close compasses adequately when leaning forward, but this must be tested for individual boats and compasses. In most cases it is not bright enough for chart reading.

Life preserver lights using a single D-cell provide up to one hundred hours (with a possible bulb change) of low-intensity light in all directions, which is often adequate for keeping a group together. They are waterproof with sturdy pins or other means of easy attachment. This type of light fixed to a broad-rimmed hat (with chin strap if necessary) is a good no-hands source of continuous all-round light for staying together, for close compass use, and for navigation warnings to slow close vessels. A faint light on a hat, however, does not eliminate the practical need for a readily accessible bright light that would unquestionably warn any vessel that might overlook the faint light. Bright warning lights are especially important when paddling in waters with many background lights, such as along populated shorelines. A weak light is easily missed in a background of shoreside lights.

As with all lights you carry, practice first to see how well they work; many low-intensity lights are not adequate for detailed chart reading. The value of red lights for chart reading while protecting night vision is overrated. Charts are difficult to read in red light, and red is not a magic color for saving night vision. Brightness is more important to night vision than color is. It is inefficient battery use to make a brighter light dim with red filters instead of using a dim white light in the first place.

In addition to a warning light, federal law requires that kayakers carry three Coast Guard-approved visual distress signals at night—although it is obviously prudent to carry appropriate signals (flares or smoke) during daylight as well, even though not required by law. Official distress signals are shown in figure 10-7. Note especially the side arm waving signal as this one requires no aids. This type of waving should be reserved for emergencies. Nighttime visual signals are flares, strobe lights (in the special circumstances discussed below), or a bright light that can be set to automatically signal SOS(• • • — — — • • •).

Bright lights that meet this last requirement also can be operated as normal steady lights that serve well for navigation warnings and camping, although they are expensive. An ordinary flashlight does not count as a visual distress signal. If you do not have an appropriate bright light (USCG-approved number 161.013 marked on it), then you must carry at least three flares. Approved hand-held flares are numbered 160.022; aerial flares are numbered 160.066.

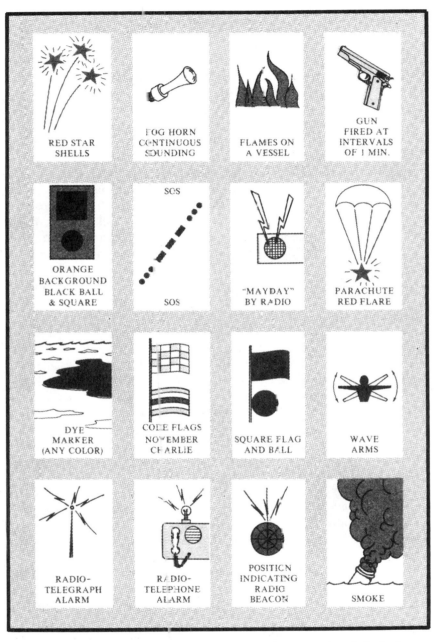

RED STAR SHELLS

FOG HORN CONTINUOUS SOUNDING

FLAMES ON A VESSEL

GUN FIRED AT INTERVALS OF 1 MIN.

ORANGE BACKGROUND BLACK BALL & SQUARE

SOS

"MAYDAY" BY RADIO

PARACHUTE RED FLARE

DYE MARKER (ANY COLOR)

CODE FLAGS NOVEMBER CHARLIE

SQUARE FLAG AND BALL

WAVE ARMS

RADIO-TELEGRAPH ALARM

RADIO-TELEPHONE ALARM

POSITION INDICATING RADIO BEACON

SMOKE

10-7. *Official distress signals on any waters. Other distress signals include a strobe light (on inland waters only); a U.S. flag flown upside down; a square shape over or under a round shape. Note the special arm wave that should be reserved for distress.*

Strobe lights (high-intensity, quick-flashing lights) require special consideration. They are an effective way to attract attention from a large distance, but they must not be used indiscriminately. Strobe lights are legal distress signals only on *inland waters*. Inland waters is a legal term in this usage, not a geographic one. It specifies those waters upon which the Inland Navigation Rules apply as opposed to the International Rules. The demarcation lines that separate these two types of waters are specified in *Navigation Rules*, as there are no simple guidelines for judging where to lie. Some coastal bays are international waters; some are inland waters inside a line drawn across the mouth of the bay. All bays, harbors, and inlets of Alaska, for example, are international waters; but major coastal ports of Washington, Oregon, and California are inland waters. Puget Sound and connecting waters, including Lake Union and Lake Washington, are called *inland waters* by the National Weather Service and the Coast Guard's licensing division, but they are international waters according to *Navigation Rules*.

The status of the waters you paddle determines the legality of a strobe as a distress signal. This is of interest, for example, if you happen to be inspected for safety equipment by the Coast Guard. More important, on inland waters a strobe can be shown *only* as a distress signal. To show it otherwise—to warn of your position, for example—is illegal with large fines prescribed. On international waters, showing a strobe light would not violate the law against false distress signals, but neither would it bring assistance from neighboring vessels, as it should, in principle, on inland waters, because the law requires all vessels to respond to distress signals.

Any nonemergency use of strobe lights must be restricted to international waters, but even there they are explicitly illegal (Rule 36 specifically states that strobe lights should not be used to attract attention). In actual practice, however, strobe lights often are used on coastal waters by fishing vessels and sailboats to attract attention. Without pursuing this unusual conflict between law and frequent practice, a small strobe light fixed to a broad-brimmed hat would serve kayakers just as well as fishing vessels and sailboats for this purpose in coastal waters. The sea state in coastal waters often requires constant two-handed paddling, so a flashing hat could be the safest option when paddling in sight of traffic. (Try to enjoy the fact that you look rather comical, rather than be embarrassed by it.)

Beyond their value as warning lights in coastal waters, strobe lights are especially valuable aids to nighttime search and rescue in any waters, once someone is looking for you in response to a distress call by radio or EPIRB. Carried for this purpose, strobe lights should be attached high on the shoulder of a life jacket. On the other hand, flares are much more effective than strobe lights for informing passing vessels that you are in trouble, even on inland waters. Many boaters on inland waters do not know that strobe lights are distress signals, whereas every boater recognizes flares as such—except possibly around 4 July in American waters, 14 July in French waters, or near New Year's Eve on any waters. For completeness, once a strobe has been successful in directing some search and rescue craft (helicopter or boat) to your position in an emergency, if you have the option, switch to a bright steady light for their actual approach and pick up. It is difficult to judge distance off a strobe light, which makes the pick up even more difficult in strong winds and seas.

If you must be towed at night, Rule 24 (h) requires that your boat be illuminated when other vessels are present, preferably with a white light from your boat that is visible in all directions (all-around light). When this is not possible, the boat towing you must shine a white light on you to identify the tow to approaching vessels—using, for example, your bright warning light, which you would always have at night. According to Rule 24 (i), the towing boat need not show the usual lights required of towboats, because it is (presumably) providing assistance, but it does share the legal responsibility that you be properly illuminated. These are not academic details; rules on tow illumination exist for a towed log as well as for a towed aircraft carrier. Any tow inhibits the maneuverability and legal status of the towing vessel. Should a collision occur that results in serious injury or property damage, infractions of the rules would be pursued relentlessly in admiralty court.

Navigation in traffic was covered in the last section. Nighttime application of the rules and guidelines presented there begins with the identification of vessels from the appearance of their lights. It is obviously fundamental that a ship's lights not be confused with those of a lighthouse. Every vessel carries running lights to identify its type, direction of motion, or special activities. Running lights are stipulated in *Navigation Rules*; they are precise and as a whole fairly complicated. It is neither practical nor necessary, however, to cover these in any detail beyond the basics, and even the basics must be simplified for practical usage in the following discussion—some exceptions and optional lights are not covered.

Except for muscle-powered craft and boats less than 7 meters long that cannot exceed 7 knots, all vessels carry sidelights (red on the port side, green on the starboard side) and a single white stern light. If you see a green light in the darkness, you are looking at the right-hand side of a vessel that is moving to your right (although the light would still be on if it were not moving); a red light marks the left side of a boat moving to the left. If you see both red and green, the vessel is coming straight at you. A single white light marks a vessel headed away from you. Although a single view of a single red or

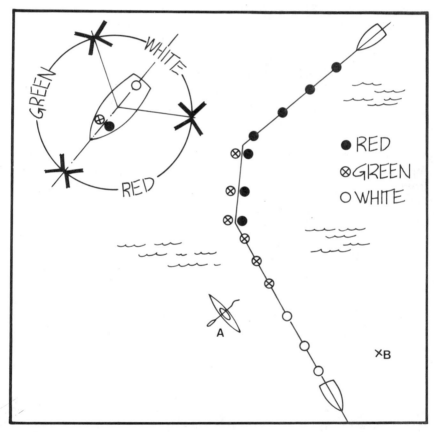

10-8. *The appearance of a vessel's sidelights and stern light from position A as it passes on the course shown. From position B, you would see a single red light throughout the passing. A power-driven vessel also would show a single white masthead light or two masthead lights if more than 50 meters long.*

green light tells the general direction of motion, it does not tell the angle at which the vessel is moving toward or away from you (see fig. 10-8). Sidelights tell more specific directions only at the moment they change. When a red or green light changes to a white light, the vessel either turned away from you, or has gone by. A red or green light that turns to both red and green means the vessel turned toward you, or you have paddled across its path.

Dividing all vessels into three categories according to length (more than 50 meters, more than 12 meters, and less than 12 meters), sidelights are required to be visible for 3 miles for big vessels, 2 miles for middle-sized vessels, and 1 mile for small vessels. In practice, however, it is not always possible to see sidelights from these limits without binoculars. Sidelights are most useful for interpreting vessel traffic at closer range.

The size and type of a vessel is specified by the presence or absence of additional lights. A sidelight alone marks a sailboat under sail; a sidelight and one white light above it marks a mid-sized boat under power; and a sidelight and two white range lights above it mark a ship. A ship's range lights deserve special attention. They are well-separated lights, with the forward one lower than the aft one. They are required to be visible from 6 miles off, which means they are always seen long before the sidelights are. Range lights are much better than sidelights for telling the direction of a ship. The ship is moving toward its lower light. Furthermore, the separation of the lights changes with the course of the ship. A ship turning toward you is clearly indicated by range lights moving closer together. When headed straight toward you they are aligned, one above the other (see fig. 10-9). Range lights are not visible from the stern, which shows a single white light for all vessels not engaged in work. The *Queen Mary* looks just the same as a 25-foot sailboat when viewed from the stern at night.

Vessels unique in nature or activity are identified with still more lights. A tug towing or pushing shows two or three white lights in a column, with an additional one or two yellow lights on the stern. Vessels engaged in fishing show two all-round lights in a column, either red over white or green over white. Small craft at anchor show either no light, or a single white light, whereas anchored ships are kept lighted with fore and aft white lights and many deck lights between them. Anchored vessels do not show sidelights. *Navigation Rules* explain these and other lights in detail for any craft from floating restaurants to minesweepers. Remember that it can be more dangerous to yourself and to others to show illegal lights (such as a single red

10-9. *The appearance of the two white masthead lights (range lights) and single stern light of a power-driven vessel more than 50 meters long passing on the course shown. Red and green sidelights also would be shown, but the white masthead lights can be seen from much farther off.*

chemical light) than to show none at all. With much traffic around, you could cause and be liable for a collision between two other vessels well away from you.

Because of precise light specifications, paddling in traffic at night can actually be safer that in the daytime. Vessel lights often can be seen at night from farther off than you could see the vessel itself during the day, and a kayaker's bright warning light is definitely more conspicuous to approaching ships than its daytime appearance is. In some cases, even piloting is easier at night. A low point of land with a lighthouse on it, for example, is easier to identify at night than during the day. The first appearance of a bright navigational light also provides a unique piloting opportunity to estimate approximate distance from the light, as mentioned in chapter 6.

Piloting at night is often limited to compass bearings to lighted aids (lighthouses, secondary lights, and buoys). Chart symbols and notations for lights are discussed in chapter 2; the *Light List*, which describes all lights, is discussed in chapter 8. The crucial element in planning nighttime navigation is predicting how far a particular light can be seen. If no lights can be seen along a specific leg of a trip, this should be known in advance and planned for. Likewise, if you do not see a light when you thought you should, it is time to stop and figure out why. With changing tidal currents, for example, it could be important to decide as soon as possible whether you have turned into the wrong bay, or have simply not proceeded far enough into it to see the light you are looking for. Most nighttime navigation questions reduce to deciding where particular lights can and cannot be seen.

The visible range of a light is determined by the height of the light, the brightness of the light, and the atmospheric visibility. From the low perspective of a kayak seat, the visible range of a light in clear weather is usually limited by the light's height, not its brightness. A light described on the chart as "Fl 4sec 25ft 13M" is one that flashes on every four seconds, is positioned 25 feet above the mean high water tide level, and has a *nominal range* of 13 nautical miles. Nominal range specifies a light's brightness by telling how far the light can be seen when its view is not limited by the curvature of the earth, that is, how far it might be seen from an airplane or the bridge of a large ship. From lower perspective, a light often cannot be seen from this distance because its view is blocked by the curvature of the earth (see fig. 10-10). The *geographic range* of a light is how far it can be seen over the horizon. As explained in chapter 6, the geographic range of a light from the seat of a kayak is given by:

$$\text{Geographic range (miles)} = \sqrt{\text{Light height (feet)}} + 1.5 \text{ miles.}$$

A light cannot be seen from farther off than its geographic range nor from farther off than its nominal range. For each light in question, it is the smaller of these two ranges that determines the visible

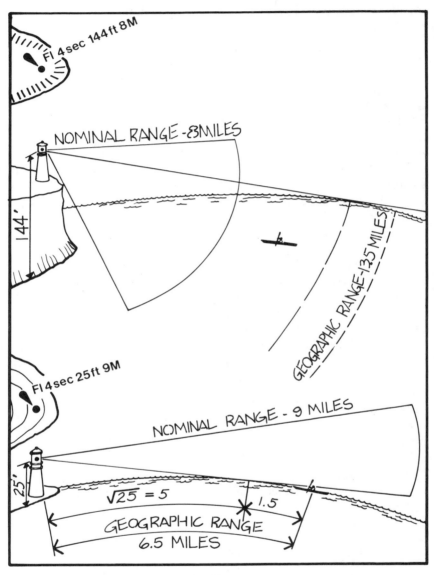

10-10. *The visible range of a light as determined from the smaller of its nominal range and geographic range. The visible range of the top light is limited by nominal range; the bottom light is limited by geographic range.*

range of the light. In the example above, the light shines 13 miles out into space (its nominal range) but it can only be seen from a kayak at a distance of 6.5 miles (its geographic range, square root of 25 plus 1.5). Geographic range must always be calculated; nominal range is charted or listed in the *Light List*.

When planning nighttime navigation, determine the visible ranges of all lights to be used and sketch these limits on the chart, as shown in figure 10-11. Also mark where lights are blocked by local ter-

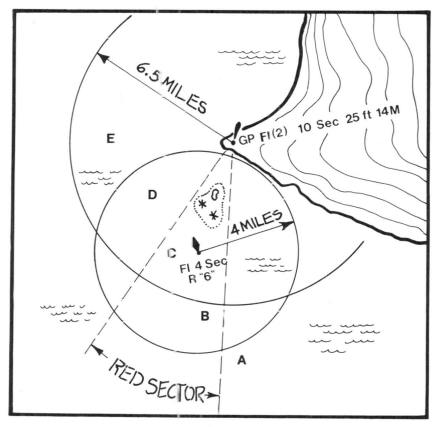

10-11. *The visible range of lights plotted on the chart show where you should expect to see them. The nominal range of the lighted buoy must be found from the* Light List, *as illustrated in figures 2-12 and 2-13. At position A no lights would be seen; at B only the buoy light; at C the buoy light and the lighthouse light appearing red, at D the buoy light and the lighthouse light appearing white; and at E only the lighthouse appearing white.*

rain and, when applicable, when they switch from white to red. Some lights have red sectors that mark rocks or other hazards in the vicinity. The boundaries of red sectors are charted as dotted lines, but it is always best to check the *Light List* for all lights you plan to use. Then draw in your intended route across these lighted arcs so you can note the locations where the lights would first appear and what their bearings should be from that point. The first appearance of a light is a check of your approximate position; the boundary of a red sector provides an approximate line of position when the color first changes.

The visible range of lighted buoys is more difficult to predict because their heights and nominal ranges are not always available—when they are available, they are more often in the *Light List* or *Local Notice to Mariners* than on charts; an example is given in figures 2-12 and 2-13. When specific data are not available, it is usually safe to assume that buoy lights are limited by nominal range to about 3 or 4 miles for buoys along the main channels. Binoculars are valuable to nighttime navigation for finding lighted buoys.

During periods of reduced visibility due to fog or rain, the brightness of a light (nominal range) becomes just as important as its height in determining visible range. Visible range is always limited to geographic range, but if the light does not reach that far through the fog, it cannot be seen. The distance a light can be seen through fog is called its *luminous range*. This depends on its nominal range and the prevailing atmospheric visibility. With some guess of the atmospheric visibility in hand, luminous range can be found from the Luminous Range Diagram in the *Light List*. In most cases, however, a simple approximation to the tabulated results is adequate. The following formula is one example:

$$\text{Luminous range} = \frac{\text{Atmospheric visibility}}{10} \times \text{Nominal range} + 1 \text{ mile.}$$

Charted nominal ranges assume a visibility of 10 miles, so the first term of the formula simply scales the nominal range according to the visibility; the additional 1 mile is a fudge factor that makes the results more accurate for lower visibilities. This formula works well for atmospheric visibilities down to about one half mile. When the visibility is less that that, it is best to refer to the Luminous Range Diagram.

In the last example (nominal range of 13 miles, geographic range of 6.5 miles), if the atmospheric visibility were 2 miles, the luminous range would be 3.6 miles (13 divided by 10, times 2, plus 1), so you would have to be that close to the light to see it, even though it was over the horizon at 6.5 miles off. Whenever you can see less than 10 miles at sunset, it is necessary to calculate the luminous range of each light before you can plot on the chart the arc of its expected visible range. The problem is arriving at some reasonable guess of the visibility. Because it is defined as how far unlighted objects can be seen during daylight, it is obviously difficult to estimate at night. Some VHF weather radio broadcasts include visibilities, but even these must be used with caution. Visibility changes with time, direction, and elevation. You might see a hill clearly, but not the shoreline just below it where the lights are located.

Nevertheless, it is important to account for luminous range even if it must be based on crude estimates of the visibility (0.5 mile, 2.5 miles, or 5 miles). If at sunset you can see an island that is 3 miles off, but not a prominent headland behind it that is 8 miles off, then the visibility is somewhere between 3 and 8 miles. If you can barely discern a shore that is 5 miles off, the visibility is about 5 miles.

One trick that works during the night is to estimate the visibility from the observed luminous range to a light that can be seen; then use that visibility to predict the visible ranges to other lights. The distance to a light is the same as its luminous range whenever it first comes into view from a distance off that is less than geographic range (6.5 miles) and nominal range (13 miles). Working the luminous range formula backward, the visibility must be about 3.5 miles (5 minus 1, times 10, divided by 13).

Another trick (explained in chapter 6) is to recognize that the visibility must be at least 1.5 miles if you can see a line between the sky and water, as this is about the distance to the horizon viewed from a kayak. These are each crude estimates of the visibility, but they are usually better than unaided guesses. With an understanding of luminous range, piloting in the fog is easier at night than it is during daylight without lighted aids, although this does not alleviate the problem of traffic in fog. Vessel lights have such a low nominal range that they are always difficult to see in reduced visibility. As on foggy days, you will likely hear traffic before you see it, so it is best to avoid traffic in the fog, night or day.

When possible, plan nighttime routes with a full moon. Moon phases are given in the *Tide Tables*, as are the times of sunrise and sunset, moonrise and moonset. Times listed in these tables are local mean times, which must be corrected for your longitude as explained in the tables. They also must be corrected for daylight saving time when in effect, although the tables do not include emphatic warnings of this. Depending on latitude and season, twilight times extend the useful daylight in the mornings and evenings by thirty minutes to one hour or more. To plan the next day's paddle, it is helpful to note the time of day when true darkness sets in or when first light appears. This can be compared to sunset or sunrise time to estimate the duration of twilight. Twilight times are the same in the morning as they are in the evening. To plan future trips, twilight times for any date can be found in *Nautical Almanacs*, even outdated ones. *Civil twilight* is the time when bright stars first appear in the evening or finally disappear in the morning. *Nautical twilight* is the time when the horizon fades into darkness at night or first appears in the morning. In clear weather, most people perceive the time of civil twilight as still daylight, and the time of nautical twilight as definitely darkness.

For extra protection during nighttime paddling, use reflective tape on your clothing and paddles. Recent developments in this product are remarkably effective. Search and rescue studies have shown that victims are often detected by reflected light from these tapes before their life jacket lights could be seen.

Navigation in the Fog

From a practical marine point of view, there are two kinds of fog: sea fog and radiation fog. It is fundamental to safety to know the distinctions between them: Radiation fog comes with no wind, and it burns off as the day heats; sea fog can come with strong winds and last for days. All fog is formed the same way. When the air temperature drops to the dew point, water vapor in the air condenses to fog. It is impossible to tell the difference between a jar of sea fog and a jar of radiation fog. Distinctions between the two types of fog lie only in the way the air is cooled and in the subsequent behavior of the fog mass and associated weather. Sea fog (also called advection fog) presents a much more serious hazard to kayakers than radiation fog.

As the name implies, sea fog is formed over offshore waters, although with an onshore wind it can penetrate far into long coastal embayments. The most common way it is formed is when warm moist air flows over cold coastal waters brought to the surface by upwelling of deep currents. Areas of dense sea fog can extend over hundreds of miles and persist for several days or longer. It moves with the prevailing winds, which is the main source of its potential danger. A calm sunny day of pleasant coastal paddling can change within hours to very hazardous conditions when a wall of cold sea fog arrives with winds up to 25 knots or more. (When paddling in coastal waters prone to sea fog, do not bury your polypropylene rain gear just because you are starting off in a swimsuit.) Sea fog along coastal waters is common in middle and high latitudes during spring and summer (check climate data in the *Coast Pilot* for specific statistics).

Sea fog is easily seen in satellite photos, so weather radio forecasts of its presence are reliable, although details of its motion are difficult to forecast. For example, when sea fog penetrates into inland waters or onto land, it often begins to dissipate when the land heats during the morning. This heating, however, also generates an onshore sea breeze, which in turn brings more fog to the shore. Thus, an important distinction between sea fog and radiation fog is that sea fog does not burn off. In contrast to paddling through radiation fog on inland waters, you cannot set off on a morning paddle in sea fog and count on it lifting as the day progresses. Even if you see the fog retreating offshore during the night or morning, you cannot count on it to stay offshore. If the wind develops in the onshore direction, it could move right back in. Also in contrast to radiation fog, you cannot assume that when you see fog approaching along coastal waters there will not be wind with it. Calm air is characteristic of radiation fog, not sea fog. Sea fog is usually accompanied by wind, although not always. Thick sea fog can occur in calm air, but areas and seasons with prevalent sea fog usually do not have many days of calm air.

Radiation fog is formed over land on clear calm nights whenever the relative humidity is high at sunset. The lack of cloud cover allows the heat of the land to radiate away overnight, which cools the air near the ground. Wind stronger than 10 knots, however, will usually prevent the formation of radiation fog because it continuously mixes the cool ground air with warmer air above it. The ideal wind for the formation of radiation fog is a light breeze of under 3 knots, just enough to lift and transport the fog without mixing it. In absolutely calm air, radiation fog will be patchy and only waist deep. Fog is unlikely on cloudy days because the blanket of clouds prevents heat loss by radiation. Although it is formed on land, radiation fog is a concern to boaters because the cool dense fog descends to fill valleys and spill out over the water. It also can obscure shoreside aids to navigation, even when the air is clear over the water. Radiation fog typically burns off as the day heats; it rarely lasts more than three or four hours past sunrise. It is most common during fall (moist months) and winter (long nights). When camping, look for radiation fog to form a few hours after dew first appears on metal objects.

It is not uncommon to begin an inland paddle during a morning (radiation) fog with confidence that the fog will lift. Nevertheless, it is always prudent to check the weather radio forecasts. Clouds might move in during the early morning, blocking the sun and keeping the day cool enough to maintain the fog much longer than usual. Also, if the afternoon forecasts call for fog (reduced visibility) during the night, they are likely to be right, even if the day is warm and clear at the time, and even if the forecasts are completely wrong about the wind speed or direction at the time. Temperature trends needed for fog forecasts are more dependable than the atmospheric pressure trends needed for wind forecasts.

Except for obvious potential hazards of strong winds and long duration that characterize sea fog, navigation in the fog does not depend on the type of fog. The same procedures and safety concerns apply in any type of reduced visibility, such as heavy rain or snow (sand storm or smoke). If you anticipate losing visibility while still underway, the first thing to do is establish your position as carefully as possible while landmarks are still in sight. If you are very far offshore, it might be best to head in closer to the beach, but this depends on the beach and the likelihood of ship traffic offshore. In some cases, it might be best to avoid rocky shorelines or coastlines with breaking waves by staying offshore. This decision depends on the circumstances, but in any event you must know where you are. Navigation without visibility is pure dead reckoning (assuming you don't have GPS), and no matter how good you are at it, your position uncertainty is only going to get worse with time once you start relying on dead reckoning. If your position is uncertain to begin with, you will soon be lost. If there is any doubt about your compass accuracy, check it with one of the quick methods of chapter 4. When paddling in a group, verify that each paddler's compass agrees.

When choosing a compass course to a shoreline or coastal destination in the fog, it is important not to aim straight toward your target. Instead, aim well off to one side of it by more than enough to compensate for any current or leeway you anticipate. Then when you reach land on the other side you will know which way to turn—something you would not know had you aimed for it and not found it when you arrived. Whether to aim toward the upwind or up-current side depends on the shoreline and lay of the land on the other side. Finding a small island in the fog, on the other hand, is a challenge to be considered carefully. Potential hazards of the waterway and its traffic must be balanced against the need to go there at that specific time. If currents are involved, recall the rules of thumb given in chapter 9 for quick estimates of set and ferry angles when currents must be crossed.

Fog calls for careful chart work. After finding your position and choosing a route, plot them both on the chart labeled with the watch time of the fix. Estimate your paddling speed, and from this figure how long it should take to reach land or the first audible aid to navigation, such as a foghorn or buoy. (Recall that bell buoys sound the same tone and gong buoys have several tones; but both are activated

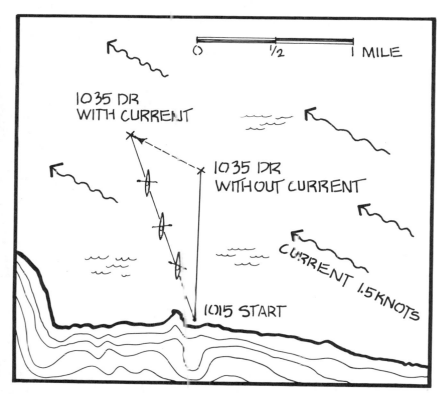

10-12. *A current-corrected dead reckoning (DR) plot. In twenty minutes, the drift in 1.5 knots of current would be 0.5 mile. To correct the plot for current, move the uncorrected position 0.5 mile downstream for each twenty minutes spent in the current.*

by wave action and consequently they might be quiet in flat, calm water.) If you must stop or change compass course underway, note it promptly on the chart. An example of a current-connected dead reckoning (DR) plot is shown in figure 10-12. Your dead reckoning track across the chart is all you have to go by in the fog, but with good record keeping it will do the job. This is the time that all your practice with dead reckoning in clear weather starts to pay off.

It is also the time to appreciate that the ultimate goal of dead reckoning is not a *point* on the chart where you *think* you are, but an *area* on the chart where you *know* you are. The difference between good dead reckoning and poor dead reckoning is just the size of this area of uncertainty. Regardless of skill, experience, or conditions, however, the size of the area of uncertainty always increases with time and distance underway when navigating by pure dead reckoning. In the fog, knowing that your average paddling speed is 3.0 knots is not enough. You also must know how well you know it. If you are confident that this average speed is right to within 0.3 knot—in other words, you think it is 3.0, but you would not bet the farm that under these circumstances it is not 2.7 or 3.3—then you must consider that your position along any proposed course line will grow uncertain by 0.3 mile each hour. After two hours of paddling without other navigational data, you must consider that you have traveled 6 miles plus or minus 0.6 mile.

Chances are, the distance you travel will be fairly close to 6 miles, because you did, after all, learn your average speed from practice. (Recall from table 5-1 that to average 3.0 knots when resting a total of ten minutes each hour, you must paddle at about 3.5 knots when underway.) In planning when you should reach land, or see a light, or hear a buoy, this uncertainty of 0.6 mile must be taken into account in order to know when to worry and when not to worry. At 3.0 knots (twenty minutes per mile) your target at 6 miles off could be reached anywhere within a paddling time of two hours plus or minus twelve minutes (0.6 times 20). A realistic estimate of your time window for arrival is fundamental to safe navigation in the fog. If you do not arrive by the end of the time window, it is time to stop and figure out why. Remember, when predicting when you should first see a light in the fog, you must first figure its luminous range from an estimate of the prevailing visibility (see Navigation at Night section of this chapter).

It is easier to estimate the effect and associated uncertainty of paddling with or against the current than it is to estimate the effects of cross currents. Paddling parallel to current, you might be quite confident, for example, that the current strength is 1.5 knots plus or minus 1 knot. As shown in the last example, the effect of your arrival time of a 1-knot uncertainty in speed made good depends on your average speed. An easy way to estimate the time window is simply to figure the transit times for the extreme possible speeds: for 2 knots and 4 knots when paddling at 3 knots, or for 3 knots and 5 knots when paddling at 4 knots. For example, suppose you are paddling with the current, and you anticipate making good 4 knots for a 3-mile run. This should take forty-five minutes. With an uncertainty of 1 knot in the current strength, however, it could take anywhere between sixty minutes (at 3 knots) and thirty-six minutes (at 5 knots). When making each estimate, recall from figure 9-11 that the net effect of a changing current can be estimated for any time period spent in the current.

Crossing strong current in the fog should be avoided whenever possible. When it must be done, recall that an uncertainty in compass course of 6° causes an uncertainty in lateral position of 10 percent of the distance paddled (fig. 4-4). After paddling 5 miles with an uncertainty of plus or minus 6° in heading, your area of uncertainty will have spread out to 0.5 mile on either side of your course line. This lateral position uncertainty must be taken into account in route planning just as your speed uncertainty is (see fig. 10-13). If the lay of the land on the other side of the crossing allows it, it might be safer to let yourself get set downstream of your target, rather than try to ferry upstream of the target without the advantage of range marks to check progress. Crossing wind presents the same concerns. As always, though, go for one side of the target, not straight toward it. (Paddling in current in the fog is clearly a case in which a GPS receiver would earn its keep.)

One advantage a kayaker has in the fog is the silence of his craft. Very distant sounds can be heard from a kayak, and although it is true that sound directions can be misleading in the fog, the problem is sometimes overstated. If a foghorn appears to be first one place then another, it could be a moving ship. On the other hand, the apparent distance to the source of a sound in the fog is, indeed, often misleading. Some sounds might even grow fainter as you approach the source, especially if any land lies between you and the source. Or a sound might vary between loud and faint with changes in wind direction, even though its distance off has not changed. Keep this potential problem in mind when trying to identify or locate sounds in the fog.

Ships and all other vessels are required by law to sound specific

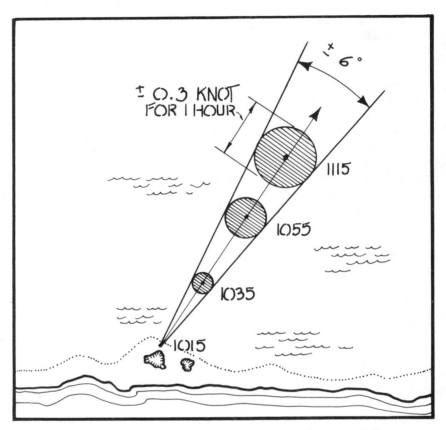

10-13. *Position uncertainty (shaded area) increases with time and distance when navigating by dead reckoning alone. The example shown is for an average boat speed of 3 knots, with an uncertainty of 0.3 knot, paddled on a compass course that is uncertain by 6°. With distant landmarks to steer by, position error is mostly due to errors in estimated paddling speed and current speed.*

signals in reduced visibility, day or night. Although you might on rare occasions hear other specialized signals from ships in the fog, by far the most common fog signal for a moving vessel is one long blast (four to six seconds long) given at intervals of not more that two minutes. Although this is technically a limit, not a specific value, most ship sounds will be repeated right at two minutes. In any event, the interval will be constant because the horns are automatically operated. This sound warns of the presence of a moving ship or other power-driven vessel more that 12 meters long. The other common signal you might hear is one long blast followed immediately by two short blasts (each one second long), again at intervals of not more than two minutes. This sound warns of the presence of a moving vessel more that 12 meters long that is somehow limited in its ability to maneuver. It could be a ship following a narrow channel or restricted to a region of deep water, a towboat pulling a barge, commercial fishing boats at work, or a sailboat under sail. Two long blasts, a second apart, repeated every two minutes is the sound of a power-driven vessel or ship that has stopped and is not moving at all.

Sound signals from ships are supposed to be audible in calm air from 2 miles off in their forward direction. When you are in front of a ship, you will have only four or five such signals (eight to ten minutes) to choose and execute some course of action. Check your compass to maintain orientation, remember the two-minute limit on the interval, and listen carefully for the next signal. Obviously, in the fog it is best not to end up anywhere near the probable path of large ships. If you do end up anywhere near traffic lanes when fog sets in, the immediate goal is to get well away from them. When the wind is blowing, ships to weather of you might be heard from farther than two miles off, but ships to leeward might not be heard until much closer. The sounds signals of vessels fewer than 20 meters long are only required to extend out to 0.5 mile, although in practice many smaller vessels do not sound any signals at all—contrary to the law.

Fog signals on aids to navigation (usually at lighthouses or other primary lights) have sounds that cannot be confused with those from ships. Typical sounds include one two-second blast every twenty seconds, one three-second blast every thirty seconds, or multiple sounds such as two three-second blasts every sixty seconds, or three two-second blasts every sixty seconds. Some foghorns are shielded and oriented to focus the sound in specific directions. This detail is not always on the chart, so it is important to check the *Light List.* When foghorns from both ships and lighthouses are in the background, the difference in their tones often helps identify them.

Other sounds are equally or sometimes more important in the fog. Dogs, people, cars, trains, and factories can often be heard from the water and used to locate land. When paddling along or toward steep cliffs (which is only safe in calm seas), you might try using echoes. Make a loud sound and count seconds until the echo is heard. Your distance off the reflective wall in miles is just this number of seconds divided by ten (the speed of sound is about five seconds per mile). In coastal waters, the sounds of swells breaking over rocks (boomers) or the sounds of surf are obvious things to listen for carefully. In some circumstances, the smells of land indicate its presence to windward.

Personal whistles can be valuable aids for keeping a group of paddlers together or for emergency signalling in the fog. They often can be heard farther than yelling, and it takes less energy to blow a whistle than to yell. Develop and practice some form of code to identify each paddler for basic communication. The standard emergency signal is SOS (••• — — — •••); an abbreviated reply might be C(— • — •), which is the standard code for YES. It is good practice to keep a whistle tied to your life jacket for such eventualities. It also can be used in an emergency at night in clear weather if your personal safety light fails. Your whistle, however, would probably not cover you legally in the requirement that *all* vessels less than 40 feet are required to carry some form of noisemaker and to sound it at intervals of not more than two minutes. A canned air horn would be required for this. Realistically, however, not many paddlers would choose to make this noise when paddling through fog in some isolated cove—the eerie silence of the fog is one of its joys that not many would choose to disrupt.

But if you are in an area with suspected traffic, or you hear a boat in the distance, then it is probably a good time to practice sounding your horn once in a while (even though it could only be sailboats or smaller powerboats idling along that might hear you). It would be almost impossible for larger ships to hear the sound over their own engines and apparent wind. Canned air horns are fairly effective for this type of signaling, but they are not dependable over long periods in a saltwater environment. Mouth-operated air horns are another option. Some of these are very effective. British models are called railroad horns or coach's horns.

The question of radar reflectors sometimes comes up in discussions of kayaking in the fog. These are metal devices designed to reflect a ship's radar and thus give the ship warning of your position. Without a reflector, nonmetal vessels do not show up very well on a radar screen. These devises work well for sailboats, because they can be positioned high in the rigging, and the height of the reflector is critical to its effectiveness. Some designs are narrow cylinders, not much larger than the typical bailing pumps used on kayaks. These styles could, in principle, be held up at arm's length and provide some reflective signal. Nevertheless, it is difficult to imagine handheld reflectors as practical aids to kayak safety in the fog. When considering any reflector, request a guarantee from the seller that they can indeed be detected. Some radar reflectors have proven worthless when tested in practice. Helium-filled balloons with crumpled metal foil inside or a honeycomb metallic surface are another concept that might be considered for possible use as radar reflectors for kayaks. Various models have come and gone from the marketplace. Again, if one is found, it should be tested by asking a passing fishing boat or other vessel to verify that they can see you on the radar. With or without radar reflectors, however, kayaks in the fog should simply stay away from the paths of larger vessels.

When you must paddle in waters near traffic lanes it pays to have a portable VHF marine radio. By monitoring the traffic control frequency (channel 13 or 14, depending on the region), you will have a good idea of the locations of ship traffic in the lanes. Ships report their positions frequently along with their speeds and estimated arrival times at various way points. In some cases, you can actually learn where you are from hearing over the radio where a ship is that you have recently seen or eventually do see or hear. The traffic reports also include frequent reports of the visibility at various locations along the lanes, which is often more valuable data than the weather radio reports given only every three hours at specific points.

On the other hand, it is unlikely that the radio would help much in the fog for contacting a ship you can hear but cannot see, or even one you did see closing in on you as it emerged from the fog. Ships cannot maneuver fast enough to do anything about a situation like that. If the ship tried to stop—its only resort when you cannot be seen—the captain or pilot would certainly report you to the Coast Guard for violating Rule 10 (impeding vessels following traffic lanes), and if they found you, that radio call would be an expensive one. It is better to just monitor the radio in these conditions, and keep the mind and paddle ready for a quick burst of energy that will get you out of trouble at the last moment.

If you do hear a ship's foghorn or engine but cannot see the vessel, it might be best to point straight toward the sound in preparation for its appearance. This orientation puts both ears onto the job equally, gives you a compass course to the sound to monitor its motion, and leaves you ready to turn right or left as called for. A group of paddlers might line up in this direction and then follow the action of the lead boat. Start the stopwatch on your wristwatch when you hear its horn, and if you do not hear the horn again within two minutes, the ship is probably headed away from you. Remember that faint sounds can be significantly amplified by cupping your hands over your ears.

Away from the hazards of traffic and dangerous waters or coast-lines, paddling in the fog is quite a pleasant experience. It is similar to walking through the silence of a snowy forest. If the opportunity arises in safe waters, paddle a compass course out into the fog and back again. It is good practice in learning to follow a compass when disoriented.

High-Seas Navigation

Long trips out of the sight of land are definitely expedition paddling. This requires special training in seamanship and navigation that is be-yond the scope of this book. John Dowd's book *Sea Kayaking—A Manual for Long-Distance Touring* discusses the topic based on the au-thor's experience of more than 2,000 miles of high seas kayaking. The solo transoceanic crossings of Franz Romer (Atlantic) and Ed Gillet (Pacific) are reviewed in the appendix of that book. Much of the navigation reduces to the same fundamentals discussed through-out this book: compass use, dead reckoning, current crossing, and navigation planning. The main difference lies in the area of piloting, as there are no landmarks at sea to use for reference. GPS electronic navigation, covered in chapter 7, should be considered the primary means for this application.

The following is only an outline of the navigation options; details are left to references in the Further Reading section. Position out of sight of land is found from the electronic instruments or by celestial navigation, although careful dead reckoning from estimated speed and compass course is always essential, as is a knowledge of the pre-vailing currents. Electronic navigation aids—other than GPS, covered in chapter 7—that can in principle be used in a kayak include radio direction finding (RDF) and hand-held calculators that are essentially small computers.

Charted radio beacons provide bearing lines out to distances of 50 to 100 miles offshore. Useful ranges to specific RDF beacons are given in the *Light List*. At the time of earlier editions of this book, hand-held units were available that could measure bearings to these beacons from a kayak. These units and this entire technology, how-ever, has essentially been replaced by GPS—it is still in place, and in principle useable, but it is far better to use GPS instead of RDF for an electronic navigation aid in kayaks or any other vessel. For now, our interest in RDF reduces to keeping in mind that in an emergency we might be able to obtain useful bearings to AM radio towers (shown on charts) using these principles. We refer the interested reader to the author's book titled *Emergency Navigation*, which covers not only this subject but many others that use no instruments or only makeshift instruments for navigation. Of particular interest to many kayakers is that book's section on steering by the stars without a compass—it is interesting subject matter even if you have a compass.

Celestial navigation is inexpensive and ultimately the most reliable means of navigation, but it requires special training and adaptions for kayak use. A lightweight inexpensive plastic sextant (such as the Davis Mark 3) is adequate for finding position in relatively calm water, to within an accuracy of 5 miles or so. The usual book and paperwork of celestial navigation, which converts the timed sextant sights of the sun or stars into an actual position on the chart, is best done with programmed calculators or palmtop computers. These small devices are not waterproof, but they can be operated through sealed clear plastic bags or other waterproof containers. Some models can be programmed to perform any customized navigation calculation at the touch of a key. They also will store and update a dead reckoning position automatically using internal quartz clocks and the speed and course entered into them. They also calculate the required almanac data on the positions of celestial bodies. using this combination of the old and the new, you could navigate across an ocean with only a shoe box full of equipment that weighs less than two pounds and requires no outside power source.

The principles of celestial navigation are covered in the author's home study courses and book *Emergency Navigation*, whose main topic is high seas and coastal navigation without instruments. All equipment is exposed and vulnerable on an ocean or coastal passage, and every mariner who ventures into these waters should be prepared to find the way to safety without the use of customary aids.

In special circumstances arrangements can be made with the French government to monitor the location of a high seas expedition using their ARGOS satellites. This does not assist on-board navigation, but it does provide a precise track of the crossing that is a strong safety supplement to the COSPAS/SARSAT satellite system used to detect EPIRB signals.

CHAPTER 11

Navigation Planning

Preparation

The resources listed in chapter 3 will help you choose the best time and place for a trip. Start with short trips in sheltered waters to test gear and practice with navigation and boat handling, and then work toward more challenging trips. It is especially valuable training to paddle in strong winds and waves near shore rather than meet these for the first time in open or isolated waters. Paddling practice just off a leeward shore (where wind is blowing toward the shore) is best; there will be larger waves to practice with, and if you capsize, you will get blown toward the land. Waves near a windward shore (where wind is blowing off the shore) are small because the fetch necessary to build the waves starts at the shoreline.

For all paddling in any waters, however, leave word of your intentions with someone ashore. The Coast Guard calls this filing a *float plan;* this precaution is fundamental to all boating. This plan, however, cannot be filed with the Coast Guard; this is not one of their services. Tell a friend or family member where you plan to go, when you plan to be back, the number of people in the party, and a description of the boats. Include contingency plans, and be sure to let them know when you have returned. Also tell them where you will be parking your car along with the make, model, and license number. On coastal routes, remember that it might be easier for you to contact the Coast Guard by marine radio than to reach your interested parties on shore directly in the case of a delay. When planning exposed routes, be sure your contact person knows how to reach the Coast Guard and explain that you might call the Coast Guard to report delays if you cannot reach them. When paddling in a group, check with the group leader to ensure that these precautions have been taken.

Once you have a proposed route in mind, even on short trips, check your exposure along it. For each leg of the route consider the potential for wind, waves, swells, current, and traffic; then note where shelter from any of these might lie. That is, look for escape routes along any exposed section. To plan each day's paddle, look up the time of sunrise and sunset (listed in *Tide Tables*), estimate your average speed along each leg, taking into account the current as explained in chapter 6, then figure the time each leg will take. When strong currents are present at some point along the route, estimate passage times carefully, trying to spend as much time as possible in favorable current. Several interrelated examples are given in the next section.

Chart preparation before departing is the key to good navigation underway. Most of what you might want to know underway can be figured ahead of time and noted on the chart. You may not have the time or the conditions that allow much chart navigation underway. Chart plotting is awkward at best in a kayak underway—some veteran paddlers simply assume that it cannot be done or that it will not be done, even if it could be, while underway; these are strong believers

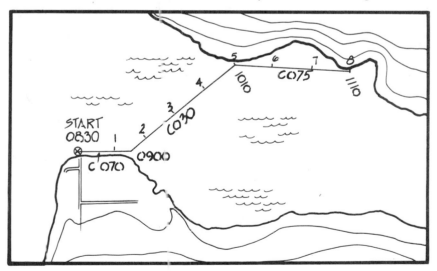

11-1. *The planned route for an 8-mile paddle at an average speed of 3 knots. Compass courses, mile markers, and estimated times can be charted before departing.*

in chart preparation. To prepare a chart, draw in course lines along each leg and label them with the compass headings. Make mile markers along each leg as shown in figure 11-1 and note the times you expect to be at various points along the route. Then when you pass these points, note the time on the chart to monitor your progress and schedule. When water depth is a factor in navigation, highlight the shelves and spits that might affect current flow, cause tide rips, or go dry at low water. Make a list or graph of the tides and currents for each day of the trip, and note the key data on the chart. In areas with extensive foreshore, remember that the land can appear quite different with changes in tide height. Compare the range of the tides with the average ranges (listed in the back of the *Tide Tables*) that define the green foreshore on the chart in order to anticipate what you will see.

Highlight potentially dangerous rocks or other landmarks that are expected to be conspicuous along the route. For longer crossings, draw in a few compass bearing lines emanating from these landmarks to monitor progress. Look for ranges along the route that will mark your position and draw these on the chart as well. Figures 11-2 and 11-3 show several examples. For prominent peaks or other features with charted elevations, draw in a few circles of equal distance off, using whatever units are convenient (degrees, centimeters along a

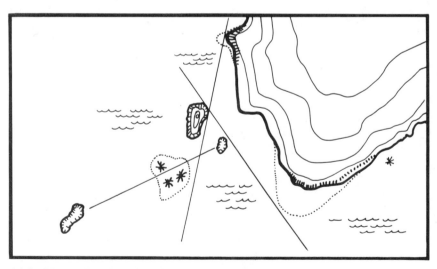

11-2. *Natural ranges plotted to locate potential underwater hazards such as the rock group and spit shown.*

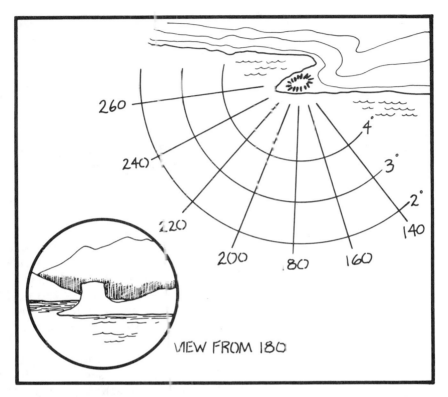

260

240

220

200 80 160

140

2°

3°

4°

VIEW FROM 180

11-3. *Charted bearing lines and circles of equal distance off are a convenient way to keep track of position in special circumstances. The circles correspond to angular heights of a kamal.*

kamal, or finger widths). With this chart preparation, it is a simple matter to keep track of where you are by just glancing at the chart and the horizon around you.

Charts must be protected from water and abrasion underway. This can be done by keeping them in waterproof clear plastic bags, soaking them in various plastic solutions (available at marine and outdoor supply stores), or by actually laminating them in plastic or transparent contact paper. For most of these options, a grease pencil (china marker) is the best way to make notes on the chart covering. As with all kayaking gear, the chosen system must be tested. In some climates, condensation can occur in chart bags, although many paddlers have used this method extensively without this trouble. Clear contact paper is convenient, but the charts do not fold well.

Although even damp charts cannot be written on with a pencil, wetness alone will not destroy a chart. Wet charts dry quickly and well by a campfire. Abrasion when wet is the bigger concern; this will destroy the chart or make parts of it illegible. Chart bags are a popular solution for both problems. Big ones are better than small ones. They allow you to expose a full day's paddle (using both sides of the bag if necessary) and leave enough chart showing that you can identify more distant landmarks. Another option is to carry a large-scale chart on one side of the bag and a smaller-scale chart on the other. It can be very difficult to unpack and refold a chart underway in wind, waves, and rain. Having a full day's paddle laid out in front of you also makes it easier to gauge your progress at a glance, if you fall off the estimated schedule marked on the chart.

Also practice reading the chart from the seat of your boat. Most cockpits are so large that charts cannot be read from a strapped down position on the foredeck; in this case the charts must be pulled back onto the spray skirt to be read. One option (see fig. 11-4) is to attach only the top edge of the chart bag to the foredeck; then it can be flopped back onto the spray skirt to be read underway or folded forward and secured in heavy seas. In complex waterways or island groups, it is often necessary to keep the chart in continuous readable range in order to keep track of where you are without interrupting your paddling. When wind and waves are not too severe, a self-fastening fabric such as Velcro® might be used to attach the chart bag to the spray skirt.

There is sometimes a conflict in deck space between chart stowage and compass mount. The compass should be in view, which means the chart cannot be on top of it. The flopping chart bag solves this problem also. These details must be worked out for individual boats. Examples are shown in figure 11-5.

When you fold a chart, you might not be able to expose a miles scale and compass rose where you want them. The miles scale (or latitude scale) is not critical if the planned course has miles marked off on it, as discussed above. If need be, a compass rose can be added to any part of the chart using transparent self-adhesive compass roses available from navigation supply stores. Even with several bearing lines drawn to key features, a chart rose might be required for bearings to other objects. For longer trips, photocopies of the relevant sections of the *Coast Pilot* and *Light List* should be carried. It also helps to carry a notebook for navigation notes along the route. Generally there is more information to keep track of than can be noted on the

BRASS GROMMET

WEBBING

SILICONE SEALANT

CLEAR VINYL

PLASTIC HOOK

SHOCK CORD

FLIP WATER-PROOF CHART CONTAINER OVER FOR CHART EXTENSION

"VELCRO"® CLOSURE

11-4. *A hinged chart pack. The pack can be flipped onto the spray skirt or secured forward in rough conditions. The elastic cord and clips at each corner allow you to hinge the pack along any edge on either side. Contact local sail or canvas makers to fabricate one of your own design.*

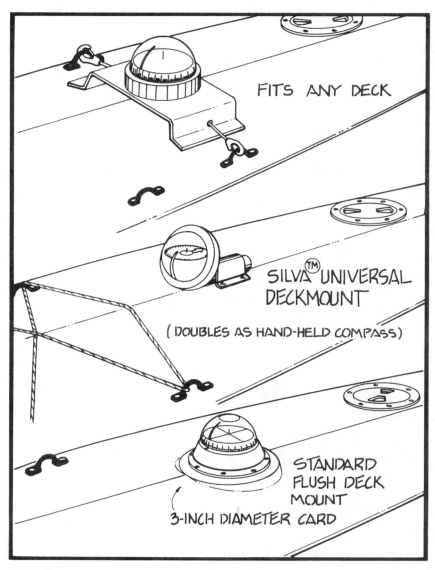

11-5. *Various ways to mount a deck compass.*

chart. This book also can serve as a log or diary of the trip to record navigational information accumulated underway. Table 11-1 is a checklist of navigational gear.

Table 11-1. *Checklist of Navigation Gear.*

_____ Nautical charts (large and small scale)
_____ Topographic maps (check for usefulness)
_____ Chart pack
_____ Compasses (deck compass and bearing compass)
_____ Watch (waterproof with stopwatch plus backup)
_____ Kamal (homemade instrument)
_____ Pencils and eraser
_____ Grease pencil with string attached
_____ Navigation notebook (preferably with waterproof paper)
_____ Large flat ruler with string attached (such as C-Thru B-70)
_____ Eyeglasses (if needed plus backup)
_____ Sunglasses
        Pertinent sections of:
        _____ *Tide Tables*
        _____ *Current Tables*
        _____ *Coast Pilot* or *Sailing Directions*
        _____ *Light List*
        _____ Special current references (if available)
        _____ Tips from tour guides (if available)
_____ Marine Weather Services Chart
_____ VHF radio plus waterproof bag
_____ List of VHF channels for marine operators
_____ Notes on VHF radio usage
_____ Weather radio (if no VHF available)
_____ Shortwave and AM radio receiver
_____ EPIRB
_____ Flare gun and flares
_____ Binoculars
_____ Bright warning light (spare bulbs and batteries)
_____ Light for chart reading (spare bulbs and batteries)
_____ Some form of compass lighting (spare bulbs and batteries)
_____ Foghorn and whistle
_____ Waterproof bag to hold this gear
_____ Heavy-duty rubber bands (to keep things organized)
_____ Highlight markers (two or three colors
        to mark charts and notes)

In many parts of the world, there are seasons when it is essential to listen to marine weather broadcasts before setting out on any trip. Even in clear weather or in areas not known for foul weather, it is still best to check the marine weather before heading out onto the water. It is the responsibility of every mariner to take advantage of the information available. Sources are listed on the Marine Weather Services Charts published by NOAA. On long trips, weather broadcasts should be monitored frequently.

A waterproof wristwatch with a stopwatch option is a valuable asset to all navigation. Some paddlers have found it convenient to carry a watch wrapped around the center of the paddle shaft in clear view at all times. They use this one for navigation to facilitate reading the time without interrupting their paddling while wearing paddle jackets, dry suits, or other foul-weather gear that might interfere with watch reading.

Examples

Shoreline Routes

Most kayaking is done along the shoreline, within a half mile or so of land, and there is good reason for this. Paddling offshore has been described by one veteran paddler as "either boring or scary." Along shore there is much more to see, and if the wind should suddenly build or the current reverse, you are not far from shelter. Nevertheless, there are still several navigational matters to consider when planning shoreline routes.

First to consider is the nature of the shore itself. If the shore is extremely steep, as along cliffs or large rocks, then it is probably not the best place to paddle. Such a shore offers no shelter, and in fact it can be a hazard because it reflects incident waves, creating steep confused seas. Even without wind waves, wakes from ship and boat traffic can create choppy water near steep shorelines. Furthermore, currents and back eddies can be quite strong along a steep shoreline. On the other hand, if the water is less than 2 feet deep along the shore it is also not the best place to paddle because of the excess bottom drag on the boat (see fig. 5-7). If you get caught paddling onto a large shallow tide flat or spit, it could take a tremendous amount of extra work to get across. To avoid either of these potential problems, study the proposed shoreline route carefully on the chart before departing. Shoreline and depth contours on the chart should reveal these features. If either feature is in the way, determine from the chart where along the shore you should angle out to go around it and note ranges or bearings that will tell when you are at that point.

Inshore rocks are another concern. Along rocky shorelines it takes a good large-scale chart to pick them out. Pay special attention to rocks that might be just under the surface (see chapter 2 on rock symbols). It pays to use a colored marker to highlight hazardous rocks on the chart when planning the route. Look for signs of barely submerged rocks as waves pass over them. If you know from the chart where to look for them, you can often spot them by the irregularities in wave patterns or slight ripples in otherwise smooth water. (On coastal routes, big swells over such rocks can be quite dramatic and proportionally more dangerous. These are sometimes detectable from residual foam streaks on the surface, even if the breaking boomer was not seen.) To identify rocks, and sometimes the lay of the shoreline itself, it is necessary to know the tide height when paddling even the simplest shoreline routes. In areas with a wide foreshore (shown green on the chart), remember that the water extends to the inshore side of the green at high water and to the offshore side of the green at low water. Determine the tide height as a function of time and note it on the chart before departing.

A kayaker must always consider the wind direction, even when paddling a close inshore route. If the wind has any onshore component, the seas will be quite choppy near shore. If you have the option, take the side with the offshore wind component, such as the east side of a north-south channel in a northeast wind. It will have the smoothest seas because the wind has no fetch on that side. In contrast, the lee side will have the full width of the channel to build waves on. Winds along channels are discussed further in this chapter in the next section on paddling in islands.

Perhaps the most common decision a kayaker confronts along a shoreline route occurs at each bay or inlet along the shore: follow the shoreline along the inside edge of the bay or paddle straight across to the next point? Straight across is the shortest route, but it might not be the fastest. In adverse current, ducking into the bay is probably best as there may be a favorable back eddy inside. On the other hand, when riding favorable current along the approaching shoreline, you might lose this advantage by ducking into the bay and even run into the adverse flow of a back eddy.

At the mouths of large bays, there is usually a shift in wind direction that also might enter into the decision. Any wind over the offshore waters tends to funnel into or pour out of the bay, which causes the offshore wind to shift to some extent toward the orientation of the bay. Wind from any direction will usually shift (to some extent) toward the beam as you cross the mouth of a bay. Head winds shift to bow winds, bow and quarter winds shift to beam winds, and tail winds shift to quarter winds. The same effect occurs at the mouth of a valley leading down to the shoreline, even without a prominent bay at its base.

In many cases, the wind also will be stronger near the center of a bay or valley than it is along the shoreline approaching it because the wind is channeled along the bay and because you lose the shelter of the shoreline as you start to cross the bay. A steep shoreline shelters the nearshore waters from wind blowing both offshore and onshore. The shoreline is in the shadow of offshore winds and onshore winds tend to rise to go over steep shores before reaching the actual shoreline.

A principal element in deciding to go in or across a bay is the nature of the point or headland that marks the far side of the bay. If you conclude from the chart and what you can see ahead that this is an area with dangerous rips that must be circumvented from outside of the rip zone, then it is best to go part way across and angle out around the rip from somewhere along the mouth of the bay. Following the shoreline around might take you directly into the rip at the next point. For large bays, a compromise might be called for, such as heading in somewhat to keep from getting too far offshore, and from somewhere inside the bay start angling back out to miss the point. This is not necessarily the fastest route, but it may be the one that feels best under the circumstances, depending on the wind and current in the bay and the potential traffic in the bay. If the large bay has much ship or ferry traffic, any route through the bay should take into account the routes of other traffic out of the bay. Check the chart for buoys or daymarks that show their route and try to cross it as promptly as possible.

When passing headlands, also keep in mind that ships or tugs passing well away from you can still influence your conditions. The long slow swells that generate will shorten and steepen or even break as they reach shallow waters on the point. A tide rip at the point that is questionably safe becomes even more of a challenge as a ship or ferry passes by.

In and around Islands

Paddling through island groups in tidal waters is a fine test of navigation skill. Island paddling is different from shoreline or coastal paddling in that you usually have more options when choosing routes and more factors to consider when making the choice. To go around an island usually requires going two ways relative to wind and current, which might not be the case along straight routes along a beach. As always, wind and current are the primary uncharted concerns, but particularly near islands there might be sparse data for the precise places you want to go—winds and currents are difficult to predict throughout the small and complex waterways through a group of islands. The task is to combine what is known with what you think will happen from your knowledge of general principles and the pieces of local knowledge you have gathered.

When circumnavigating an island you must first decide which way to go around. The right choice can make the difference between fun and drudgery. Tidal currents, for example, change directions about every six hours. In idealized circumstances, it might be possible to paddle up one side of an island riding a flood current and then paddle back down the other side riding an ebb current. Going the right way could be fast and easy; going the wrong way might not even be possible. Currents, however, are rarely of the same speed or duration on opposite sides of an island. Furthermore, wind speed and direction might be more important to progress than currents are, or it could be that the relative direction of wind and current is the main concern. Current flowing against wind must always be noted with caution, as discussed in chapter 8.

Sometimes the choice of rounding direction is obvious; other times it takes careful planning in anticipation of conditions you cannot see or of conditions that have not yet developed. Local knowledge can be critical. Check with someone who has done it or read all you can find about the area first. The adventure of spontaneous exploration is an attractive feature of kayaking; but it is not wholly consistent with good navigation. Rounding a large exposed island or rounding individual islands of a group that are each surrounded with fast channels and many points of tide rips requires more planning than a simple look at the chart might imply. Without doing your homework, it is possible to get stuck halfway around looking for a campsite where none is to be found, as you wait out the current or adverse winds. Good navigation planning should minimize surprises that threaten your convenience as well as your safety.

Ideally, the wind would be either calm or behind you throughout the roundings. But winds change as the weather changes or as the local terrain changes, and even without changes in weather or terrain, winds often change with the time of day. In many areas the wind is calm in the morning and builds as the day heats. The general direction of the building wind—called a sea breeze even on island waters—is usually known locally and is often given in *Coast Pilots*. In very broad terms, these winds blow from the area of most water toward the area of most land. (Remember: a north wind is from the north; a sea breeze is from the sea.) Sea breezes increase in strength fairly rapidly starting about midmorning, peak about two hours after midday, and die off completely at sunset. Sea breezes can build routinely to over 20 knots in some areas. On a smaller scale, winds through channels and islands tend to follow the curves of the waterways, because channeled waterways usually have elevated shorelines that channel the wind as well as the water. Exceptions occur only near large bays or valleys along the channel as discussed in the section on shoreline routes.

Planning must include current and wind, although wind is just as likely to be the factor that must be considered first. You can get out of adverse current more frequently than adverse wind, and over a long run adverse wind can do more damage to your time schedule and arm muscles. Currents are eventually going to change; winds might not. It is valuable to know if the source of wind is a weather pattern or a sea breeze. Weather pattern winds can last anywhere from a few minutes to a few days. Wind in the morning or at night is not from a sea breeze. If it was calm in the morning and blowing from the seaward direction in the afternoon, it is probably a sea breeze that will go away at night.

Sometimes choosing a route calls for a choice between adverse winds versus adverse current (two evils) or between favorable wind versus favorable current (two blessings). From the discussion of chapter 5, it is easy to see that any wind over 15 knots has more effect on speed over ground than any current under 1 knot does. Going downwind, for example, a 15-knot wind will push you along at nearly 2 knots without any paddling at all. A route with a solid true wind of 15 knots behind you in slack water is definitely faster and easier than a calm route with 1 knot of favorable current, especially if there are any waves to surf. The contrast is even more dramatic on adverse routes. To make good a speed of 3 knots against a true wind of 15 knots, you must paddle as hard as you do to go 4.5 to 5 knots in calm wind, depending on the waves produced by the 15-knot wind (see fig. 5-6). Put another way, you would have to paddle two to three times harder. Any calm route with adverse current under 1.5 knots would be clearly favored over any slack route with head winds over 15 knots. Each situation must be evaluated individually. Even stronger adverse currents might be favored over just 10 knots of head wind along shores that offer some shelter from the main current flow around the island. You might also make one type of choice for the beginning of a route but prefer other standards for the end of a day's paddling.

When winds are not a critical factor, choose the route and schedule the rest times that will put you in the best current for the most time. If the currents are bad at some point in both directions, check the chart carefully to see which route might offer the most opportunities for getting out of the current: bays and coves with back eddies or routes with shallow shorelines. In some cases, however, an isolated area of strong current can completely determine the route and timing of the trip.

As an example of these points, consider the circumnavigation of the hypothetical island shown in figure 11-6 during times of strong currents and strong afternoon sea breezes. From various resources it is known that the winds are calm all around the island in the mornings, but in the afternoon the east side is exposed to strong easterlies, and the northeast side has strong southeasterlies along the shore. The east and west sides have weak currents at all times; the northeast side has weak ebbs but strong floods, and the channel along the southwest side has very strong floods and ebbs with no shelter from the current. Assume it takes a day to paddle around the island, and you can start in the early morning from any of the points A, B, or C. What would be the best choice for this trip?

A peak flood during midmorning that turned to ebb at midday would be ideal for rounding the island to port (counterclockwise) starting from point A. The eastern side would have no wind or current at the start; paddling along the northeast side, the wind and current would build behind you; and you would round the potentially hazardous north point near slack water as you turned into shelter from the strong east wind. The west side would be slack and calm as the ebb increased in the channel ahead. You would meet the channel along the southwest side at peak ebb for a nice ride home.

On the other hand, if you did not figure the sea breeze into the route, but simply stood at point A in the morning looking at the calm air and water flowing northward along the channel—or even checked *Current Tables* for the southwest channel—you might be tempted to head around to starboard on a rocket ship ride up the southwest side. You would feel good about the choice until well around the north

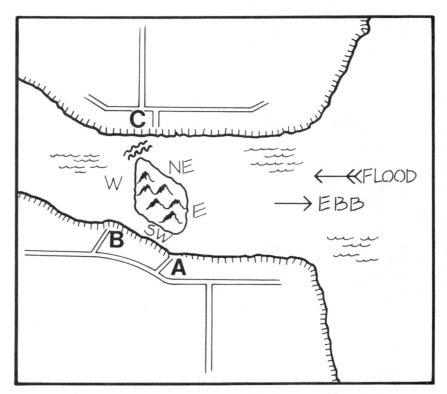

11-6. *A hypothetical island exposed to both wind and current.*

point because you would get there early with the fast current. But somewhere along the northeast side things would start to get bad, and get bad fast. The building ebb would be straight into the building head winds, and the rest of the trip would be a lot of work, if not dangerous. For some boats and paddlers, maintaining course and speed with strong wind on the beam (the east side of this trip) is just as much trouble as strong head wind is once the waves build.

Point B is not even an option for starting a circumnavigation with the midmorning flood. You could not head off on a port rounding with the channel flood building against you, and if you started off to the north, the channel would be ebbing by the time you got around to it—after fighting the easterlies along the east side. You would be stuck at point A. Point C is a possible starting point, but not a good choice because you could not escape strong east wind along the east side. On the other hand, a midafternoon flood would make point C the best choice (to starboard) and point A the worst choice (in either direction).

When circumnavigating a lake along its perimeter, wind direction is the only concern because there is no current in landlocked lakes. A lake running north-south that takes about a day to paddle around, for example, might have a persistent northerly sea breeze building over it in the afternoon. In this case, starting from the south end in the morning would put the afternoon wind behind you for the return leg. A phone call to local sailing organizations that use the lake could provide such wind information if not known ahead of time.

Islands along exposed coastal waters present additional hazards of the seas along their seaward sides. Fast channels at the ends of coastal islands might even generate breaking waves on the ebb cycle. The steepest waves occur when an ebb flow out of the channel meets the onshore ocean swell. A coastal channel between islands might not be passable even when the current direction is favorable.

Keeping track of position as you go around an island takes extra care whenever there is little to be seen in the background away from the island. The view from close inshore along bays and coves is often restricted to the island itself. Although there is obviously no doubt you are on the edge of the island, after some paddling along a round island it is easy to lose track of the side you are on. A close watch on the compass and a few notes on the charts as you go around will solve the problem and avoid throwing off your schedule.

Another more detailed example of planning around wind and current is given later in this chapter.

Open-Water Crossings

With no wind and no current, long crossings of open water (ending up well offshore in the process) are mostly a matter of watching out for traffic and paddling a compass course. Examples are paddling across a large sound, strait, or lake or paddling from point to point across a large bay. To optimize the chances of light wind, it is usually best to plan long crossings for early morning, before sea breezes build. On crossings that take a couple of hours or more, any current present is likely to change with both time and place. With little to see in the background, it is often difficult to monitor the effect of the

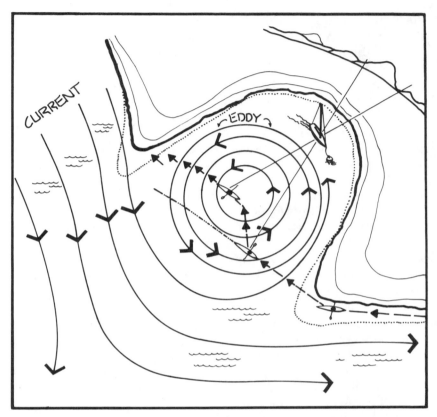

11-7. *The use of a natural range to monitor progress across a bay. A course jog into the eddy center gets this paddler out of adverse current, which was detected from the range.*

current. In some cases, it might be necessary to just make your best estimate of the current and how it is going to change en route and ferry accordingly. When your target is not in sight as you depart, back bearings to the shore or point you leave from will help you gauge the current during the start of the crossing. Crossing currents by ferrying was discussed in chapter 9. When crossing with a group, it is best to keep the group together.

When crossing large bays within fairly clear sight of land at all times, progress across can often be checked with ranges. Even when details of the horizon are difficult to discern, it might be possible, for example, to watch an anchored boat off your beam relative to the terrain behind it. If the boat does not move relative to the background, you are not making progress (see fig. 11-7); you might as well head into the bay and take the longer route, closer to shore, where the adverse current is less or even favorable. You may not have to go all the way into shore; your lack of progress farther out might have been due to adverse current that extends only a short way into the bay. With such a convenient natural range to watch (the anchored boat with a peak behind it), you could tell how far into the bay you must go to get out of the current. When you start making progress on the anchored boat, you know you are getting out of the bad current.

In a case like this, if you run into much flotsam as you head into the bay, it is further confirmation that you might have been paddling in an eddy current. Often there are bits of bark, branches, seaweed, or various kinds of rubble trapped in the centers of large eddies. The outer edge of a prominent eddy—farther offshore in the last example—also is marked by flotsam in many cases, trapped in a line along the edge. This outer edge also is often marked by a conspicuous change in the texture of the water whenever the wind is blowing roughly parallel to the current flow (see fig. 8-16). Water flowing into the wind is rougher than that flowing with the wind. This is just a microscopic example of how opposing wind and current enhance waves, even when the waves are just ripples.

As with coastal paddling discussed below, however, paddling into open water is as much a matter of safety and boat handling preparation as it is navigation preparation. Safety and boat handling are covered in several of the references in Further Reading. Matt Broze and George Grouseth's column on safety in *Sea Kayaker* magazine is an excellent reference. They have described many accidents and potential accidents, including the conditions that led to them and how they might have been avoided. These incidents and analyses and more are presented in their book *Sea Kayaker's Deep Trouble*, listed in Further Reading.

Coastal Routes

Although the name "sea kayaking" is often applied to paddling a seaworthy kayak in any waters, coastal paddling, when actually exposed to the open sea, is an advanced part of the sport. Many paddlers find adequate enjoyment and challenge in waters well sheltered from the open sea. Trips into coastal waters should be planned carefully and done in the company of experienced paddlers. A kayak is a unique craft, made for the ocean. With it you can go places and see things that are not accessible by other means.

Coastal paddling, however, can call upon all the kayaker's skills in seamanship and navigation (see Washburne's *Coastal Kayaker* in the Further Reading section. Although the sea can be and often is as calm as an inland lake, it can change rapidly into hazardous waters of strong winds and big waves. Strong winds can develop quickly from offshore or onshore—afternoon sea breezes are quite strong along some coasts, especially near the openings to bays and canyons. Either wind direction could pose a problem. A strong offshore wind could force you into open water or a strong onshore wind could blow you into a dangerous surf or a rocky coastline. Even in calm air and flat water, large swells from distant storms can arrive, turning a gentle beach into a hazardous surf zone within a matter of hours. Frequent monitoring of marine weather broadcasts is essential in coastal waters. The sea state as well as the weather is forecasted for coastal waters every six hours.

Escape routes are often the primary concern along coastal routes. Landing sites were discussed in chapter 10. When planning an extended run along a beach, pick several landmarks to use for navigation along the way, and prepare the charts accordingly. Carefully monitor progress to avoid getting stuck halfway between two protected escape points. Piloting is especially important along a coast because coastal currents are difficult to predict. It is also difficult to predict progress against wind and waves if they should develop.

Even paddling downwind, it is difficult to know ahead of time what your ultimate course made good will be in big seas. The seas are made up of irregular wind waves built upon smooth rolling swells. Wind waves grow and subside with the wind, and they move in the direction the wind is blowing. The height and direction that swells move, however, are not related to local winds; swells are the wave remnants of distant storms. When swells and waves run in different directions, the seas are confused and difficult to predict. It is not easy to know ahead of time what course through them will be the safest to paddle, even when you are headed generally downwind. It might be that the course that is easiest to paddle is angled in toward a dangerous coastline.

Always keep in mind that escape routes might close with the onset of bigger swells or swells from a new direction. A rock passage or river bar that was smooth in one sea state could have large breaking waves in another. An escape route also can close with a change in wind speed or wind direction or with a change in tidal current flow. An ocean entrance in calm water across a bar near slack water can be blocked in less than an hour by breaking waves on a building ebb flow out of the river. Changes in tidal current flow or tide height also can block exits through rock passes or remove the shelter of a tombolo.

A storm predicted to arrive late in the evening might have associated swells that arrive many hours or even a day earlier. The advancement speed of swells is derived from their parent wave speed in the distant storm. Within a storm, wave speeds build toward the wind speed as the storm develops, but the storms themselves move across the ocean at much lower speeds. Consequently, swells outrun the storm that produced them, arriving well before the storm itself—the storm might not even come to your area, or it might be dissipated by the time it does arrive. Even without an increase in wind, when new swells are first detected consider what is happening along shore where you plan to get out even though these new swells pose no present threat to paddling offshore. Large swells will break in any confined or shallow water.

Navigation in coastal waters is no different than in sheltered waters; each of the points listed in the earlier examples applies to coastal waters. There is just more at stake along the coast, in more frequent instances. Skills in piloting dead reckoning, and chart reading are required, but these are not the only prerequisites. Practical knowledge of weather and oceanography is more critical in the ocean, and paddling in or through large waves requires more skill in boat handling.

It is also important to know your resources. The *Coast Pilot* includes extensive information on coastal weather. In coastal waters, strong winds do not require a storm. Thirty-knot northerlies lasting for days off the California coast are common in the summertime, and they occur without storms or frontal systems, under clear skies or in dense fog. Strong sea breezes are another example of potentially dangerous winds that do not require bad weather systems. Local weather occurrences such as these are discussed in the *Coast Pilot*. Figure 11-8 shows an example of sea-state statistics from the *Canadian Sailing Directions*.

Listen to the weather broadcasts and watch the sky and wind direction. When bad weather is forecasted, it is usually out there. It is dangerous to assume the forecasts are wrong simply because reports of present weather are wrong. The occasionally uncertain aspect of a forecast is not the existence of bad weather—this is clearly seen in satellite photos and verified by ship or other weather-station reports—but the precise arrival time of the weather system. Because of the

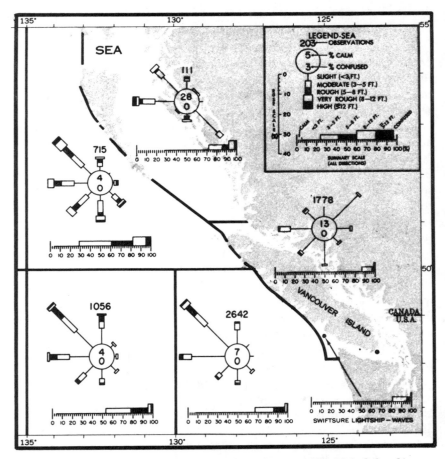

11-8. *Significant wave height statistics along the coast of British Columbia during June, July, and August, from the* Canadian Sailing Directions. *Significant wave height is the average height of the highest third of all waves; the average height of all waves is 0.6 times the significant wave height. There is a separate diagram for swells.*

potential uncertainty in the arrival time, successful planning around the weather can depend on your ability to judge this timing on your own. (This is less of a problem on the east coast than on the west coast, because weather systems move from west to east, and they are monitored by many more weather stations on land getting to the east coast than they are over water getting to the west coast.)

Throughout most of the northern temperate latitudes, fair wind is from the northwesterly quadrant and foul wind is from the southerly quadrant. To go from far to foul, the wind must go from northwest to south, and it does so in most cases by shifting to the left (a backing shift), i.e., from northwest to west, to southwest, to south. Consequently, the approach of foul weather is often first detected by a backing shift in the wind direction, accompanied by lowering clouds. As you start a coastal passage, watch carefully for this shift by noting precise wind directions as opposed to the simple awareness that the wind is, say, westerly. If you notice, for example, that the wind has shifted in the last few hours from 270° to 255° on the compass, be aware that this is one of the first things you might expect to see if you were going to lose good weather in the next half day or so.

A wind shift alone, however, is not a positive indicator along a coastline. Along a coast the wind direction often shifts seaward (blowing more toward the land) as a sea breeze builds on a clear day. This effect can confuse the interpretation of a wind shift. Sea breezes, however, usually occur in clear skies or under fair-weather cumulus clouds, so watch the clouds as well as the wind direction. (Cloud caps building on coastal peaks near midmorning means air is rising up the peaks, and this air often comes from sea breezes.) A backing shift is a better sign of an approaching weather system when there is not a building sea breeze.

In areas of prominent sea breezes, an approaching weather system might be detected by the absence of a sea breeze on a clear day or a gradual dying off of the winds in the afternoon when they should be building. Sea breezes occur because the rising air over the warmer land creates a local low pressure region that pulls in air from the higher pressure over the water. As the low pressure of a bad weather system approaches the coast from offshore, the pressure difference driving the sea breeze disappears and the wind dies. Even in the absence of this particular process, fair winds often die off from the northwest and then fill in from the south some time later, rather than smoothly backing around as they build. In general, a dying fair-weather breeze in the afternoon when it should be building, accompanied by lowering clouds or new kinds of clouds, also could be a sign of approaching bad weather—the lowering clouds inhibit the heating of the land that drives the sea breeze. This calm period before the new winds fill in is often described as muggy or unusually still. (When paddling in a long waterway with steep hills on either side, be prepared for the wind to fill in from the opposite direction after going calm in this manner.)

Because storm winds predicted for the evening or next day might arrive earlier when these signs are present, when conditions create doubt about making it to the next escape point, it could be better to head back or make alternative plans. Also, any prominent fog bank seen approaching from the sea is most likely moving in because the wind is blowing it in that direction, even if the wind is calm where you happen to be at the time. Consider the potential for strong wind *and* fog when making plans in this situation. Important distinctions between sea fog and radiation fog were discussed in chapter 10. In any waters, it is always better to wait out bad weather on shore than to tough it out on the water.

The above has been just a brief overview of some of the weather factors that should be taken into account in route planning. For those interested in pursuing this important knowledge, please refer to the Starpath Weather Trainer software program. This extensive resource and training tool is applicable to all vessels, large and small, but it was written with the specific needs of kayaks always in mind. It is the best resource available for learning the natural signs of weather and how to interpret them, as well as how to relate these observations to the official forecasts obtained by radio or other means. See www.starpath.com for more information and demonstrations of how to obtain very useful weather information from the Internet.

Planning around Wind and Currents

Here we consider a more detailed example with built-in hazards to illustrate their analysis, even though *this would not be a typical place to choose for first experiences in kayak touring*. Consider the hypothetical place shown in figure 11-9, which we will assume to be inland waters, but not sheltered from the westerly direction, where there are some 50 miles of open water leading to the ocean. It is also an area with strong tidal currents. Checking the *Tidal Current Tables,* we find that there are secondary reference stations providing current information at each of the positions marked by a circled "x." The only chart available for the entire region is at a scale of 1:80,000 (about 8 miles per handspan); but more detailed charts (1:25,000 or about 2.5 miles per handspan) are available for the Cannery Cove and Fast Pass areas. Both of these areas require these detailed charts for safe navigation. The place is hypothetical, but numerical values (distances, winds, currents, etc.) and available descriptions of the place are realistic.

Our round trip must start Friday A.M. and finish Sunday P.M. at Apple Point; we would like to visit Bird Island, Cannery Cove, and

Dunkin Hot Springs, spending at least four hours at each place; we do not mind paddling at night if we have to, but would prefer not to. We could camp, if necessary, at just about any place we could get ashore in this region, with the exception of the beach along the south part of Big Island, beneath the bluff, indicated by hatch marks. Question: Is this a reasonable trip plan, and if so, what would be the

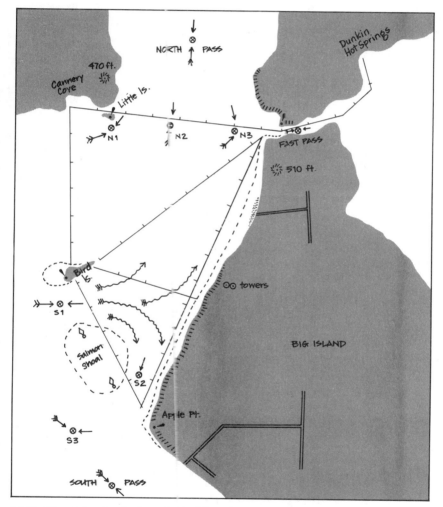

11-9. *Chart sketch of a hypothetical kayak trip in exposed waters. Circled "X"s mark the location of tidal current reference stations. Tracklines are marked in 1-mile intervals.*

best route? We like to cruise along at about 2.5 knots average in flat water, but we can paddle a knot or so faster for a few hours if we have to. (Note that if your steady cruising speed is 3.0 knots and you average about fifteen minutes per hour for breaks, your net average speed is about 2.3 knots; see Table 5-1.) We also like to paddle, so we don't mind paddling more than just the shortest routes among these places. Indeed, the goal of the trip is to cover some ground and get time on the water; we are not necessarily looking for a guaranteed completely leisurely trip, but we also don't want to tackle more than we can handle. It is usually valuable, by the way, to clarify your goals as a regular part of the planning. If one person wants a workout and another just wants to get away, the trip has potential conflicts built in that might spoil its success.

In planning any trip, a first consideration is its total length. (In the process of measuring this, it is easy to draw individual legs of the route and mark them off in miles right on the chart. I find this very helpful for keeping track of position underway. Compass courses also can be marked on each leg for further convenience, as well as predrawn bearing lines to prominent features to be used for piloting.) The point to point round-trip distance in this case is some 44 miles. At just 2 knots, it would take 22 hours to cover the distance in still water. With some sixty hours allotted for the trip, of which sixteen or so should be spent sleeping and at least twelve spent sightseeing, we still have ten hours to spare for eating and other necessities. This might appear ample margin, but with strong currents involved and the usual preference for sleeping at night, we are not at all finished with even the feasibility study. The trip could still be anywhere from not possible to a cake walk.

A check of the *Tide Tables* appendix tells us that sunrise will occur at 6 A.M. and sunset at 7:45 P.M., where these times have been adjusted to account for daylight saving time and for our longitude. Equally important are the twilight times, which must be obtained from the nautical almanac, or estimated from the table shown in figure 11-10. For our example, we will assume that nautical twilights occur at 5 A.M. and 8:45 P.M. As a rule in normal atmospheric conditions, it is totally dark only from evening nautical twilight to morning nautical twilight. In our case, we can expect fairly good light from about 5:30 A.M. till about 8:15 P.M. (2015 on a twenty-four-hour scale).

A key point to our timing is the location of Dunkin Hot Springs inside of Fast Pass. The *Coast Pilot* warns all small craft to check the Current Tables since currents in the narrowed part of Fast Pass can

Duration of Bright Twilight (Sunset to Civi Twilight = Civil Twilight to Sunrise) (evening) (morning)				
Latitude	0° N	20° N	40° N	50°N	60°N
June 21	22 min	25 min	33 min	45 min	107 min
Sept 23	20 min	22 min	27 min	32 min	41 min
Dec 21	23 min	24 min	31 min	38 min	58 min

Duration of Dimmer Twilight (Civil to Nautical Twilight = Nautical to Civil Twilight) (evening) (morning)				
Latitude	0° N	20° N	40° N	50°N	60°N
June 21	26 min	29 min	42 min	66 min	all night
Sept 23	24 min	26 min	32 min	39 min	50 min
Dec 21	26 min	28 min	34 min	42 min	57 min

11-10. *The length of twilight. At civil twilight it is typically dark enough to see the brightest of stars, and at nautical twilight it is too dark to see the horizon. During mid-June, the total twilight period is seventy-five minutes long at latitude 40° N. Most observers would agree that in clear weather it is still "daylight" at thirty-three minutes past sunset, but sometime near forty-two minutes past sunset, everyone would agree it is "dark."*

reach speeds of 8 knots. Without skillful eddy hopping along the edges, which we are not interested in doing, we cannot enter this pass against an ebb. Furthermore, because the currents are so strong at peak flow, we can expect turbulent water even in mid-stream, so we don't even want a rocket ship ride through the pass on a flood. We want to traverse this pass at slack water and even then we want to do it carefully and expeditiously. But we do want to do it; Dunkin Hot Springs is a don't miss place in this part of the world. We must simply plan around getting in and out of there.

Tidal currents for Fast Pass and other points in the region for the allotted days are shown in figure 11-11. The current pattern is complex, so it will take a couple of hours to prepare a table like this one using standard current tables—maybe one hour if you don't make

FRIDAY MAY 22

N1			N2			N3			Fast Pass		
0402	S		0415	S		----			0624	7.5	E
0854	3.6	E	0831	2.3	E	0701	1.7	E	0941	S	
1302	S		1350	S		----			1303	71.	F
1600	3.0	F	1630	2.0	F	1640	2.3	F	1645		S
2013	S		2026		S	----			1924	7.1	E

S1			S2			S3		
			0222	0.9	E			
0432		S	----			0909	3.2	E
0852	1.6	E	----			0909	3.2	E
1203		S	1342	1.6	E	1336		S
1527	1.4	F	----			1541	0.7	F

SATURDAY MAY 23

N1			N2			N3			Fast Pass		
0506		S	0519		S	----			0404		S
0942	3.4	E	0919	2.2	E	0749	1.6	E	0716	7.6	E
1344		S	1432		S	----			1032		S
1640	3.0	F	1710	2.0	F	1720	2.3	F	1350	7.1	F
2040		S	2053			----			1728		S

S1			S2			S3		
			0309	1.0	E			
0532		S	----			0439		S
0945	1.5	E	----			1002	3.0	E
1249		S	1435	1.5	E	1422		S

SUNDAY MAY 24

N1			N2			N3			Fast Pass		
0629		S	0642		S	----			0501		S
1002	3.6	E	0939	2.3	E	8.09	1.7	E	0807	7.5	E
1400		S	1448		S	----			1121		S
1709	3.5	F	1739	2.3	F	1749	2.6	F	1437	6.9	F

S1			S2			S3		
			0352	1.0	E			
0633		S	----			0540		S
1034	1.3	E	----			1051	2.6	E
1334		S	----			1507		S
1652	1.2	F	1524	1.3	E	1706	0.6	F
2031		S	----			2133		S

11-11. *Tidal current times and speeds in the vicinity shown in figure 11-9. At station location N1, the water is slack at 04:02, at which time it starts to ebb. The ebb increases to a peak speed of 3.6 knots at 08:54 then begins to decrease. At 13:02, slack again as it turns to a flood. Slack times at N3, just outside of Fast Pass, cannot be predicted because of the influence of the pass. S2 also has unusual behavior explained in the text. We expect daylight during this period to extend from 05:30 to 20:15.*

mistakes. Reference points N1, N2, N3 are secondary stations, meaning the *Current Tables* provide only corrections at these points. We must correct both the times and the speeds at each point, and the corrections at each point are different. The primary hourly data are given at the center of the North Pass. The same is true for points S1, S2, and S3, relative to hourly data at South Pass.

Before looking into this current pattern, note that many places around the world that have complex currents where there is much commercial boat traffic will have available government or commercial current references (beyond the standard *Current Tables*) that show hourly current arrows and speeds throughout the region. These aids greatly alleviate the detective work that we will have to do here. They are called by various names: current charts, diagrams, atlases, or guides. Sometimes, however, these aids do not provide all the details kayakers might care about in this particular region; for example, they do not show several important points that we can glean from using the actual government station reports.

Once the data are accumulated (as shown in figure 11-11), we can sit back and think about it. Station S2, for example, is a strange one. The tables do not list any information, but refer to a footnote (called endnote) that says the current always ebbs here, meaning always flows south, regardless of what nearby currents are doing. They also say the maximum speed of the ebb at this point occurs five hours and fifteen minutes later than at South Pass and its average speed is about 0.4 times the peak ebb at South Pass. The key to understanding this is the location of Salmon Shoal. We must conclude that the flood enters from the west and diverges when it hits Big Island, as shown by the wavy arrows we have drawn in ourselves—these were not on any chart. Thus the "flood" through the underwater channel at S2 flows in the same direction as the ebb does. This shoaling is all underwater, so standing at Apple Point looking west over the water, you would have no way at all to guess this current behavior. We learn it (guess it?) from doing our homework.

Looking at the currents between Little Island and Fast Pass (N1 to N3) we notice another important point. The current differs significantly as you head west across the mouth of North Pass, especially on the ebb. Or more to the point, the current is very strong around Little Island. We should even anticipate that it might be stronger still in that part that gets compressed behind Little Island. Here is an example where neither the chart nor the *Coast Pilot* warns of tide rips in the vicinity, but we should nevertheless expect rips of fast turbulent water in this region. There simply can't be almost 4 knots of current turning a corner around a small island without causing a hazard to kayaks. We must treat this as a dangerous area at maximum current flow. With just 10 or 12 knots of wind blowing against this current, the area will be covered with white caps.

Another feature to note is the lack of correlation between currents in Fast Pass and those just outside of the pass. There is some agreement with the time of maximum ebb on Saturday and Sunday, but even this does not hold on Friday. There is particularly no correlation between slack in the pass and slack in the channel, just a mile or two outside of it; it is, in fact, just the opposite. The pass is nearly at peak flood when the approach to it is slack. This, however, should not be a surprise. In most narrow passes with strong currents and large bodies of water on either side, there is not, in general, any correlation between current speeds or times in the pass with individual currents or tide heights on either side of the pass. Without specific current predictions for a narrow pass, one must always approach it very cautiously, knowing only that you will not know what is going on in the pass till you get there. Fast Pass is a major waterway, however, as many such passes around the continent, so specific predictions are available.

There are no predictions in between the north stations and the south stations, so we must interpolate these currents, assuming a more or less smooth, continuous flow. For example, at about 0900 there is 3.6 knots of ebb at N1 flowing southwest and at the same time 1.6 knots of ebb at S1 flowing west. We are reasonably safe, then, to assume that there will be about 2.6 knots of ebb flowing about southwest at the point halfway between N1 and S1 at 9 o'clock on Friday. We also can assume that the flood will be fairly weak along the Big Island shore, where it fans out to the north and south.

We also must remember that these currents are only the best predictions possible without our knowing ahead of time what effects wind, atmospheric pressure, and unseasonable river run-off might cause. As a rule, we might guess that very near the actual station locations, these predictions will likely be accurate to within some 20 percent in the speeds and some twenty minutes in the predicted times. In rare cases, they could be off by 50 percent in speed and over an hour in time. The effect of the wind is the easiest to put numerical guesses on. If the wind blows in a steady direction for half a day or longer, it will add an additional current to the tidal flow of some 2 to 3 percent of the wind speed, flowing in the direction of the wind. A day-long 20-knot northerly in this region, for example, would add some 0.6 knots to the ebb and take away about 0.6 knots from the flood. The ebb cycle would be longer and the flood cycle shorter than predicted in this case, but they would still peak at about the same times. Excessive river run-off is signaled by a brown or gray color to water that should be blue or green. River run-off always adds to the ebbs and reduces the floods.

The chart shows a shallow shelf along the west side of Big Island extending out some 0.2 to 0.5 mile. If we must proceed against current, we can paddle on this shelf for some relief; when paddling with the current along this shore, we may well want to stay off this shelf for a better ride. As a rule, currents are weaker in shallow water. They also change directions earlier in the shallow water of a shelf than they do in the deeper water just off the shelf that carries much more momentum with it. Our small scale chart (1:80,000) does not tell much about Bird Island, other than its shape and its navigation light, and the presence of a shoal to the west of it. The *Coast Pilot*, on the other hand, tells us that the island is very low on the east side, with the western wide part rising steeply to an elevation of 75 feet. It also warns that the shoal to the west of the island has dangerous tide rips on a strong flood. To determine what they mean by a "strong" flood we must go back to the *Current Tables* and check the primary station at South Pass. Checking the tabulated average value of the flood at South Pass (which covers an eighteen-year period) we find it is 2.0 knots, whereas the South Pass floods on our weekend will be some 3.0 knots. We have a strong flood, indeed, and should keep these flood rips in mind when we paddle around Bird Island looking for its namesakes.

The *Coast Pilot* is also the best readily available source of climatic weather data. It obviously can't promise what will actually happen, but it does summarize what typically happens at this time of year. If there is a local marine weather service, a call to them would be a strong supplement to the *Coast Pilot*, but professional weathermen will rarely go out on a limb and offer a guess more than three days in advance— especially in places like this one, where on one weekend the sky can be clear, the water flat, the air calm, and the fish a'jumpin'; with the next weekend bringing pea-soup fog, 30 knots of wind, and seas considered big to 80-foot boats.

Weather information is spread throughout the *Coast Pilot:* statistics in the appendix, overviews in the introductions, and local effects in the individual sections for specific places. For our region, we learn that fair wind here is from the north or west, with storms typically bringing easterlies or southerlies. On clear days, we can expect a building westerly sea breeze that might reach 20 knots or so by late afternoon at this time of year, but if this is the only wind, it will be calm in the mornings. These waters are known for early morning radiation fog on calm clear spring days (the kind of fog that burns off by mid-morning), but since the area is exposed to the ocean, we also should be prepared for sea fog blowing in from the west, and this type of fog will not burn off. If fog is present or forecast, it will be important to monitor the weather broadcasts. They are generally accurate about fog conditions, even if they might be off in the wind forecasts in this area of complex terrain.

The steep cliff right along the southern beach of Big Island will offer good shelter from easterlies and even some from westerlies as the wind rises to go over the cliff. A strong westerly with 50 miles of fetch, however, will certainly bring big seas onto the shore in the late afternoon, which would put surf all along that beach and make landing difficult. As nearly always, we must think about the wind as well as the current in planning this route. We must think about the wind's effect on us and its effect on the sea. We know we have strong currents to reckon with, and could have strong winds as well. When strong winds oppose strong currents, we have the additional, even bigger concern of steep seas.

Referring to figure 11-11, we can enter Fast Pass on Friday, if we choose to go there first, at about 0941 in the morning or 1645 in the afternoon—the times are mentioned to the minute to identify them in the table, but they are certainly not that precise. In fact, we want to be there at least thirty minutes early to cover cases where the Pass goes slack earlier than predicted. Narrow channels with strong peak currents do not stay slow very long at slack; if we were late for slack in the afternoon with the Pass turning to an ebb, things could get bad very fast. We could get stuck camping outside the pass and have to wait until 1032 on Saturday to get through in daylight—all that time wondering what was going on at Dunkin Hot Springs, just around the corner.

It is some 12 miles from Apple Point to Fast Pass, so leaving at first light (0530) only gives us some four hours to make it up there for the first slack, or early part of the flood. With the current along the beach ebbing against us at a knot or so, we can't safely make this without leaving well before daylight. We should go someplace else first. We could go to Bird Island first; it is 5 miles off as the crow flies (about two hours in slack water), but we would have to plan around a building ebb setting to the south as we proceed across. We could then hang around Bird Island to as late as 1400 or so and set off for the 1645 slack at Fast Pass riding a building flood to the north. This also fits into the anticipated winds: light in the morning and an afternoon westerly to help push us to the northeast.

I wouldn't head straight from Apple Point to Bird Island, however. There will be some 1.6 knots of ebb setting to the west as we approach the island at 0830, and nothing but open water and stronger current to the west of it. The safest bet would probably be to paddle north along the beach, staying on the shelf to avoid the building southerly ebb, and then ride the ebb back down and across to the island. We could carry on the beach leg clear north of Bird Island and not lose much time, since we will be going across to it at some 4 knots once we get into the ebb. In this case it is much better to paddle a few extra miles than risk being set off into nowhere—all the time wondering what was going on back at Dunkin Hot Springs.

The planning so far looks good. We leave at first light, make it to Bird at 0930 to 1000 at the latest; look around there until about 1400; and set off for Fast Pass in favorable current and likely good wind. A strong westerly or southerly would only help us; a strong easterly would probably call for heading more directly back to Big Island and then north in its lee. It would be more work, but still doable. A strong afternoon northerly against the strong flood would be the major threat to our getting north from the open waters of Bird Island. In this case, we would have to head straight back to Big Island—not much danger if we are blown to the south on this route—and then claw our way north, not counting on making the 1645 slack, but camping as far north as we feel like going. A manageable setback in our plans.

With anything but a strong northerly, the trip north would be a good ride. The current starts flooding at 1203 at Bird Island, but does not peak out at the north until 1640. We will have almost 2 knots of flood behind us as we approach the Pass. We will be in the flood for almost a complete half cycle, which means our net current boost will be approximately 0.6 times the average peak current along the route (see figure 9-11 and related discussion). The average peak is about 2 knots in this case, so we will effectively paddle north with an extra 1.2 knots or so throughout the leg. The 8-mile run should not take much longer than two hours even with little help from the wind. Nevertheless, with possibly weaker than predicted currents and a safety margin of thirty minutes at the pass—this slack is turning against us, so we don't want to be late—if there is no favorable wind, we probably should not leave later than about 1330.

Assuming we get in on Friday, there is only one daylight slack on

Saturday (1032) and then only one again on Sunday (1121). If we do not get out on Saturday, we will have to skip Cannery Cove, which we would not want to do if we were that close to meeting our goals—unless, as Fletcher Christian decided, we just don't want to leave Dunkin Hot Springs at all. To get out, though, we must be waiting and watching the water just inside Fast Pass by about 1000 Saturday (this slack is also turning against us if we are late), which means getting out of Dunkin by at least 0830 for the 4-mile run to the pass—even though we will have an ebb pushing us toward the Pass from Dunkin.

The crossing to Cannery Cove also works out well with the currents. We anticipate exiting the Pass at about 1100, which puts us about halfway through the decreasing side of the ebb cycle in the channel. It is about 8 miles or some three hours in still water over to Cannery Cove, which would mean arriving there at about slack, just as we would like because of the anticipated rips at Little Island if we were to arrive there in strong current. Looking ahead, however, we must now check the Sunday weather forecasts carefully. Because of the strong afternoon floods, once we get to Cannery, we will have to stay there till Sunday. At Cannery Cove, we are the farthest from our final destination, and it is mostly exposed paddling on the way back. We should only proceed on if the weather forecast for tomorrow is a good one. We could probably handle northerlies or westerlies, but southerlies or easterlies would be bad news.

Assume the forecast is for light air, so we head on over. This calls for a somewhat more realistic evaluation of the trip across the channel. We will be setting off in a fairly strong ebb (probably averaging about 1 knot to the south). If we paddle due west at 3 knots, we will get set about 2 miles to the south by the time we reach the vicinity of Little Island. We should either crank in some ferry angle on departing (about 20°) or just not worry about it, knowing we will eventually get set back to the north as the flood starts to build. In any event, it pays to know what is likely to happen and then watch it develop. In these waters, a surprise should be a nice orca visit, not an unplanned trip to Japan. If we choose to look around Little Island today, we should do it as soon as we get there, because it could be dangerous after about 1500 (3-knot flood at 1640). Alternately, we could check it out about 0630 Sunday morning.

Since the current floods strongly to the north all afternoon Saturday, the best bet is to spend the night in the Cannery area and ride the morning ebb (1002) back to the south on Sunday morning. This will be a four- or five-hour open water crossing and with all going well we will be right on schedule. We must just bear in mind that the ebb sets more to the southwest than to the south through most of this passage. We could ever get tricky and ride the ebb down to Bird Island, leaving about 0800, heading about 15° to the east of the island to compensate for the southwesterly set, arriving about lunch time at Bird; picnic and play around there till about 1600 and ride the unusual flood around Salmon Shoal straight to Apple Point, arriving well before dark for a perfect textbook landing.

We have concentrated on currents and winds, as they usually require the most creative planning. Other matters, however, are also important in the end. These include a careful study of the detailed charts for the Fast Pass, Dunkin, and Cannery Cove areas (checking for landing sites, shelves, etc.); checking the general region of the trip for access points to civilization in case of emergency, such as the road to the beach on Big Island; checking with the phone company or some other reference to learn the VHF channel for the local marine operator, if any—you might get stuck and want to call home to report a delay. Again it is always better to wait out bad weather on shore than to tough it out on the water.

Appendix A: Sources

Sources of Charts, Publications, and Equipment

NOAA Chart Catalogs list authorized chart dealers in the region covered by each catalog. Catalogs are online (See Appendix B) as is the list of dealers nationwide. The appendix to any volume of the *U.S. Coast Pilot* includes a complete list of addresses for all agencies that provide maritime information or publications.

Charts and publications may also be obtained directly from the National Ocean Service's Distribution Division. Mail orders should be sent to: Distribution Division (N/ACC3), National Ocean Service, 6501 Lafayette Avenue, Riverdale, MD 20737-1199. Orders should be accompanied by a check or money order payable to NOAA, Department of Commerce, or by providing Visa or MasterCard information. Remittance from outside of the United States should be made by either an International Money Order or a check in U.S. funds drawn on a U.S. bank. Chart catalogs, which include a listing of authorized sales agents, are free upon request. Telephone orders may be placed (Visa or MasterCard accepted) to (301) 436–6990, (800) 638–8975, or by Fax to (301) 436–6829.

Information on Canadian topographic maps is available from: Canada Map Office, Surveys and Mapping Branch, Department of Energy, Mines, and Resources, Ottawa, Canada K1A 0E9. Available publications include: Topographic map catalogs, a list of authorized dealers outside of Canada, and pamphlets ("How to Use a Map" and "Maps and Wilderness Canoeing").

Information on American topographic maps is available from Eastern Distribution Branch, U.S. Geologic Survey, 604 South Pickett Street, Alexandria, VA 22304 (for regions east of the Mississippi River, including Minnesota, Puerto Rico, and the Virgin Islands) and from Western Distribution Branch, U.S. Geologic Survey, Box 25286, Federal

Center, Denver, CO 80225 (for regions west of the Mississippi River, including Alaska, Hawaii, Louisiana, Guam, and American Samoa). Indexes of maps as well as numerous related pamphlets are available. Topographic map symbols are in a pamphlet called "Topographic Maps," produced by the National Mapping Division. Aerial and satellite photos are also available.

Sources of Waterproof Flashlights

ACR Electronics, Inc.
5757 Ravenswood Road
Ft. Lauderdale, FL 33312
Phone: (954) 981–3333
Fax: (954) 983–5087
www.acrelectronics.com

Mag Instrument, Inc.
1635 South Sacramento Ave
Ontario, CA 91761
Phone: (800) 289–6241
www.maglite.com

Pelican Products, Inc.
23215 Early Avenue
Torrance, CA 90505
Phone: (310) 326–4700
Fax: (310) 326–3311
www.pelican.com

Radio Shack
200 Taylor Street Suite 600
Fort Worth, TX 76102
Phone: (817) 415–3200
Fax: (817) 415–3240
www.radioshack.com

Tekna Design Group
334 E Street
Chula Vista, CA 91910
Phone: (877) 275–8403
www.teknascuba.com

Appendix B:
Overview of the Internet

The Internet is a worldwide network among computers throughout the world. Any two computers can be linked this way, but the key links are provided by a few specific large computers that act as hubs in the net. The network itself is simply conventional telephone wires that connect various sites, but the key to the success of the net is the computer protocol and software that has evolved to allow communications among the participants.

The network was originally established for communications between scientists, so many of the computers on the network are associated with universities and other research institutes. Part of the original goal was to provide ready access to research materials and references throughout the world. Computerized indexes that allow convenient access to various references and data bases have been developed. In some senses, the Internet can be viewed by users as a computerized card catalog to a library of information.

The original communications goal of the net has led to the development of an elaborate and extremely efficient system of electronic mail. Worldwide and nearly instantaneous communications are possible at no extra cost beyond the Internet setup itself. This allows users of similar interests to share their knowledge readily with others.

The E-mail system led to the development of "user groups" or "newsgroups" of people with similar interests who want to hear what others are discussing. They set up a common address and compile a list of topics under current discussion. Newsreader software accesses the latest postings and lets readers mark in their computers what they have read and allows them to post their own comments on the subject. Thousands of such newsgroups exist now. Many involve serious research and teaching discussions, but others now are pure entertainment.

The newsgroups are one of the key resources in all areas of research and general interest on the net. Just about any question you might imagine about just almost any subject can eventually be answered by someone on the net. It has been said that everyone is only a few connections away from any other person in the world via the Internet. Send out a message looking for some answer and it will seep its way through the net to find the person who knows what you want to know.

The great diversity of the network, however, brings with it a great diversity of information, not all of which is useful or even valid. There is a distinct responsibility of the user to filter out the value of data received, just as one would with any diverse source of information.

Tools and connections required

The basic tools needed are a computer, a phone modem, a phone line, an Internet account, and Internet software.

Computer

For practical, efficient use of the Internet, one needs a newer computer. Anything purchased since 1997 or so should meet the goals. Some older machines might work, but not efficiently, and they may limit the various presentation media now available. On the Internet now exist essentially all forms of media: text, audio, graphics, video, and various multimedia combinations of these.

Modem

Modems are the devices that connect two computers via telephone lines. The main specification of modems that applies to the use of the Internet is the speed of data transfer. Presently, the state of the art in readily available commercial units is 56.6 kilobaud, meaning 56,000 characters per second can be transferred over the phone lines. Much faster, but more expensive, connections are available through cable and telephone companies. Check with your local Internet provider for the latest information.

Phone line

The use of the Internet requires a telephone line. It is much preferred that this be a dedicated line, not shared with other parts of the building, since any interruption will corrupt the data transfer. For home use, however, this can be your regular residential phone line. The phone calls made on Internet connections will all be local calls (in or near most major cities), even though they ultimately reach around the world. Hence phone billing is not a major concern, unless many lines have to be installed for multiple simultaneous users. There are numerous options available for larger installations that use computer networks and more advanced Internet connections.

If your phone line has call waiting service it must be temporarily shut off during modem connections.

Internet account

Internet accounts are available from commercial vendors throughout the country. Major cities usually have many options. The Internet itself is the best way to find the local Internet providers. From a friend's connection or from the library, do a search (see below) on "Internet providers." These companies act much like local phone companies. They may or may not charge a moderate set up fee and then bill monthly for access to the Internet. As of early 1999, the typical cost for service is $10 to $20 per month. These companies also typically provide the necessary software to access their services.

Commercial vendors such as AOL and CompuServe have Internet connections, but they have historically been more expensive and less efficient than direct Internet accounts. Some offer a so-called free trial period of ten hours or so, but then require a credit card number in order to log on. If you quit using it after just a few hours, be sure the host is very clear that you have quit. Don't just stop using it or you will be charged for the next month as if you are still on.

Internet software

It used to be that several separate software programs were required to access the Internet most efficiently, and many "old timers" still prefer to use separate programs for various features. But these days, all software needed is included in each of the two main Web browser packages, Netscape or MS Internet Explorer. The types of software involved includes:

1. **A communications program** designed to link your computer to the Internet. Now this is typically done with a built-in MS Windows program or some Macintosh equivalent.
2. **A worldwide web browser** such as Netscape or MS Internet Explorer. These two competitors are fighting for dominance as we go to press, but Microsoft's control over the Windows environment

definitely gives them an edge . . . not to mention that Netscape has just joined camps with AOL, the significance of which is not at all clear to the end user looking for the best product for Internet access. Regardless of the politics and finance, they both provide remarkable services to the user. Only time will tell which software will be around in a year or so.

3. **A newsreader program** that accesses, organizes, and communicates with newsgroups. Again, separate programs such as Free Agent are popular with some, while others use the built-in newsreaders of Netscape and MS Internet Explorer.

4. **An E-mail program** that coordinates E-mail communications. Eudora is an example of an excellent independent mail program, but there are thorough E-mail functions in both of the browsers as well.

5. **A file transfer program** such as Cute FTP facilitates the moving of computer files (documents, pictures, etc.) from one computer to another, but the basics of these operations can also be carried out with the browser programs.

Again, separate programs used to be the norm, but now just one integrated suite of programs does the job. You typically get a CD from which you click "setup.exe" and all is done for you.

Finding materials

The Internet offers access to information in the form of text documents, graphic pictures, and audio and video presentations, as well as actual software programs that can be downloaded into the user's computer. The virtue of the system is the elaborate interlinking of the resources with cross references and hotwords that navigate the screen directly from one source to another, often times from one part of the world to another ("hotword" is usually blue and underlined—click it and it does something).

Web browsing

This is the most popular and easiest way to find and extract data. Web browsers include various search engine links built right into them. Popular search engines have names such as: AltaVista, Yahoo, Excite, etc. Be sure to try more than one. They are competitors, and they each operate slightly differently. Enter any key word and you will get tons of leads. Web browsing is sometimes called "surfing the net" (there is an unlimited and ever increasing jargon associated with this technology). Browsing means just starting with some question or key word to get to some reference, and from there following the various hotword links to visit various sites on related subjects.

Newsgroup questions

Post a message in an appropriate newsgroup (if it's not appropriate, someone will likely tell you, and if it's a thoughtful person, they will suggest where to find the right one). There are many groups related to boating (navigation, weather, paddling, GPS, outdoor clothing, etc. Enter a keyword or two in a group search program (discussed below).

Subscribe to the group by simply adding it to the list of groups in your software. This indicates no commitment to participate. You can simply read what others post and nobody knows you are there. Generally your software will mark the messages you have read and then signal you when a new one has appeared. If you suspect participants in one group might have information about another group, you can always post a question in one group such as "Does anyone know of newsgroups or Web pages that discuss use of topo maps?" (there is, by the way, an excellent one provided by San Diego State University TREES program at earthview.sdsu.edu/trees/topohans.html).

The main search engine for content in newsgroups is at www.dejanews.com. Such a Web address is called a universal resource locator (URL). Within a newsgroup, the series of comments and questions on a specific topic is called a "thread."

Some newsgroups are moderated and have some structure to them. These are generally the most useful for serious application. Others are completely unstructured and anything goes. Good results, however, can be found in both categories. If you don't find what you want with Web browsing, newsgroup searches and postings (asking a question) are the next step, and a very powerful one at that. Here are a few newsgroups of interest to kayakers:

rec.boats.paddle: this is the main newsgroup at present for kayakers.
uk.rec.boats.paddle: this is the UK counterpart, although these are all international.
ott.rec.canoe-kayak: this is the Canadian counterpart.
Here are just two sample related groups:
rec.kites: this includes discussion of kites pulling kayaks.
rec.backcountry: one of many on camping and outdoor life.

If you are interested in cameras, diving, weather, whatever, there are many people around the world ready to share their expertise and experience with you. When you set up your newsreader program it will automatically download the entire list; just do a search of it for keywords to find groups of interest.

Mail lists

Some moderated newsgroups are structured as an automatic bulk E-mail service. Every message sent to it goes to all subscribers via their E-mail address. These messages show up in your E-mail software as opposed to your newsreader programs. These are also places you can post questions related to the topic of the group. They are supposed to be devoid of advertising. After some response to a question is received, one communicates directly with a person via E-mail rather than using the group list. Note that this source is best used with discretion because you can otherwise end up with tons of E-mail everyday. Whenever you sign up (subscribe), note how to unsubscribe, and if you are getting too much junk mail, simply unsubscribe. When good, though, and very restricted to a keen interest of yours, new mail from this group can be a highlight of the day.

A navigation mail list along with an archive of navigation shareware can be found at www.roninhouse.com/navigation.

Selected Web sites for kayakers

The following are a few sample links to get you started. Almost certainly, some will change in time—it is part of the process. But once you get the hang of surfing around, they can be found again. Also, check out our home base at www.starpath.com. We include a thorough list of up-to-date links on all aspects of small-craft navigation and marine weather. There is also a newsletter of recent events and changes in navigation and Internet sources. Note that a period at the end of the addresses is not part of the Web address.

Magazines, clubs, and associations

Magazine sites have illustrated online articles and many useful links, including latest lists of associations and clubs. Sometimes an individual's personal list of favorite sites becomes so useful that it is referenced by these major sources:

Sea Kayaker: www.seakayakermag.com

Wave~Length Paddling: www.wavelengthmagazine.com

Atlantic Coastal Kayaker: www.qed.com/ack/index.htm

Canoe and Kayak: www.canoekayak.com

Association of North Atlantic Kayakers (ANORAK): members.aol.com/gokayak/anorak

Trade Association of Paddlesports (TAPS): www.gopaddle.org (they include most kayak dealers and equipment outlets, along with newsletters and calendars of events).

Navigational matters

Try these sites:

- The USCG main index page has leads to all aspects of Coast Guard activity. It is a large and multifaceted site with interwoven links. Nevertheless, it is an excellent resource, getting better every day. See www.uscg.mil.

- The USCG Navigation Center page on GPS. The Navcenter has more specialized information. See www.navcen.uscg.mil/gps.

- A useful "Primer on GPS" plus more information on the subject with links can be found at www.aero.org/publications/GPSPRIMER/index.html.

- To learn about the radio regulations from the FCC, see FCC on VHF licenses at www.fcc.gov/wtb/aviation&marine/fctsht14.html.

- Canadian Marine Navigation Services (Local Notices and Light List) can be found at www.notmar.com/eng/index.html.

- If you have an interest in what the future will look like in marine navigation, check this out—Universal Shipborne Automatic Identification System Transponder at www.navcen.uscg.mil/marcomms/ais.htm.
- All about nautical charts is the subject of the US Marine Chart Division

(of NOS of NOAA) at chartmaker.ncd.noaa.gov/ocs/text/mcd.html.
There you can see chart catalogs, lists of latest editions, local dealers,
opportunity to buy online, etc.

• USCG Local Notices to Mariners are posted at www.navcen.uscg.
mil/lnm.

• Rules of the Road, including free download of a convenient illustrated presentation of the Rules, plus links to related sites, can be
found at www.starpath.com/navrules.htm.

Marine weather

There are many marine weather sites and they change fairly often.
We have compiled the best and try to keep them up-to-date at
starpath.com/links/marlinks.htm. Samples include instant, very convenient text reports and forecasts (from Ohio State University), actual
buoy reports of near-live data (from Florida State University), weather
maps for those who want that detail (from National Weather Service),
and other unique resources such as cloud images from satellites, climatic analyses, tropical storm data, and so forth. Just about anything
you might want to know about the weather.

Contact the author

Finally, if you have any questions about this book or related matters, do not hesitate to contact the author at dburch@starpath.com. It's
global out there, we might as well take advantage of it.

Further Reading

The following list is not intended as a thorough bibliography on these topics. Many fine books and publications that are not included here exist.

Some of the U.S. government publications listed below are available from Superintendent of Documents, U.S. Government Printing Office, Washington, D.C. 20402, they're if not available at booksellers or libraries—see www.gpo.gov and look for "online bookstore," or call their order line at (202) 512–1800. Products from Starpath School of Navigation are available from www.starpath.com (800–955-8328). To learn about other Globe Pequot Press books and where they can be purchased see www.globe-pequot.com.

Marine Navigation

Bowditch, Nathaniel. [1802] 1995. *American Practical Navigator: An Epitome of Navigation,* Pub. No. 9. Washington, D.C.: NIMA (formerly DMAH/TC). The official encyclopedia of marine navigation. A massive book that includes extensive tables and the most thorough glossary of marine navigation terms. The entire book and glossary are online at 164.214.2.59/Navigation/index.cfm. They are also available on CD from Starpath.

Brogdon, Bill. 1995. *Boat Navigation for the Rest of Us—Finding Your Way by Eye and Electronics.* Camden, Maine: International Marine and McGraw-Hill Book Co.

Burch, David. 1986. *Emergency Navigation.* Camden, Maine: International Marine and McGraw-Hill Book Co. Covers makeshift navigation in all conditions, with extensive discussion of steering by the sun and stars without a compass. Excellent general training for backcountry navigation as well.

———. 1999. *Home Study Course on Inland and Coastal Navigation.* Seattle: Starpath School of Navigation. Oriented toward larger craft, but most of the content and practice problems are useful to kayakers as well.

Cockcroft, A. N. and J.N.F. Lameijer. 1996. *A Guide to the Collision Avoidance Rules.* 5th ed. Oxford, UK: Heinemann Newnes. This is the author's favorite treatment of the Nav Rules.

Eyges, Leonard. 1989. *The Practical Pilot— Coastal Navigation by Eye, Intuition and Common Sense.* Camden, Maine: International Marine and McGraw-Hill Book Co. Much the same spirit as our own book with regard to piloting, with other examples and some variations.

Maloney, Elbert S. 1996. *Chapman Piloting, Seamanship, and Small Boat Handling,* 62nd ed. New York: Hearst Books. Usually called just "Chapman's," this is the most popular treatment of these subjects among recreational and professional mariners.

Smith, Richard A. 1994. *Farwell's Rules of the Nautical Road.* 7th ed. Annapolis: Naval Institute Press. A popular and thorough investigation of the Nav Rules. Definitely oriented toward larger vessels.

———. *Federal Requirements for Recreational Boaters.* (COMDTINST M16760. 2/85). Washington, D.C.: U.S. Government Printing Office.

———. 1990. *Navigation Rules, International-Inland* (COMDTINST M16672.2B). Washington, D.C.: U.S. Government Printing Office. New edition expected in 1999. Any printing prior to 1999 is out of date in several areas. See Appendix B for Internet sources through which to find up-to-date editions.

Marine Weather

Ahrens, C. Donald. 1998. *Essentials of Meteorology.* Belmont, CA: Wadsworth Publishing Co. A popular college text.

Burch, David. 1999. *Starpath Weather Trainer* software. Seattle: Starpath Corporation. A complete home-study course and resource on all aspects of marine weather written with kayakers and ship captains in mind. Covers everything from the natural signs to latest satellite and internet technology.

Environment Canada. 1993. *Marine Weather Hazards Manual—A Guide to Local Forecasts and Conditions* (in British Columbia). Vancouver, B.C.: Gordon Soules Book Publishers, Ltd. This book is out of print, but well worth tracking down if you paddle in these waters. See related book by Lange.

——. 1998. *Wind, Weather & Waves—A Guide to Marine Weather in the Great Lakes Region.* Elmwood, Ontario: Whirlwind Books. Excellent cloud pictures and discussion along with much detail on weather on the Lakes.

Gedzelman, Stanley David. 1980. *The Science and Wonders of the Atmosphere.* New York: John Wiley and Sons. College textbook, out of print, but worth finding in a library for students of weather.

Kotsch, William J. 1983. *Weather for the Mariner.* Annapolis: Naval Institute Press.

Lange, Owen S. 1998. *The Wind Came all Ways—A Quest to Understand the Winds, Waves, and Weather in the Georgia Basin.* Vancouver, BC: Environment Canada. Examples are all from waters around Southern Vancouver Island, but if you want to learn about wind and terrain, this is an excellent resource.

National Oceanographic Data Center NOAA. Quarterly. *Mariner's Weather Log.* Washington, D.C.: U.S. Government Printing Office.

Watts, Alan. 1979. *Instant Weather Forecasting.* New York: Granada Publishing.

——. 1975. *Instant Wind Forecasting.* New York: Adlard Coles, Dodd, Mean and Co.

Oceanography

Bascom, Willard. 1980. *Waves and Beaches.* New York: Anchor Books. Out of print, but a classic on the subject.

Bigelow, Henry B., and W.T. Edmondson. 1977. *Wind Waves at Sea,*

Breakers, and Surf. H.O. Pub. No. 602. Washington, D.C.: U.S. Naval Hydrographic Office. Ou: of print.

Britton, Graham P. 1981. *An Introduction to Sea State Forecasting.* Ed Kenneth E. Lilly, Jr. Washington, D.C.: National Weather Service NOAA.

Duxbury, Alyn C., Allison Duxbury, and Keith A. Sverdrop. In press. *An Introduction to the World's Oceans.* 6th ed. New York: McGraw-Hill Publishers. An excellent college textbook.

Pierson, W. J., Jr., G. Neuman, and R. W. James. 1971. *Practical Methods for Observing and Forecasting Ocean Waves,* H.O. Pub. No. 603, Washington, D.C.: U.S. Naval Oceanographic Office.

Thomson, Richard E. 1981. *Oceanography of the British Columbia Coast.* Ottawa: Special Publications of Fisheries and Aquatic Sciences 56.

Sea Kayaking and Canoeing

Broze, Matt, 1998. *Sea Kayaking Safety.* Seattle: Mariner Kayaks. See this and other articles on safety and flotation at www. marinerkayaks.com.

Broze, Matt, and George Gronseth. 1997. *Sea Kayaker Deep Trouble — True Stories and Their Lessons from Sea Kayaker Magazine.* Camden, Maine: Ragged Mountain Press.

Davidson, James W., and John Rugge. 1983. *The Complete Wilderness Paddler.* New York: Vintage.

Dowd, John. 1997 *Sea Kayaking—A Manual for Long-Distance Touring.* Seattle: University of Washington Press. The excellent book remains the classic treatment of the subject.

Fons, Valerie. 1986. *Keeping it Moving—Baja by Canoe.* Seattle: The Mountaineers Book.

Foster, Nigel. 1997. *Sea Kayaking.* Brighton, East Sussex: Fernhurst Books.

Garepis, Demece. 1999. *Sea Kayaking: Northern California.* Camden,

Maine: Ragged Mountain Press.

Hanson, Jonathan. 1997. *Complete Sea Kayak Touring.* Camden, Maine: Ragged Mountain Press.

Hutchinson, Derek C. *The Complete Book of Sea Kayaking.* 4th ed. Old Saybrook, CT: The Globe Pequot Press.

———. *Derek C. Hutchinson's Guide to Expedition Kayaking—on Sea and Open Water.* 3rd ed. Old Saybrook, CT: The Globe Pequot Press.

Ince, John, and Hedi Kottner. 1992. *Sea Kayaking Canada's West Coast.* Vancouver, B.C.: Raxas Books.

Lindemann, Hannes. 1982. "Alone at Sea," in *Great Voyages in Small Boats, Solo Trans-Atlantic.* Camden, Maine: International Marine Publishing Co.

Ramwell, J. J. 1980. *Sea Touring—An Informative Manual for Sea Canoeists.* 4th ed. England: J. J. Ramwell, privately published.

Seidman, David, and Singer Andy. 1997. *The Essential Sea Kayaker.* Camden, Maine: Ragged Mountain Press.

Stuhaug, Dennis. 1998. *Kayaking Made Easy—A Manual for Beginners with Tips for the Experienced.* 2nd ed. Old Saybrook, CT: The Globe Pequot Press.

Washburne, Randel. 1998. *The Coastal Kayaker's Manual—A Complete Guide to Skills, Gear, and Sea Sense.* 2nd ed. Old Saybrook, CT: The Globe Pequot Press.

———. 1990. *Kayaking Puget Sound, the San Juans, and Gulf Islands.* Seattle: The Mountaineers Books.

Wyatt, Mike. 1990. *The Basic Essentials of Sea Kayaking.* Old Saybrook, CT: The Globe Pequot Press.

Index

Boldface numerals indicate pages on which illustrations occur.

About the Author

David Burch is director of the Starpath School of Navigation in Seattle, Washington, and he has taught marine navigation to more than 15,000 students since the school's establishment in 1977. He received the Institute of Navigation's 1985 Superior Achievement Award for outstanding performance as a practicing navigator.

Burch has written for several boating magazines, including *Sea Kayaker*, on the subject of marine navigation and weather. He is a former Fulbright Scholar and a former member of the graduate faculty at the University of Washington; he holds a Ph.D. in physics from the University of Texas. With more than 65,000 miles of blue-water sailing and navigation experience behind him, Burch devotes his time to teaching and writing about navigation. A recent project is the *Starpath Weather Trainer*, a home-study computer course that teaches marine weather.